MARGIN

MARGIN

HOW TO CREATE THE EMOTIONAL, PHYSICAL, FINANCIAL, & TIME RESERVES YOU NEED

Richard A. Swenson, M.D.

Richard A. Swenson M.D.

NAVPRESS

BRINGING TRUTH TO LIFE

NavPress Publishing Group

P.O.Box35001, Colorado Springs, Colorado 80935

The Navigators is an international Christian
organization. Jesus Christ gave His followers
the Great Commission to go and make disciples
(Matthew 28:19). The aim of The Navigators
is to help fulfill that commission by multiplying
laborers for Christ in every nation.

NavPress is the publishing ministry of The Navigators. NavPress publications are tools to help
Christians grow. Although publications alone cannot make disciples or change lives, they can help
believers learn biblical discipleship, and apply
what they learn to their lives and ministries.

Cover photograph: Dan Westergren

Some of the anecdotal illustrations in this
book are true to life and are included with the
permission of the persons involved. All other
illustrations are composites of real situations,
and any resemblance to people living or dead is
coincidental.

Unless otherwise identified, all Scripture in
this publication is from the *Holy Bible: New
International Version* (NIV). Copyright © 1973,
1978, 1984, International Bible Society. Used
by permission of Zondervan Bible Publishers.
Other versions used include: the *New American
Standard Bible* (NASB), © The Lockman Foundation 1960, 1962, 1963, 1968, 1971, 1972,
1973, 1975, 1977; *The New Testament in Modern
English* (PH), J. B. Phillips Translator, © J. B.
Phillips 1958, 1960, 1972, used by permission
of Macmillan Publishers Company; and the
New King James Version (NKJV), copyright
© 1979, 1980, 1982, 1990, Thomas Nelson Inc.,
Publishers.

Printed in the United States of America

Contents

For Linda

*It's hard to imagine this book—or life—
without your presence and love.*

List of Figures and Graphs

Acknowledgments

This book was ten years in the making, which means that a number of deserving people have waited a long time for their official acknowledgment.

Bill Tomfohr, perhaps more than any other, kept the work alive in the early years. For preliminary ideas about the theme of margin, credit goes to Ralph Suechting. I wish to thank those who read portions of the book during the formative process for their comments and criticisms: Bill Thedinga, Walter Schultz, Dan Johnson, Hector Cruz, Mike Simpson, and Jim Eggert.

Many contributed in various other ways, including practical and sensitive expressions of encouragement: Everett and Genevieve Wilson, Ruth Swenson, Caroline Miller, Aggie Wagner, Donna Knipfer, Chuck and Becky Folkestad, Dave and Judy Hatch, Hazel Bent, Betty Cruz, Gail Thedinga, Mary Schultz, and Michael Bailey. In addition, I remain grateful to family and friends around the world who have demonstrated their sustained and prayerful interest in this project.

I owe a great debt of gratitude to Don Simpson, whose counsel was always as accurate as it was gracious. As editor, Steve Webb was both an enthusiastic supporter of the author and a faithful advocate for the reader. Knollwood Lodge was initially timely and later essential for allowing special arrangements to write in that beautiful, secluded winter retreat.

My wife, Linda, has been encourager and critic, copy editor and typist, reader and researcher—in short, collaborator throughout the entire decade. This work would have been abandoned long ago without her help. Our two sons, Adam and Matt, have been more than patient, but are nevertheless pleased at the prospect of having their parents returned to them.

My margin has been devoted to writing for a very long time. It will be an uncommon joy to devote it once again to my family.

Marginless Living

The conditions of modern-day living devour margin. If you are homeless, we direct you to a shelter. If you are penniless, we offer you food stamps. If you are breathless, we connect the oxygen. But if you are marginless, we give you yet one more thing to do.

Marginless is being thirty minutes late to the doctor's office because you were twenty minutes late getting out of the hairdresser's because you were ten minutes late dropping the children off at school because the car ran out of gas two blocks from the gas station—and you forgot your purse.

Margin, on the other hand, is having breath left at the top of the staircase, money left at the end of the month, and sanity left at the end of adolescence.

Marginless is the baby crying and the phone ringing at the same time; margin is Grandma taking the baby for the afternoon.

Marginless is being asked to carry a load five pounds heavier than you can lift; margin is a friend to carry half the burden.

Marginless is not having time to finish the book you're reading on stress; margin is having the time to read it twice.

Marginless is fatigue; margin is energy.

Marginless is red ink; margin is black ink.
Marginless is hurry; margin is calm.
Marginless is anxiety; margin is security.
Marginless is culture; margin is counterculture.
Marginless is reality; margin is remedy.
Marginless is the disease of the 1990s.
Margin is its cure.

PIECES OF BROKEN HUMANITY

It was my lunch hour on a beautiful autumn day, but I did not mind. A bloody towel clutched over a bloody face revealed the need.

At seventy-six, John was slim, fit, and active. Following retirement and a heart attack, he determined to take care of himself and have fun at the same time. It was Wisconsin in the summer and Florida in the winter, but mostly it was golf every day.

As his wife was otherwise occupied, John challenged Glen to eighteen holes. Approaching the first hole, John drove his ball down the middle of the fairway and then moved to the side. Glen prepared his ball, lifted the club, and swung vigorously. The ball, however, came off the toe of the club, angling hard to the right. At a speed exceeding one hundred miles per hour, it struck John in the left eye. Blood instantly came gushing out as his eyeball dropped into his hand.

By the time they arrived at the clinic, Glen was still as white as a sheet. The injured John, however, was obviously enjoying himself—even though covered with blood.

"I guess Glen never knew I had an artificial eye," he twinkled. "I popped it out to make sure it wasn't broken. I didn't really mean to scare him like that."

Rarely a day goes by that I don't pick up some pieces of broken humanity and attempt to put them back together again. In John's case, the wounds turned out to be humorous, and his lacerated eyebrow was easily sutured. Unfortunately, not all my patients have stories that are humorous. And not all "broken pieces" are so easily repaired.

Some people come in for broken legs; others, broken hearts. Some have irritable colons; others, irritable spouses. Some have bleeding ulcers; others, bleeding emotions. And compounding these wounds, many patients show signs of a new disease: marginless living.

How often do I see the effects of marginless living? About every fifteen minutes. Into my office on a regular basis comes a steady parade of exhausted, hurting people. The reason these patients come to me, however, is not to discuss their lack of margin. They don't even know what margin is. Instead, they come because of pain. Most don't realize that pain and the absence of margin are related.

Seeing people in pain is my job. As a matter of fact, I am continually surrounded by pain, for this is the context of medical work. Helping hurting people is the part of medicine I most enjoy. It is a privilege. At the end of a long day it is a satisfying feeling to know that I have alleviated the pain burden of the world just a little. The trouble is, pain today seems to be in an inflationary cycle. While it is true that I enjoy alleviating pain, I could do with a little less work.

THE UNEXPECTED PAINS OF PROGRESS

That our age might be described as painful comes as a discomforting surprise when we consider the many advantages we have over previous generations. Progress has given us unprecedented affluence, education, technology, and entertainment. We have comforts and conveniences other eras could only dream about. Yet somehow, we are not flourishing under the gifts of modernity as one would expect.

Why do so many of us feel like air-traffic controllers out of control? How can the salesman feel so stressed when the car is loaded with extras, the paycheck is bigger than ever, and vacation lasts four weeks a year? How is it possible that the homemaker is still tired despite the help of the washing machine, clothes dryer, dishwasher, garbage disposal, and vacuum cleaner? If we are so prosperous, why are the therapists' offices so full? If we have ten times more material abundance than our ancestors, why are we not ten times more content and fulfilled?

Something has gone wrong. Our society has been attacked by pain. If you know what pain wounds look like, you will see them on all your friends. To be sure, there are as many different kinds of pain as there are reasons for pain. Most people associate the doctor's office with the pain of organic disease. But this is not the only suffering physicians have to deal with. There are, for example, the pains of self-destructive behaviors, of abuse and poor parenting, of pollution, of unrestrained sexual permissiveness, and even the pains associated with prosperity itself.

This "new morbidity" is a fascinating and disturbing study. But it is not the focus of this book. Instead, this book is dedicated to exposing and correcting the specific kind of pain that comes from marginless living. Why? Because we find ourselves in the midst of an unnamed epidemic. The disease of marginless living is insidious, widespread, and virulent.

THE NEW UNIVERSAL CONSTANT

The marginless lifestyle is a relatively new invention and one of progress's most unreasonable ideas. Yet in a very short time it has become a nearly universal malady. Few are immune. It is not limited to a certain socioeconomic group, nor to a certain educational level. Even those with a deep spiritual faith are not spared. Its pain is impartial and nonsectarian—everybody gets to have some.

Do you know families who feel drawn and quartered by overload? Do you know wage earners who are overworked, teachers who are overstressed, farmers who are overextended, pastors who are overburdened, or mothers of young children who are overwhelmed? Chances are the pathogen of marginless living is largely responsible.

One would think that physicians, the acknowledged pain experts, would be both forewarned and forearmed. Not so. As a profession, we suffer deeply from the absence of margin. Consequently, I know of the extent and seriousness of this condition from three sources. First, I have observed it in the lives of my patients. Second, I see its effects in the lives of the interns and residents I teach. Third, I know of the weight of marginless living because for a long time it sat on my chest. Ten years ago I paid the ransom and purchased back margin, a decision that has cost me a great deal of money. Yet it was one of the wisest purchases I ever made. I have no regrets.

WHY ALL THE FUSS?

Because most of us do not yet know what margin is, we also do not know what marginless is. We feel distressed, but in ill-defined ways. We can tell life isn't quite what it used to be or perhaps not quite what we expected it should be. Then we look at our cars, homes, and color televisions with remote control and conclude that our distress must be in our imaginations.

Others deny vehemently that anything is wrong. "Life has always been hard," they say. "People have always been stressed. It is simply part of living. There has always been change to cope with. There have always been economic problems, and people have always battled depression. It is the nature of life to have its ups and downs—so why all the fuss?"

I'm not the one who's making the fuss; I'm only writing about it. I'm only being honest about what I see all around me. I sit in my examining room and listen. Then I report what I hear. Something *is* wrong. People are tired and frazzled. People are anxious and depressed. People don't have the time to heal anymore. There is a psychic instability in our day that prevents peace from implanting itself very firmly in the human spirit. And despite the skeptics, this instability is not the same old nemesis recast in a modern role. What we have here is a brand-new disease.

To be sure, the pains of the past were often horrible beyond description. To have your wife die in childbirth, your children crippled with polio, your cattle ravaged by tuberculosis, and your crops leveled by locusts is not the common definition of the good life. But those were the pains of the past, and most of them are gone. Unfortunately—and unexpectedly—the pains of progress are now here to take their place. Prominent among them is the disease of marginless living.

THE FOCUSING VALUE OF PAIN

No one likes pain. We all want to get rid of it as soon as possible, in any way possible. But physical pains are usually there for a reason, to tell us something is wrong and needs to be fixed. Emotional, relational, and societal pains, too, are often indicators that all is not well. As such, they serve a valuable purpose. They help us focus.

Modern-day living, however, opposes focusing. Surrounded by frenzy and interruptions, we have no time for anything but vertigo. So our pain, it turns out, is actually an ally of sorts. In the hurt is a help. Pain first gets our attention—as it does so well—and then moves us in the opposite direction of the danger.

If you were my patient, you would come to me already focused on your pain. You would want me to explain it and would hope I could make it go away. My responsibility would be to listen to your symptoms, diagnose your problem, offer a prescription, and encourage you in the direction of health. And because drawing diagrams often helps us to understand, I might write it all on a prescription pad for you to refer to and remember. It would look something like this:

```
┌─────────────────────────────────────────┐
│         RX: From the Desk of            │
│       Richard A. Swenson, M.D.          │
│   ═══════════════════════════════════   │
│                                          │
│   Symptom: PAIN                          │
│                                          │
│   Diagnosis: OVERLOAD                    │
│                                          │
│   Perscription: MARGIN                   │
│                                          │
│   Prognosis: HEALTH                      │
│                                          │
│   Therapeutic Goal: HEALTHY RELATIONSHIPS│
│                                          │
└─────────────────────────────────────────┘
```

IS THERE A CURE?

If we focus and work to understand, is this painful disease of marginless living curable? Is health possible? Of course it is. But the kind of health I speak of will seldom be found in "progress" or "success." For that reason, I'm not sure how many are willing to take the cure. But at least we all deserve a chance to understand the disease.

THE
PROBLEM:
PAIN

The Pain of Progress

Erick Ostrom was born in Sweden in 1894 and came to the United States in 1912 at the age of eighteen. No one is quite sure why he came, for Grandpa never wanted to talk about it. Not knowing the language and having only a third-grade education, he sometimes slept in theaters while going from job to job. A few years later he married Anna, whose love and gentleness buffered but could not prevent the hardness of life. The Ostroms had six children, losing two of them in infancy—the causes of their deaths unknown. Grandpa would tell of transporting one of the dead infants in a blizzard to the neighboring town, burying her there in the frozen ground.

During the Great Depression, Grandpa developed tuberculosis. He was in and out of the sanitarium for the next eleven years, had one of his lungs removed, and was never again to reach one hundred pounds. The doctors told him he probably contracted the disease from the fumes in the steel mills. To make ends meet, the children began working while Anna cleaned houses and took in washing. After his release, the family tried farming, but the cows got sick and Grandpa got sicker.

Although he lived to the remarkable age of eighty-four, life was always hard for Grandpa. It never did get easy. Neither did he expect that it would, or should.

If my grandfather could have asked for whatever he wanted to make his life easier and more fulfilling during those difficult years, he would have requested health for himself and his family, and that his babies would not die from unnamed diseases. He would have wished for education, a warm home in the winter, and a reliable supply of safe and healthy food. He might have requested a good team of horses, good seed, and fertilizer. Perhaps he would have wished to visit his family in Sweden.

All of these advantages have been granted in America today. Yet the formula for happiness has proven to be more elusive than the simple bestowing of these benefits. Somewhere the equation has broken down. Food plus health plus warmth plus education plus affluence have not quite equaled Utopia. We live with unprecedented wealth and all it brings. We have leisure, entertainment, convenience, and comfort. We have insulated ourselves from the unpredictable ravages of nature. Yet stress, frustration, and oftentimes even despair unexpectedly accompany our unrivaled prosperity.

PROGRESS AND PANDEMONIUM

While visiting our family recently, an eleven-year-old friend from a large city announced, "There's an epidemic going on down there. I think it's pandemonium."

We live in a troubled age. We have more questions than answers, more problems than solutions. Few know where we are headed, but universally acknowledge that we are careening along at breakneck speed.

How can this be? Aren't we advancing, improving, evolving? Aren't technological development and social learning bringing us an ever better world? That progress might be in trouble today is unexpected news, for we always assumed it could do the job. Never did we suspect that pandemonium and progress would one day walk on stage together, or that pain and progress would one day join forces against us.

People everywhere are in anguish, and progress does not seem to care. It is time to reexamine our assumptions.

ONWARD AND UPWARD

Exactly what is progress? Simply stated, progress means proceeding to a higher stage of development. *"The idea of progress holds that mankind has advanced in the past . . . is now advancing, and will continue to advance through the foreseeable future*," explains historian Robert Nisbet. "From at least the early nineteenth century until a few decades ago, belief in the progress of mankind, with Western civilization in the vanguard, was virtually a universal religion on both sides of the Atlantic."[1] Progress was automatic, the inevitable function of chronology. Thus, saying we had lived from 1950 to 1970 was synonymous with saying we had *progressed* two decades. The flow of progress was assumed to be inherently positive.

Progress is so natural and axiomatic an idea that twentieth-century Westerners can't conceive of life without it. The modern mind has been so reared under its assumptions that devising alternative scenarios seems impossible. If not progress, then what? Regress? Who in their right mind would advocate regress? Even the connotations of these words are laden with bias. Progression is forward; regression is backward. Enlightenment versus darkness. Perfection versus primitivism.

Most of us, no doubt, trust the idea of progress more than we realize. It is the train we all boarded for the ride to the good life. "*We have faith in progress*," observes philosopher Nicholas Wolterstorff. "Until recently, the general public . . . regarded modernization as a *good* thing, typically giving it the honorific title 'development.' Development was touted as the cure to a multitude of human miseries."[2]

Is there a disease? We will soon have a remedy. Is there poverty? We have enough wealth to go around, and a social program or two will solve the problem of the poor. Is there an energy shortage? We will find new technologies to harness the power of the nucleus and to capture the sun. Is there famine? We will use fertilizers and hybrid seeds to conquer hunger. In our most idolatrous moments, we actually began to assume that the solution to any problem could be confidently entrusted to progress. Thanks to its blessings, we came to perceive the future as a safer place to live.

FAILED FAITH

For a while, it appeared progress was going to lead us to the mountaintop, and we were euphoric in anticipation. One after another, progress paraded before us its spectacular successes, prominent among which were an incredible array of technical achievements that test the limits of imagination. We can now transplant both the heart and lungs and get you out of the hospital in six days. We have robots that work, pop machines that talk, and trains that hover. From atom smashers to earth movers to "smart" bombs, it is an amazing age. "The broad populace has naively come to believe," explains religion professor David Hopper, "that technological novelty is identical with progress."[3]

Then, almost without warning, failures began to take their place on stage alongside the successes—first a few, then more, and now many. When you ignore them, they intensify. When you try to explain them away, they double. As a result, faced with a torrent of disconcerting evidence, many people once loyal to progress are defecting. Formerly uncontested, the tenets of progress are now openly challenged. "Everything now suggests, however," writes Nisbet, "that Western faith in the dogma of progress is waning rapidly in all levels and spheres in this final part of the twentieth century."[4]

Our enthusiasm for both progress and the future has moderated. For some, it has disappeared. "How does it happen that serious people continue to believe in progress," asks historian Christopher Lasch, "in the face of massive evidence that might have been expected to refute the idea of progress once and for all?"[5]

Polls reveal many Americans no longer believe their children will have a better life than they did. We are not sure whether progress is a cause for celebration or a reason to run and hide. Many are not quite sure they want to enter the future linked hand in hand with it. When we discovered an unexpected pain so often accompanying each new development, our hope for the promise of tomorrow understandably waned.

After all, we did not have acid in our lakes or holes in our ozone layer until progress gave them to us. Margin was as abundant as prairie grass until progress took them both away.

RUINOUS IMPROVEMENTS

It is not my intention to denigrate the value of progress's achievements. We have all benefited greatly. As a physician, I understand the tremendous advantages of immunizations, antibiotics, and anesthesia. We all marvel at the power of communications and the speed of transportation. The print media has vastly increased access to learning. Wealth has permitted opportunities far beyond the imagining of our great-grandparents.

The United States in particular has been a prodigy from the womb of progress. Our technology is celebrated, our medicine awe-inspiring, our universities prestigious, and our research of consistent Nobel-Prize quality. Knowledge of our language is desired the world over. In many ways the Church is large, wealthy, and strong. Our freedoms set a standard for other nations to compare themselves to.

Yet as visible as these achievements have been, our faults demand a glaring prominence of their own. If we lead the world in successes, we also lead in far too many failures. Through much of the last decade, we had the developed world's highest rates of divorce, teenage pregnancy, illicit drug abuse, crime, homicides, AIDS, litigation, functional illiteracy, national debt, and foreign debt. We even make more garbage than anyone else.

If progress is so wonderful, why are we plagued, as Lasch accuses, by such "a baffled sense of drift"? Why do we drink and drug to forget our problems? Why are we divorcing and suing at such rates? Why are people killing themselves—and others—in such numbers?

Forty years ago our nation's schoolchildren were being disciplined for talking, chewing gum, making noise, and running in the halls. Today, the biggest discipline problems are rape, robbery, assault, vandalism, and drug abuse. Is this then what we might call forty years of progress? Over those forty years we have had more education, more wealth, more science and technology, more medical care, more media and communications—in short, more of everything. Does this mean we have "proceeded to a higher stage of development"?

Eighty years ago we had no national debt. Today, we have a multitrillion-dollar debt that keeps running away from us like an escaping convict.

One hundred years ago we had fresh air and clean lakes. Today, much of our atmosphere is hazardous and our water polluted.

Two hundred years ago we had lush forests and thick prairies. Today, our forests are threatened by acid rain, and our prairies are being flushed down the Mississippi.

CRISIS TO CRISIS

With the aid of progress, perils now encircle us. No matter which direction we turn, yet another crisis stares us in the face. Not only has progress been unable to solve these crises, it has not even been able to slow them. Thus, as British economist E. F. Schumacher observed, the modern world finds itself "tumbling from crisis to crisis."

We are immersed in a crime and prison crisis; a drug-abuse crisis; a national-debt and international-trade-deficit crisis; a savings-and-loan and banking crisis; a health-care system and Medicare crisis; a sexually-transmitted-disease crisis, including AIDS; an adolescent-suicide crisis; a liability-and-litigation crisis; an ethics crisis at every level of personal and public life; and the inexorably deepening environmental crisis. Our families are relentlessly torn apart by divorce, abuse, incest, and teen-age pregnancies. Our educational system remains woefully deficient. Inner cities are war zones. Breakdown on a large scale is now within our reach.

"Each day we awake to a world that appears more confused and disordered than the one we left the night before," complains social critic Jeremy Rifkin. "Every time we think we've found a way out of a crisis, something backfires. The powers that be continue to address the problems at hand with solutions that create even greater problems than the ones they were meant to solve."[6]

All of this is not to say, of course, that crises are a new arrival, unique only to modern-day America. Still, one would have expected progress to bring us fewer rather than more.

FOR THE RECORD

Thirty years ago, the record of progress was still relatively intact. Of course, there were the expected problems and setbacks, but gains and the promise of prosperity always offset them.

Then came the 1970s. Apocalyptic talk flowed heavily, as energy and OPEC threats distressed us and economic news was glum. Eco-logical degradation stuck a pin in our global eye, while fear of nuclear annihilation chilled the air. Those were days custom-made for somber prophets. Their warning bells alerted the world, touching off a prognos-tication free-for-all that persists to the present.

Leading the charge was *The Limits to Growth* by Dennis Meadows and fellow researchers. This first report of the Club of Rome used world-system computer models developed at Massachusetts Institute of Tech-nology to examine the question of exponential growth in a finite system. "If the present growth trends in world population, industrialization, pol-lution, food production, and resource depletion continue unchanged, the limits to growth on this planet will be reached sometime within the next one hundred years," they concluded. "The most probable result will be a rather sudden and uncontrollable decline in both population and industrial capacity."[7]

Millions of copies were sold in over thirty languages, and the book sparked an international debate. Though the Meadows team was praised for the scope of their innovative work, their methodology was criticized for incomplete data, inaccuracies of mathematical models, missing economic variables, and failure to account for regional differences. Many of their conclusions were later revised or retracted. Nevertheless, the ground was irreversibly broken by a landmark study. The fight was on.

Two years later, the Club of Rome struck again: "Suddenly—virtually overnight when measured on a historical scale—mankind finds itself confronted by a multitude of unprecedented crises," warned systems researcher Mihajlo Mesarovic and engineering professor Eduard Pestel in *Mankind at the Turning Point*. This second report of the Club of Rome used revised computer models to conclude that "mankind's options for avoiding catastrophe are decreasing, while delays in implementing the options are, quite literally, deadly."[8]

Economics professor Robert L. Heilbroner contributed a provocative analysis of our future in his widely discussed *An Inquiry into the Human Prospect*: "The outlook for man, I believe, is painful, difficult, perhaps desperate, and the hope that can be held out for his future prospect seems to be very slim indeed. . . . The answer to whether we can conceive of the future other than as a continuation of the darkness, cruelty, and disorder of the past seems to me to be no; and to the question of whether worse impends, yes."[9]

For the most part, progress did not fare well in the seventies. True, there were optimistic predictions coming from such heavyweights as Harvard's Daniel Bell (chairman of the Commission on the Year 2000; a "moderate optimist") and Herman Kahn (founder of the Hudson Institute; an "enthusiastic technological optimist"). But even these respected futurists wavered in subsequent years.

The 1980s seemed to bring respite. Sustained economic prosperity throughout the Western world alleviated some of our problems and masked many more. Faith in our cleverness at finding solutions was reinforced by this financial balm. Yet somehow the problems kept building, even if now they had been pushed off center stage: two problems and one solution, two more problems and one more solution. Crime, drugs, pollution, AIDS, debt—prosperity, it turned out, was more placebo than penicillin.

The prophets, for the most part, softened their rhetoric. Some took a different tack, what I call the transitionist approach: Yes, life is traumatic, but these are only birth pains. The squeeze through society's pelvis is unexpectedly wrenching, but a fresh new life will be awaiting us in the natal world. According to this scenario, new trends and power shifts will be enormously disruptive but must be tolerated. The information age is here, like it or not. Decentralization and demassification will result in a wildly pluralistic society, so we might as well begin to appreciate the value of pluralism. And if all goes well, cooperation of the human community will replace conflict.

This, of course, is a mixture of futurology and crossing one's fingers. In *The Third Wave*, Alvin Toffler placed his considerable influence behind such a transitionist idea. The caution in his optimism, however, is evident: "Often, as Second Wave institutions crash about our heads, as crime mounts, as nuclear families fracture, as once reliable bureaucracies sputter and malfunction, as health delivery systems crack and industrial economies wobble dangerously, we see only the decay and breakdown around us. Yet social decay is the compost bed of the new civilization."[10] "One of the most important things we can give to our kids," Toffler advises parents in a later interview, "is the sense that they live in a world being born, not a world dying."[11]

John Naisbitt reinforced the transitionist theory in his megapopular *Megatrends*: "We are living in the *time of the parenthesis*, the time between eras. It is as though we have bracketed off the present from both the past and the future, for we are neither here nor there." Naisbitt goes on to argue that this traumatic transformation zone "is a great and yeasty time, filled with opportunity" if one can only leverage it correctly. He concludes with this exclamatory: "What a fantastic time to be alive!"[12] If you enjoy convulsions.

THE NINETIES: OPPORTUNITY VERSUS ANGST

These prognostications, however abbreviated, give some flavor of the debate that has carried us into our current decade. Hundreds of additional prophetic opinions have been generated by the remarkable circumstances of the latter twentieth century, and indeed, we are not starving for opinions. As we close in on the end of a millennium, there is much excitement, not a little anxiety, and certainly a lot of press.

It makes for fascinating reading and sleepless nights. Yet when all the data is analyzed, it becomes apparent that our crystal ball remains filled with fog. No one knows for sure what will happen. Will we collapse? Will we thrive? Will we transition? One fact, however, *is* certain: Something historical is happening in our lifetime.

Given that modernity has become such a paroxysm, for us to have survived as long as we have is, in itself, an accomplishment. Now, where are the planners who will lead us into the unknown? Which prophet should we listen to? There are many, but their words argue among themselves. As the forecasts fly, they collide. What for one futurist is an opportunity, for another is angst. For every up, there's a down; for every levo, a dextro.

TOO MUCH PAIN

My advice is to stay away from the futurists who predict destruction and then recommend it, too. They describe the future but cannot bring themselves to judge it. Instead, whatever seems inevitable they endorse. The rest of their text is spent telling us why we must conform.

Such value-devoid passivity is an approach I would not recommend. There are too many dangers. There have been too many failures. There has been far too much pain.

Analyzing progress and social trends from the macroscopic view, as we have done thus far, lends a valuable perspective. But we do not see pain as clearly from this distance as we do when it sits in front of us. Pain comes alive when it talks—even more so when it cries. My initial observations about progress, pain, and margin came not from the distance of the macroscope but instead from the closeness of my examining table. One patient at a time, one story at a time. I worry about the deteriorating statistics, but numbers don't feel pain. It is the face I see behind each statistic that motivates me to write.

These patients are depressed, stressed, and exhausted. Some are desperate. Their jobs are insecure. Their farms have been repossessed. They are over their heads in debt. Their marriages are in trouble. Their sons are using drugs, and their daughters are getting pregnant.

These patients don't know what to do or where to turn. They have no social supports, no roots, no community. Their stomachs won't stop burning. They can't sleep at night. They think about drastic solutions. The public blames the medical profession for giving too many tranquilizers and antidepressants. But what would you do? Doctors like to see healing as the result of their work. Yet today we often must be content with far less. There are so many things wrong with people's lives that even our best is only a stopgap.

Mental torment hurts. Stress hurts. Overload hurts. Crime and violence hurt. Debt hurts. Divorce hurts. Poor parenting hurts. Abuse hurts. Sexual diseases hurt. Alcoholism hurts. Drug addiction hurts. Abortion hurts. And when you add up all the hurts, we hurt more than we used to.

WHO IS AT FAULT?

The promise of progress has soured into epidemic personal, relational, and environmental pain. I have spent the last ten years of my life striving to understand what went wrong and why. A full explanation is beyond the scope of this book, but I do want to touch on four points germane to our discussion.

Progress Sabotages Margin

There can be little doubt that the ubiquitous contemporary absence of margin is directly linked to the march of progress. Those cultures with the most progress are the same as those with the least margin. If you were wondering why there is a chapter on progress in a book on margin, this is the reason. Margin has been stolen away, and progress was the thief. If we want margin back, we will first have to do something about progress.

We *must* have some room to breathe. We need freedom to think and permission to heal. Our relationships are being starved to death by velocity. No one has the time to listen, let alone love. Our children lay wounded on the ground, run over by our high-speed good intentions. Is God now proexhaustion? Doesn't He lead people beside the still waters anymore?

"Something has been stolen from us that we can't quite name," accuses Norman Mailer.[13] Who plundered those wide-open spaces of the past, and how can we get them back? There are no fallow lands for our emotions to lie down and rest in. We miss them more than we suspect.

Certainly one cannot blame all the pains of the world on lack of margin. But it is fair to say that the lack of margin is a much greater component of our pain than most realize.

Progress Leads to Stress

The automatic development of a society under the tutelage of progress leads to stress, overload, and complexity. This is closely related to the point made above, but distinct enough and important enough to warrant separate mention. I will explain more in the chapters that follow. For now, suffice it to say that progress, as currently defined and practiced in American culture, flows strongly in the direction of increased pressure on the individual and on the system.

Progress Has Unanticipated Consequences

We do not know what we do not know, and we cannot foresee the unforeseen. We can never fully anticipate the future—it will always hold surprises. Progress has been victimized by this improvidence and, at times, devastated by it. For example, we did not know acid rain would result from burning fossil fuels. We did not know mobility would disrupt family and community stability. We did not know inner-city housing projects would turn into ghetto war zones. We did not know thalidomide would deform babies. We did not invent suburbs to throw our traffic patterns into chaos.

"Many of the crises of the present have *positive* origins," explain scientists Mesarovic and Pestel in *Mankind at the Turning Point*. "They are consequences of actions that were, at their genesis, stimulated by man's best intentions."[14] Best intentions, however, do not guarantee problem-free outcomes. And because unanticipated consequences are so common and so vexatious, we can never fully trust even the brightest sounding intentions.

Progress Has Been Based on Faulty Premises

In its specifics, the definition of progress varies from culture to culture and from age to age. Within contemporary American society, however, our notion of progress was first defined and later dominated by money, technology, and education. Each of these areas is of value, but none of them cares much about our transcendent needs. That indifference constitutes a fatal flaw.

Americans have a widespread perception that inextricably associates our overall well-being with our material and cognitive status. This, in fact, is how we measure progress. If we earn a Ph.D., get a raise, and buy a new house, we are "better-off." But what about the depressed schoolteacher, the recently divorced executive, the suicidal adolescent, or the octogenarian being force-fed in the nursing home? By what economic and cognitive parameters do we measure their "progress"?

In our enthusiasm to improve material and cognitive performance, we neglected to respect the other more complex and less objective parameters along the way. The social, emotional, and spiritual contributions to our well-being were, and continue to be, overlooked and underestimated. Not only are they more difficult to measure, but we apparently believed they would simply "improve" along with everything else. Or else, in our rush for the future, we didn't care.

So when the family began to crumble, we did not know what to think of it. When mobility began to tear apart community, we took little notice. When psychological stress and pain appeared on nearly every doorstep, we attempted to invalidate it. Our paradigm does not know how to accommodate this type of data. If you are better off, then how can you be worse off? Since you have progressed, you cannot feel sick. As long as the stock market is up and houses are bigger, you must be doing well—even if you're not.

"All that 'endless progress' turned out to be an insane, ill-considered, furious dash into a blind alley," accuses Nobelist Aleksandr Solzhenitsyn.[15] Until we can find a way to integrate the social, emotional, and spiritual into our notion of progress, we are destined to race into one blind alley after another.

Did progress betray us? Not really. We should never have expected material and cognitive well-being to carry us very far. We should have known from the start there was more to life than that. Until we understand what progress is and isn't (that is, should be and can never be), we will remain trapped in a paradigm that is not taking us where we need to be going.

OUR SHARE OF THE BLAME

To lay all the blame for our considerable woes on progress is neither accurate nor fair. Humans are also culpable. Progress is only guilty of what it is guilty of; the rest of the blame belongs to us. If progress gave us the gun, we pulled the trigger. If progress gave us wealth, we contributed avarice. It was progress that showed us the atom, but we who dropped the bomb. Are we really building a better world—or simply nourishing evil?

By putting progress in the hands of our fallenness, we have magnified nearly every human flaw. We have put armaments in the hands of our hostility, litigation in the hands of our cynicism, affluence in the hands of our greed, the media in the hands of our decadence, advertisements in the hands of our discontent, pornography in the hands of our lust, and education in the hands of our pride. These have not been stabilizing developments. Trying to solve man's problems by giving him more power is like trying to tame the wolf by letting it play with the lamb.

REGAINING CONTROL

Should we jettison progress and start over? That would not be wise. We do not really wish to abandon its many benefits. But neither do we any longer wish to endure its many complications. "As the twentieth century draws to a close," summarizes Lasch, "we find it more and more difficult to mount a compelling defense of the idea of progress; but we find it equally difficult to imagine life without it."[16]

Is there perhaps another option available to us? Can we put progress on probation while we work out its many problems? Two actions would be required of us for this approach to succeed: First, we must regain control of progress; and second, we must redirect it.

To control progress will not be easy. If we decide to put on the brakes, which pedal do we push? If we want to call "foul," which referee should we approach? To what authority does progress submit? The answer is: None. There are no brakes, no referees, no authorities. As one social critic complains, "Progress itself goes on progressing; we can no longer stop it or turn it around."[17]

After gaining an autonomous strength, progress has built up a good head of steam; it does not depend on us to push it along. The trouble is, it no longer *responds* to us either. "The very progress which we first applauded has now become a problem," observes economist Bob Goudzwaard. "The production system, initially a willing servant laboring to end our misery, seems to have taken charge."[18] Has the servant become greater than the master?

Progress calls the shots. When it wrestles, it wins. If progress and pain are linked, well, a little pain never hurt anyone. If progress and margin are enemies, well, what is margin? So what if we are all stressed? So what if the divorce rate is 50 percent? So what if my backyard is polluted?

We are addicted, and progress knows it. We now do *its* bidding. Before we can subjugate progress, we must first break the addiction. Contentment and simplicity, as described in part 3 of this book, will help. Abiding by scriptural teaching concerning money, possessions, education, and priorities will help immensely.

As we subjugate progress, we make it subservient to our greater goals and needs, especially relationships. We once again practice economics "as if people mattered." We once again agree that things do not own us and are not even very important. We once again assert that jobs are only jobs, that cars are only organized piles of metal, that houses will one day fall down—but that people are important beyond description. We once again assert that love stands supreme above *all* other forces, even to the ends of the universe and beyond.

If, however, we fail in our attempts to break the addiction and to subjugate progress, we had better put on our crash helmets and brace ourselves. The train continues gaining speed, and no one is at the controls. Progress is leading us to a threshold, but when asked, will not tell us which threshold we near. As sociologist Robert Bellah and colleagues have pointed out; "Progress, modernity's master idea, seems less compelling when it appears that it may be progress into the abyss."[19]

A MATTER OF (RE)DIRECTION

I am not abandoning all faith in progress. I am not for regress. But I am for redirection. The abyss is not my favored destination.

If you are traveling from Chicago to New York and instead find yourself in Houston, the sensible thing to do is to stop the car, consult the map, and turn in the right direction. In the same way, if we have traveled down the road of progress and now find ourselves in a situation where relational, emotional, and spiritual pain are pandemic, where stress and overload rule our daily schedules, and where margin as a component of living has virtually disappeared, we do not need to apologize for stopping and redirecting ourselves.

In turning deliberately onto the broad road of wealth, education, and material possessions, we have left behind the better way, covered by the dust of our hurry. If we had followed the signposts of that narrower road by acting justly, loving mercy, and walking humbly with our God, we wouldn't now have the anguish we find ourselves buried under.[20]

HOLD THE TRAIN

Perhaps we should not go any further until we have accomplished this redirection and defined progress in more wholesome terms. Perhaps we ought to defer the future for a while until we have developed a satisfactorily integrated model to guide our journey. Under the new understanding of accounting we would not call it progress if we gained in wealth but lost in relationship; we would not call it beneficial if we improved in estate but injured the psyche; and we would not call it profitable if we achieved a promotion but lost spiritual integrity.

Until we find ways to guard our mental and spiritual health as well as our "social ecology" (that is, our interrelational environment), we will only compound our troubles and further destabilize our future. As Bellah has warned: "Unless we begin to repair the damage to our social ecology, we will destroy ourselves long before natural ecological disaster has time to be realized."[21] Only when progress begins to show discipline and restraint, as well as a respect for the inward and transcendent needs of human beings—including our need for margin—will we again be able to trust it.

RIGHT RELATIONSHIPS

Progress's biggest failure has been its inability to nurture and protect right relationships. If progress had helped here, I would have no quarrel with it. But it didn't help. So we must either teach it to use new tools or put it on the sideline.

As we have already seen, progress builds by using the tools of economics, education, and technology. But what are the tools of the relational life? Are they not the social (my relationship to others), the emotional (my relationship to myself), and the spiritual (my relationship to God)? None of the tools of progress has helped build the relational foundation our society requires.

Margin knows how to nurture relationship. In fact, margin *exists* for relationship. Progress, on the other hand, has little to say about the relational life. Even our language gives us away. When we talk of progress, we do not mean social, emotional, and spiritual advancement. Instead, the word is reserved in our common usage to mean material/physical and cognitive/educational gains.

In analyzing our age, commentator after commentator will demonstrate how much better-off we are. Yet, invariably, they are talking about money, energy, transportation, housing, communications, technology, and education. People, however, have relational needs that go much deeper. And while all the focus was on the material and cognitive, our relational environments suffered from neglect.

FIVE ENVIRONMENTS

MOST OF OUR *PROGRESS:*
1. Physical environment (wealth, technology, health—the material world)
2. Cognitive environment (knowledge, information, education—the intellectual world)

MOST OF OUR *PAIN:*
3. Social environment (family, friends, neighbors, church—the societal world)
4. Emotional environment (feelings, attitudes—the psychological world)
5. Spiritual environment (the eternal and transcendent—God)

While the *progress* we boast of is found within the material and cognitive environments, most of the *pain* we suffer is found within the social, emotional, and spiritual. The material and cognitive environments are unquestionably important. They also have an advantage in that they are more visible and thus more highly pursued. Scripture teaches us, however, that the social, emotional, and spiritual environments are more important. *A crucial task for our society today is to reverse the order of emphasis and visibility of these environments.*

How might we know that the relational environments are where God would have us concentrate? Simply put, these are the same areas Christ spent His time developing and where His teaching is focused.

Where do you think God would have us search for answers regarding drugs, crime, divorce, suicide, depression, teenage pregnancies, sexually transmitted diseases, and litigation? In the material and cognitive realms, or in the relational ones? Our society tries in vain to remedy these problems using the popular notions of progress—appropriating more money (that is, material/physical answers) and setting up more classes (that is, cognitive/educational answers). But insufficient funds and lack of education are not the problems. The problem is lack of love.

With the establishment of a proper emphasis, all appropriate needs will be met. Should we fail in this task, however, progress will only bring us increasing pain. Our wallets will get fatter, our houses bigger, our cars faster, and our brains smarter. Yet when we neglect the most important priorities, our final reward will fittingly be all the unhappiness money can buy.

MEASURING PROGRESS

Progress—tempting, willful, arrogant, divisive, unruly, godlike—what shall we do with you? We have trusted your guidance and followed your lead. In many ways, you've tried to build a successful world. But you have been getting us into trouble of late. We need to stop doing the things that get us into trouble and start doing better things.

"The whole point," contends Schumacher, "is to determine what constitutes progress."[22] What *should* constitute progress? Suspending our "chronological arrogance," let's stay with the British and back up to the days before progress had much momentum. Two centuries ago, an eloquent statesman stood before England and battled tirelessly—and successfully—the evils of slavery. William Wilberforce served in Parliament for forty-five years, universally honored for his integrity.

In his influential writings, Wilberforce makes several references to the importance of progress. Yet it is not progress in wealth, education, and power that he speaks of, but instead, progress in virtue. This, he suggests, could be measured by "the fear and love of God and of Christ; love, kindness, and meekness toward our fellow men; indifference to the possessions and events of this life compared with our concern about eternity; self-denial and humility."[23] It does not sound much like our current definition of progress, but it *does* sound hopeful.

Discerning Christians have long known that God is not impressed with our wealth, education, or power.[24] Nevertheless, we have labored willingly in those fields. What if, instead, we were to begin measuring our progress not by our wealth but by our virtue; not by our education but by our humility; and not by our power but by our meekness?

Graduate degrees and GNPs will never usher in the Kingdom—only love can do that. And love brings us back to Wilberforce: "Above all, measure your progress by your experience of the love of God and its exercise before men."[25]

The Pain of Problems

A few years ago, I attended a late-night delivery by a very young-looking twenty-two-year-old mother. As I was the faculty member "on call" and was simply assisting the resident with the case, I had not met the family before.

This was Brenda's first baby. She was acting bravely despite her obvious discomfort. An occasional cry escaped as the contraction peaked. Then she would close her eyes in exhaustion and await the next wave of pain.

The nurse who both coached and comforted Brenda would occasionally glance over to the window ledge where the husband sat watching television. Brenda had a long second stage of labor, and we were in the room for over two hours. But I never heard him utter a sound.

The resident and nurse were doing most of the work with the patient, so I just stood back and watched. Then I leaned against the wall and watched. Then I sat down and watched. I was tired. But despite my tiredness, I was also fascinated by the increasingly bizarre social event that was unfolding in the room.

It was around midnight. Brenda's labor happened to coincide with the end of one slasher-type movie and the beginning of another. The final hour of the first movie was filled with violence. I counted at least ten different extended sequences of knifings, bloody machine gun fights, and exploding cars and boats.

The nurse and I looked at each other and rolled our eyes in disgust. Should I use my authority to demand that the set be turned off? I thought about it for a while and then decided the husband might pull out his own submachine gun and blow me away. Anyway, the first movie was mercifully wrapping up, body bags all over the place.

By this time, the baby's head was crowning. Brenda was still fairly well controlled, but her cries were getting louder and lasting longer. Another ten minutes, I figured.

Still no response from the husband, who was settling in for the beginning of the next movie. On the television screen, a mother, father, and small child were strolling down a big-city street when they stopped to watch a clown act. Suddenly, one of the clowns grabbed the little boy by the hand and took off running across the street. With the boy yelling "Daddy, Daddy!" the clown leaped into the back of a waiting van, the father in pursuit. Just as the vehicle started to pull away, the father tore open the back door. The clown inside shot the father pointblank in the face. Blood was everywhere.

Just then—*exactly* then—Brenda screamed and the baby was born.

Go back inside, little one, I thought. *You really don't know what kind of world awaits you.*

DIFFERENT GAME, DIFFERENT RULES, DIFFERENT STAGE

As this baby will surely grow up to discover, we live in a problem-laden world. If these problems would stay in one place, perhaps we'd have a better chance at solving them. But progress has given them wings. And with the advantage of speed, problems are harder to hit than a swooping bat at midnight.

Not only have problems picked up speed, but so has history itself. The flow of history is now the flood of history. The "throughput" of change, information, and people has accelerated explosively. Despite our best attempts to manage the sweep of events, history has escaped. Now we count ourselves fortunate if we are even able to track it, let alone predict it, interpret it, or manage it.

In the past, as we have already noted, progress implied upward and onward, and we developed a linear, ascending way of thinking.

Somewhere in the last few decades, however, we took a quantum leap off the straight line. The astounding acceleration of change and the increasing complexity and interrelatedness of issues have time-warped us into a new era. "If failure to grasp this fact impairs one's ability to understand the present," observes Alvin Toffler, "it also leads otherwise intelligent men into total stupidity when they talk about the future. It encourages them to think in simple-minded straight lines."[1]

Despite uninformed claims to the contrary, we live in an unprecedented day with unprecedented problems. We have been disarticulated from our own past and do not yet know how to deal with the present, let alone the future. Having been selected to live out this great drama, we are playing a different game by different rules on a different stage than any other people in the history of the world.

SKEPTICS AND STOICS

That we live in an unprecedented era with unprecedented problems would seem to be self-evident, yet I have difficulty convincing people of this. When I explain the concept, nine out of ten do not have the slightest idea what I am talking about.

Many of these people can be characterized as *skeptics*. Attempting to understand the reason for their skepticism, I finally realized that most in our modern age are simply not trend-perceptive. The vast majority see only the little bits and pieces around them that reach back to last week and forward to tomorrow. From this vantage point, skeptics insist our situation is not unprecedented because "there is nothing new under the sun."

The *stoics* also disbelieve. They especially disdain the whining and sniveling of the weak who complain incessantly about life's problems. When you discuss the unprecedented difficulties of the age with them, a challenge invariably results: "I don't believe life is any different now. Sure, that little newborn baby might have a difficult life—but people have *always* had problems and always will. If you went back to the 'good old days,' you couldn't stand it for a week. You'd come flying back to the 'troubled' twentieth century in a flash!"

THE GOLDEN FRAME OF NOSTALGIA

Too often the discussion of contemporary problems ends up being detoured by this same debate about the past. People assume that expressing concerns about today's world implies a preference for yesterday's world. But this is a detour I don't wish to make.

Comparisons with the past are risky. Our tendency is to select what we wish to remember and conveniently forget the rest. "Christians in particular are prone to abbreviate the historical record, pruning from the past that which is messy," explains Notre Dame historian Nathan Hatch. "By a subtle and often unconscious process we pick out of the historical tapestry only those strands which reinforce our own points of view."[2] Or, as Jackie Gleason quipped, "The past remembers better than it lived." So when I say that our age is difficult and our problems are unprecedented, it does not mean I am pining for a romanticized past. It only means that our age is difficult and our problems are unprecedented.

In fairness to the skeptics and stoics, I will concede that comparisons between times present and times past do reveal several similarities:

▶ We have problems, and our ancestors had problems.
▶ Our problems are painful, and our ancestors' problems were painful.
▶ We have some advantages in our lifestyle, and our ancestors had some advantages in their lifestyle.

All of this is true—so far as it goes. But where we differ radically from our ancestors and indeed, even from our own recent past, is that suddenly, almost overnight, an entire new wave of social, technological, and economic experience has descended upon us. It is as if history sneezed, and we have been thrown into a different trajectory.

The list in figure 3.1 illustrates how, in a very pervasive sense, our day is unique. Many readers will scan the list and think, "There is nothing very special about these issues." But this is only true for those who are not trend-perceptive, who think in terms of three weeks instead of three decades.

Figure 3.1—Unprecedented . . .
a partial list

Speed of travel	Power of computers
Information age	Litigation levels
Collapse of information float	Specialization
Speed of communication	Number of scientists/researchers

Technological advances	Energy utilization and dependence
Shrinking world	Nuclear waste-disposal problems
Tightly coupled world system	Destructive power of weaponry
National indebtedness	Electronic money
International indebtedness	Mobility
Corporate indebtedness	Complexity
Personal indebtedness	Media pervasiveness and power
Pervasiveness of pollution	Population congestion
Vulnerability to terrorism	Traffic congestion, land and air
Overpopulated prisons	Availability of illicit drugs
AIDS	Abortion
Aging populace	Disintegration of extended family
Prevalence of divorce	Changing role of women
Disappearance of traditions	Daycare for children

Each item listed has played a significant role in making our era different from all those that preceded it. And when we factor in the interrelatedness of issues, the dimensions involved, and the speed of change, then unprecedented becomes too mild a word.

To help us understand it better, let's explore how the claim "unprecedented" is both a statement of history and, importantly, a statement of mathematics.

LESSONS OF HISTORY

History is a valuable teacher. Yet when I maintain that we live in an unprecedented era, it implies that the lessons of history will only be marginally successful in framing our questions and suggesting our remedies. Having navigated ourselves off the map, we do not know what is around the next bend. Furthermore, we cannot depend on the lessons of history to tell us, for history, too, has never been here before.

"One of the reasons we have not been as good at understanding change as we might have been," explains futurist Harry Clay Blaney III, "is that we are taught about a past world as if it were still existing; we are preparing ourselves for a world we no longer face. Even now our schools teach about the world of past decades and largely ignore the present let alone the future."[3]

I am certainly not intending to deprecate the tremendous value of a historical perspective. I am aware that to disqualify history, even partially, is at best presumptuous and at worst idiotic. We should all be warned, however, that at this particular juncture, an analysis of the past could be more misleading than revealing when it comes to understanding the uniqueness of our day and the dangers of tomorrow.

Many historians will get their hackles up, and I cannot say I blame them. It is a wild idea. However, it is born of an analysis, not of straight lines or cyclical theory, but of mathematical exponentiality.

THE EXPONENTIAL CURVE

One major reason our problems today are unprecedented is because the mathematics are different. Many of the linear lines that in the past described our lives well have now disappeared. Replacing them are lines that slope upward exponentially.

Figure 3.2

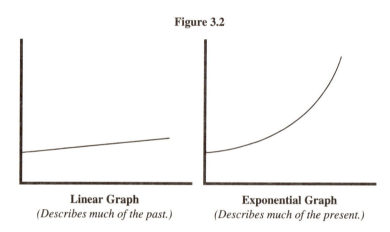

Linear Graph
(Describes much of the past.)
    Exponential Graph
(Describes much of the present.)

These figures help us to understand what is happening in our society in a *quantitative* way. The linear graph on the left represents how most of life used to unfold. In contrast, an increasing amount of today's experience is better described, even if approximately, by the exponential curve on the right.

Because there is little in our day-to-day lives that changes exponentially, we tend to think and plan with a linear mind-set. The sun rises and the sun sets. Twenty-four hours is still only twenty-four hours. Week after week, everything seems about the same.

Meanwhile, largely unnoticed by us, history has shifted to fast forward. If linear still best describes our personal lives, exponential now best describes much of historical change. The significance of this is incalculable, yet the typical American, not knowing how to think in exponential terms, consistently underestimates it.

To illustrate how rapidly exponential numbers accumulate and why they are so hard for us to envision, long-range forecaster J. Scott Armstrong gave a graduate class of twenty business students the following puzzle: If you folded a piece of paper in half forty times, how thick would the result be? The answers given were as follows:

Answer	Number of Students
Less than one foot	13
Greater than one foot, up to one mile	5
Greater than one mile, up to 2000 miles	2
Greater than 2000 miles	0

The correct answer is that the paper would be thick enough to reach from here to the moon![4] Such an answer is more than unexpected—to most of us, it is incomprehensible. This is why it is so hard to appreciate the radical quantitative dimensions of contemporary change. Yet unexpected or not, incomprehensible or not, changes that—at least for a time—follow an exponentially increasing curve are what we must often now contend with.

The appendix contains many graphs demonstrating such exponential change. This compilation of graphs is diverse—from population to prisoners, from advertising to air travel, from divorce to debt. Even a glance will provide abundant evidence that the circumstances of our age *are* different from anything previously encountered. Once we grasp this quantitative uniqueness, we will be in a much better position to understand what is happening in the world around us.

LIMITS

Because so much in life has now shifted to exponential terms, the issue of limits has suddenly become an important one. We coast along for decades on the slow-growth portion of the exponential curve without encountering significant limit problems. Then, suddenly, we hit our head on the ceiling.

Previously, there was abundant margin in the world system, and we did not have to worry about limits. We could grow, expand, and waste as much as we wanted without worry. This is no longer the case. We have met or exceeded limits in scores of areas, but we do not know how to pull back. How do you slow a careening world when the throttle is stuck wide-open?

All things have limits—people, governments, buildings, bridges, brains, and organizations. Even more subjective things such as friendships, creativity, or adaptability have limits. If we are well within boundaries, we can be expansive and growth-oriented. When approaching a limit, however, the rules change.

If a car goes twenty miles per hour, there will be few problems. If, however, that car goes two hundred miles per hour, all kinds of dangers arise. Cars have limits.

In a similar way, progress has limits. Some limits are external (for example, environmental, material, economic) while others are internal (for example, psychological, social, spiritual). Since we are impinging on many of these limits, much of our life experience is now traveling through uncharted territory. And because margin is closely related to the issue of limits, most of it has disappeared.

EXPONENTIALITY AND PROBLEMS

Up to this point I have not necessarily implied that exponentiality is a negative phenomenon. Just because something changes exponentially does not mean the development is automatically painful. In fact, such rapid changes can be positive (as in the accumulation of interest on your bank account), mixed (as in the rapidly increasing numbers of elderly), or negative (as in the astounding rise in health-care costs). This "negative" category is what should concern us. For when we apply the principles of exponential growth to our *problems*, we find ourselves quickly mired in deep trouble. Crisis points are reached almost overnight.

When we realize that exponentiality approximates the growth pattern of such problems as national debt, health-care costs, complexity, the prison population, births to unmarried women, the number of divorces, litigation rates, bank failures, and bankruptcies, then it becomes clear that we are in trouble. (Again, see the appendix.) And it is trouble of a dimension foreign to human experience. Maybe we can solve the problems, maybe we can survive, maybe we can even thrive. But the simple truth is—no one knows.

THE S-CURVE

Obviously, the mathematics of human experience can't actually go to infinity. All things stop before that, even explosions. For example, if previous exponential curves for projecting human longevity and vehicular speed had continued, by the year 2000 humans would be able to live forever and travel at the speed of light.[5]

When most exponential slopes approach the impossible, they begin to level off again. This often results in a slope called the logistic curve, or the "S-curve." (The pure exponential curve, in contrast, is called the "J-curve.") The point at which the exponential curve begins sloping into the S-curve is called the turning point. Predicting where this turning point will occur is important but difficult. If it comes early we will be okay. But if it comes late, acceleration alone will cause widespread breakdown in many of our social systems.

Figure 3.3

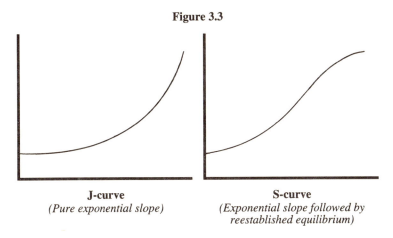

J-curve
(Pure exponential slope)

S-curve
(Exponential slope followed by reestablished equilibrium)

Realizing that the S-curve lies ahead gives us some respite from our anxiety. And this respite is valid. But we should not be complacent. That we have leaped off the linear and onto the exponential is a very significant phenomenon, a historical disruption. A disruption of this magnitude makes it an exciting day in which to live—in a frightening sort of way.

ISOLATE OR INTEGRATE?

There are two ways (at least) to address our many problems. The first way is to *isolate* each one, treating each as a single independent entity. If we were to apply this strategy to our long list, each individual problem would no doubt be solvable. Dealing with one problem at a time is not a bad strategy with which to approach life, particularly a very complex life. The analytical, reductionistic strategy is, in many instances, the correct approach. We dissect and analyze, and once we can wrap a plan around the difficulty, we go for it.

The second approach, to *integrate* them all together, is an entirely different proposition. Here we use a wide-angle lens instead of a microscope. Stepping back, back, back . . . until the integrated picture comes into view, we learn some things we did not suspect when studying only isolated problems. Seeing everything together and connected gives us a more accurate assessment of the immensity that confronts us. It is this perspective that is so troubling about our modern-day situation.

This sort of integration, though essential, is seldom done because it is very difficult. Yet if we wish to accurately understand the uniqueness of both our day and our problems, it is an effort we must make.

Let me illustrate why this is true. If a patient comes to the clinic with diabetes, I can usually control the problem. But if I discover this same patient also has heart disease, renal failure, and pneumonia, the prognosis is much different, that is, much worse. So simply saying the patient has diabetes is a significant thing to say, but we have not learned much about the whole patient. We must know the integrated picture, and we must understand the context of the disease. In some contexts, diabetes is manageable. In others, it is fatal.

Space shuttles can also have fatal diseases. Possibly the most complicated piece of machinery ever built, the *Challenger* had a million components when first assembled. Had we examined each individual piece of technology separately, we would have seen hundreds of thousands of flawlessly constructed and assembled parts. A marvel of human engineering. And yet it blew up. Therefore it was not a marvel—it was a disaster. The disaster, however, is only understood when the faulty O-rings are factored in with the other 99.9999 percent of perfectly functioning parts. The disaster, in other words, becomes apparent only when the analysis integrates all the technology together to discover how one flaw doomed the entire project in a tragic fireball.

One cannot even begin to assess how future forces will interact without factoring in each piece of important data. Futurists and forecasters understand the significance of integration. "The integrative thrust of futures studies constitutes, in fact, one of their most distinctive characteristics," explains international studies professor Barry Hughes. "And they are *integrative*, not just encompassing. 'Systems thinking,' popularly defined in the expression 'everything is connected to everything else,' has characterized most futures work."[6]

Yet, for the most part, integration is absent from the contemporary American landscape. Scientists, physicians, educators, analysts—all perhaps would adhere to integration in principle but practice its opposite. Information overload causes us to burrow ever deeper into specialization, subspecialization, and then supersubspecialization, thus effectively burying ourselves with our own problem. This is not to say that specialized analysis cannot yield useful information. But reducing all of life into ever smaller particles is taking us in the wrong direction. "What has failed at every level—from the society of nations to the national society to the local community to the family—is integration," observe the authors of *Habits of the Heart*. "When the world comes to us in pieces, in fragments, lacking any overall pattern, it is hard to see how it might be transformed."[7]

STEAMROLLED BY HISTORY

When we finally do open our eyes to the totality of what confronts us, it is frightening. It hurts, like looking at the sun. There is too much to take in. How do you talk about something this big other than in generalizations? Forced by dimension alone, back we go to debating just one problem, one detail, one statistic. Yet we must resist returning to the one-at-a-time strategy. We could, for example, be drawn back to discussing how acid rain might be decreased with more widespread use of flue-gas desulfurization scrubbers. And that might be a valuable discussion in one context. But it would also be like arguing over who's going to kill the cockroach in stateroom 219 as the *Titanic* nears its iceberg.

Even if we do not have the courage or vision to understand life in an integrated way, life *happens* to us integrated. Whether we like it or not, history will steamroll us with the whole, not with particles.

A MORNING IN THE OFFICE

Now, let's apply what we have learned about integration and see how it changes our perceptions. Come with me to the office. Look over my shoulder and see what pain looks like. Not the headache or bruised-knee kind of pain, but the kind of pain that swallows up human beings.

In medicine, there are two ways you can get through the day. One is to see each patient as an isolated problem and do all you can before the fifteen minutes are up. Then you move on to the next patient. This, in fact, is the way physicians usually work.

The other mode is the integrative approach, and it is much more time-consuming. But if you are serious about understanding the patient's pain, integration is essential. You back up and try to see the whole. You try to see the patient in the context of the patient's past and probable future. You look at the mental status, lifestyle, and health habits. You look at the family, the social-support network, and even the society.

Taking that approach on this Monday morning, see if you don't agree: something here disturbs.

Monday, 9:30 a.m.—Room 7
JACKIE: Postpartum Exam
Jackie is in for her six-week postpartum check. A twenty-one-year-old single mother of three, she left her husband at age sixteen but has not yet divorced him, despite living with another man since then.
    Her current boyfriend uses marijuana regularly.

Monday, 10:00 a.m.—Room 8
SONYA: Birth-Control Pills
A twenty-eight-year-old divorcée with four children, Sonya is requesting birth-control pills even though she doesn't have a sexual partner. There is a medical history of gonorrhea and pubic lice. She hasn't menstruated for twelve months since stabbing herself in the abdomen during an unsuccessful suicide attempt.

Monday, 10:15 a.m.—Room 9
CINDI: Prenatal Care
Cindi is a twenty-year-old unwed woman about to deliver her first baby. Herpes, chlamydia, and pelvic inflammatory disease have complicated the pregnancy.

Monday, 10:30 a.m.—Room 10
GWEN: Broken Arm
Gwen needs an X-ray. After she reported her boyfriend to the police for pushing drugs, he beat her up. While trying to run away, she fell and broke her arm. Gwen is now twenty-one. When she was only three, her mother died of an overdose of heroin. Her father was later shot to death by his girlfriend.

If, on this particular morning in May, I were to use the "assembly line" approach, nothing remarkable would have struck me. My first four patients consisted of a postpartum exam, contraceptive counseling, a prenatal visit, and a broken arm.

But I stepped back and opened my eyes a little further. Then my morning looked different. Using the lens of integration, these same four young women carried as baggage the painful problems of teenage pregnancies, unwed mothers, single parents, divorce, domestic violence, homicide, suicide attempts, unemployment, lack of education, drug overdoses, welfare, depression, cohabitation, illicit drug abuse, sexually transmitted diseases, and pelvic inflammatory disease.

Yes, it is a satisfying feeling to know that you have alleviated the pain burden of the world just a little bit. But it would be even more satisfying to know that the world you were working on was progressing in a better direction.

CONTEMPORARY ACCOUNTING

Perhaps you are still not convinced. "After all," you argue, "we have so many *benefits* to living in our modern day. Surely we can learn to live with these problems. If we counted up all the good and measured it against all the bad, we would *still* come out ahead. Besides, aren't we supposed to focus more on the positive things and not spend all of our time worrying about the negatives?"

Yes, of course we should always be grateful for the benefits. Yet problems are real, and they must be dealt with. Christ certainly lived a life of grace and gratitude—but He also dealt with problems head on.

There is an exceptionally dangerous trap here if we are not careful. It lies in the accounting method commonly used to calculate positives versus negatives. If, in analyzing this labyrinthine snarl we call the twentieth century, we were to use standard accounting methods, we would add up the credits and subtract the debits. A positive net balance indicates that a gain has been realized. Unfortunately, this summation method applied to contemporary conditions is misleading. Modernity is not cooperating with the accountant.

If we listed all the positives, we would have a very long list. There can be no question that we enjoy many advantages over previous generations. The trouble is revealed, however, when we begin to tabulate the negatives. Here we find a daunting list of problems that threatens the viability of our entire society. *If the negatives are sufficiently dangerous, they cannot be offset by the positives, no matter how beneficial the positives are.* You cannot simply subtract the negatives from the positives and look at the sum. The negatives must be accounted on their own.

To illustrate this principle, suppose we have a train with 500 cars bound for an impoverished Third-World village. Four hundred of these cars are loaded with all the bounty science has to offer: medicines, microscopes, computers, automobiles, televisions, telephones, libraries, food, and recreational equipment. An additional fifty cars are filled with tons and tons of gold. The remaining fifty cars, scattered throughout the length of the train, contain deadly viruses, pollutants, poisonous gases, heroin, cocaine, and nuclear weapons poised to explode should they be jostled inadvertently.

Now, what shall we say about this train? Is it a "good" train or a "bad" train? It has 450 "good" cars compared to only fifty "bad" cars. Will it bring blessing to the impoverished village it is headed for, or will it bring pain and disaster? Do we recommend it or condemn it?

Progress and the train have much in common. Progress, like the train, brings us many benefits but, at the same time, many problems. For progress to be simultaneously profitable and painful is annoying. Nevertheless, this coexistence of positives and negatives is exactly where we find ourselves. The positives bless, but the negatives can kill.

The *Challenger*'s positives outnumbered its negatives a million to one. Yet in seventy-three seconds, it was gone.

CRITICAL MASS

A serious question now presents itself: Is there a critical mass of problems beyond which a society—or, for that matter, an individual—will be destroyed no matter how wonderful the benefits it enjoys? If so, what is that critical mass? Are we approaching it? Have we reached it?

The first question I have already answered. Yes, there is a critical mass, for *if the negatives are sufficiently dangerous, they cannot be offset by the positives no matter how beneficial the positives are.*

What is that critical mass? Undetermined.

Are we approaching it? Without question.

Have we reached it? Possibly.

It is true that humankind has always had problems and always will. It is not true, however, that yesterday's problems and today's problems are automatically the same. To assert that all problems have equal weight is not only foolish but dangerous. No one has ever stood where we stand, nor has anyone ever faced what we face. We live in a paroxysm, and it is still uncertain as to whether it is a paroxysm we can survive.

When we integrate our criminal activity, urban war zones, street gangs, drug addiction, skyrocketing prison population, national debt, foreign trade deficit, corporate and consumer debt, savings and loan and banking crises, record closing of hospitals, soaring costs of health care and college education, deteriorating education, sexually transmitted diseases, hundreds of thousands of AIDS cases, alcoholism, family breakdown, divorce, teenage pregnancy, single parenting, child abuse, collapse of our child-protection system, increasing stress, complexity, overload, anxiety, depression, suicide, pollution, litigation, crumbling infrastructure, "death-oriented hopelessness" of the contemporary arts, and the vanishing of both tradition and community, we find that the specifics, the dimensions, and the threat are all very different today than ever before.

"As I've come to feel a deep sense of urgency about the Future Forces at work today, I've decided to do all I can to communicate to you the pressing need for action," writes Princeton pollster George Gallup, Jr. "If swift, forceful steps aren't taken to defuse the political and social time bombs facing us, we may well find ourselves on a track that could lead to the destruction of civilization as we know it."[8]

Many of the problems we have today are not new. "What *is* new," continues Gallup, "is the intensity with which they demand our attention." He concludes his book *Forecast 2000* with a warning shared by many futurists: "I'm sufficiently convinced that our society is heading in a dangerous direction that I feel compelled to sound a note of extreme urgency."[9]

SOME IMPLICATIONS

In my efforts to show how our contemporary problems are without precedent, I have escorted you through what is perhaps uncharted territory, land mined with concepts such as exponentiality, S-curves, integration, and accounting methods. In simplified terms, what are some implications of this discussion?

Margin—Our margin is negatively influenced by both the number and size of our problems. The *more* problems we have, the *less* margin we have. And the *larger* our problems become, the *smaller* our margin becomes.

Humility—Our problems are so unprecedented that we must never be complacent or self-assured concerning our ability to solve them. Just because we have solved our problems in the past says nothing about our ability to solve them now. We have never had problems like these before.

Quick catastrophes—Because the math is so different, problems can go from small to immense almost overnight. Indeed, many have—as, for example, the savings and loan fiasco. And, historically speaking, the disappearance of our margin happened in the blink of an eye.

Vigilance—Having learned about exponentiality, we now understand that our problems are growing much faster than we had previously believed. Having learned about integration, we now understand that our problems are far more interconnected than we perhaps thought. And having learned about contemporary accounting, we now understand that the danger of our problems can't always be offset by the many positives we enjoy.

It is a day for vigilance. If something historic is happening, the Church should not be the last to know.

The power of evil—When exponential growth is applied to money, power, speed, communications, and technology, society might be benefited—but so is evil. Evil today has more power at its disposal than ever before.

My greatest worry about our prospects for the future stems from a full awareness of the following linkage: (1) Mankind is fallen and capable of limitless acts of evil, and (2) progress exponentially increases the power available for the purposes of evil.

Think about it.

Relational collapse—A frightful consequence of the dramatic changes of the last few decades is how rapidly and thoroughly the relational life has come unglued. It has amounted to not only a social revolution but also an unprecedented social catastrophe. And yet it has been largely ignored by many futurists. The common focus of most long-range forecasting is the economy, resources, energy, pollution, population, education, and technology. But what about relationships? Neglecting to factor in the state of the relational life is surely incomplete integration. Our society could easily succumb to internal dissonance long before the external threats become fatal.

Nearly all indices of the scripturally prescribed relational life have suffered major setbacks over the last three decades. Marriage—worse; parenting—worse; the extended family—worse; the sense of community—worse; social-support systems—worse; church commitment—worse; church unity—worse; and one-anothering in the church—worse. And it happened seemingly overnight. Little wonder our pains are so acute.

THE DISAPPEARANCE OF MARGIN

Whatever happened to margin? It was steamrolled by history. Let's go back and see how this happened.

First, we start with margin. As noted, progress is the enemy of margin, and they have competed from the start. While margin can usually be counted upon to stay in one place, progress is always on the move—otherwise it would not be progress. After a time, progress turned over the speed controls to exponentiality, and we shifted into overdrive. Limits were hit with frightening suddenness. The speed and complexity of these developments were unprecedented, causing widespread confusion and pain.

Margin, the space that once existed between ourselves and our limits, was an early casualty. When you reach the limits of your resources or abilities, you have no margin left. So as history and progress picked up speed, we hit limit after limit. Slowly, margin began to disappear. Then when exponentiality took over the controls, margin vaporized.

Now that we have exceeded so many of our limits—personal, emotional, relational, physical, financial—we have no margin at all. Yet because we don't even know what margin is, we don't realize it is gone. We know that something is not right, but we can't solve the puzzle beyond that. Our pain is palpable, but our assailant remains unnamed.

Much of this pain is in our relational life: to self, to others, to God. We *miss* margin in many areas. But we *require* it in our relationships. We need to get it back.

When we have no margin and our limits have been exceeded; when we are besieged by pain, stress, and overload; when our relational life is ailing; when it seems the flood of events is beyond our control; then problems take on a different dimension. One at a time they are perhaps manageable. But they just won't stand in line. Instead, they grow from problem pile into problem mountain and then all fall on us at the same time.

NOT GLOBALONEY

After looking at our problem mountain—whether global, societal, or individual—and doing the work of integration, there are four judgments we can make: *Our problems are real* (not artifacts), *they are systemic* (not superficial), *they are serious* (not globaloney), *and they are unprecedented* (not a simple continuation of what we have always known).

If we are strong, we can confront our problems—even if they are real, systemic, serious, and unprecedented. If, however, we have been bled to death by stressful, marginless living, we may be defeated before we even start.

It is hard to solve the problems of the world when you can't even make it through the next day.

The Pain of Stress

Many of the annoyances of modernity do not yield to quick analysis. We wouldn't exactly label them evils—more like frustrations or nuisances. They are more like heartburn than homicide. You can't really pick out a villain, yet you have a headache anyway. Sometimes you suspect there must be a computer virus hiding deep inside the center of the earth, clogging up all its gears. Maybe that's why so many things continue to backfire after all these years. It's confusing: We have all this information but still can't seem to figure out what we need to know to solve our problems.

Why does the airplane keep arriving late—wouldn't you think they'd have that worked out by now? Why can't the person using the sophisticated computer seem to clear up my magazine subscription? Why doesn't the Internal Revenue Service know the answers to its own questions? What causes people to shoot at total strangers on the freeway? Whatever happened to friendly clerks? Why does the addition of yet one more program at my local church sound like a penalty rather than an opportunity? Why is it we don't feel confident that when the world awakens tomorrow, we will all be one day closer to victory?

YET ANOTHER POLLUTANT

High levels of stress follow as naturally after progress as does exhaust after traffic. It is a byproduct of our age, yet another societal pollutant. Nearly every patient I see leads a life influenced in some way by inordinate levels of stress. Pick up any periodical at the public library—on farming, business, psychology, health, teaching, religion, sports, fashion, or family—and see if it doesn't contain an article mentioning the subject. "Death and taxes aren't the only sure things anymore," comments one such periodical. "Stress has become an inevitable part of life for most people."[1]

Four out of five Americans report a need to reduce stress in their lives. Because these painful stressors are so ubiquitous and our coping skills so poorly developed, many resort to tranquilizers. Why, in such a prosperous age, is it necessary to sedate so many?

"More and more tranquilizers, stimulants and other 'happy' pills are handed out every year, but they serve only to hide the cause of the problem," comments world-renowned surgeon Christiaan Barnard. "We have to find and remove or reduce the stress."[2] The negative aspects of stress disable not only our personal lives and the lives of our families but the workplace as well. According to the American Institute of Stress, stress-related illnesses cost the American economy $100 billion annually.

OUR RESPONSE TO CHANGE

Hans Selye, the late Canadian endocrinologist and "father" of stress research, defines stress as *the nonspecific response of the body to any demand made upon it*."[3] This definition is contrary to the popular thinking that defines stress as an unpleasant circumstance, such as tax time or a screaming baby. Stress is *not* the circumstance, it is our *response* to the circumstance. It is not "out there" but rather *inside us*.

It makes little difference if the situation we react to is a positive one, such as buying a new home, or a negative one, such as bankruptcy. Although the ultimate consequences of frustrating stress can be very different from those of rewarding stress, nevertheless, the initial adaptive response mechanism is similar in both cases. Merely encountering the word *stress* should not connote a positive or a negative feeling (though it probably does). The word only describes an entirely normal psychophysiological process without which we would die.

Our bodies are constantly adapting to the environment. This adaptation is a marvelous process, more intricate than we imagine. It involves the brain and nervous system, the heart and circulatory system, the liver and spleen, the adrenal glands and immune system, and many other organs as well. An incredibly sophisticated communication network functions continuously at a low level. It is on perpetual standby alert, monitoring for sudden changes in the environment. At times of increased need the system surges, preparing us for any necessary response.

This stress system is important and, in fact, vital. When it is overactive, however, damage can result. While stress itself need not be destructive, the overstimulation of an uncontrolled stress response may be both painful and destructive.

Stress then is the name given to the normal internal physiological mechanism that adapts us to change. *Distress* is the negative, destructive aspect of this mechanism, and *eustress* is the positive, constructive aspect of the adaptation response. *Hyperstress* describes a condition whereby the system is stimulated too often for too long. *Stressors* are those environmental changes that set in motion the adaptation response.

EUSTRESS, DISTRESS, HYPERSTRESS

Many of us, often without realizing it, use stress to our advantage. This eustress energizes us. It is what football players call "psyching up" before a game. Eustress is what makes us especially creative before a deadline, when concentration and efficiency are so much easier. It is what a doctor uses in the middle of the night to shake off somnolence when an ambulance brings in an accident victim. Or what sleeping mothers use when they hear an infant gagging in the next room and they have to be instantly awake. This is what employers consciously induce in a work environment to make employees alert and productive—a kind of creative tension. Some people love this feeling, thrive on it, and almost become addicted to it.

When the stress response becomes negative or destructive, it is acurately called distress. This is what most of us mean when we use the word *stress*. We are really referring to the negative aspects of stress, or distress.

An excessive volume of stress is called hyperstress. The volume is important because how we deal with stress depends on how much of it we are confronted with and what type of personality we have. If the amounts are manageable, we can learn to avoid distress and possibly turn it into eustress. If, however, the amounts are at hyperstress levels, then stress reduction is more important than stress management.

Clarifying Stress Terms

STRESS: the normal internal physiological mechanism that responds to and adapts us to change

DISTRESS: the negative, destructive aspect of stress

EUSTRESS: the positive, constructive aspect of stress

HYPERSTRESS: a condition whereby the stress response is stimulated too often for too long

STRESSORS: those environmental changes that set in motion the stress adaptation response

NO ONE TO SLUG

When we encounter a stressor, our body reacts with a cascade of neurohormonal changes. The brain releases CRF (corticotropin releasing factor), which immediately arouses the entire central nervous system. In turn, the central nervous system triggers at least three reactions: the sympathetic nervous system releases adrenaline and other similar hormones; the pituitary gland releases multiple hormones, including ACTH (adrenocorticotropic hormone), which causes the adrenal glands to put out the hormone cortisol; and the brain releases natural painkillers such as endorphins. As a result of this rapid deployment, we are instantly more alert, have more oxygen and sugar available, and shunt more blood to the brain and muscles. Such a reaction is called the "fight or flight" phenomenon. It perhaps served humankind well for most of our history, but today, notes cardiologist and stress expert Robert Eliot, "Nature's plan is seldom appropriate, for there is no one to slug and there is no place to run."

Dr. Selye classifies the stress response or General Adaptation Syndrome as having three phases: the Alarm Stage, the Resistance Stage, and the Exhaustion Stage. The Alarm Stage is the "fight or flight" phenomenon noted above. Following the Alarm Stage comes the Resistance Stage, a period of vigilance and resistance. Such vigilance cannot be sustained for long, however, and the Exhaustion Stage follows.

Once we understand this sequence, the implications may begin to clarify some of our own behavior patterns. If we trigger the response too frequently, we will be in states of alarm or resistance too often. This overdosing on our own adrenaline has potentially serious adverse consequences.

If the stress reaction is resolved in a way that results in success, no apparent damage is noticed. If, however, the result is failure or frustration, multiple pathologies may ensue: tissue aging occurs at the cellular level; the immune system may malfunction, leading to infection or cancer; cardiovascular catastrophies, such as stroke, heart attack, or arrhythmias, may occur. We feel the pain, and the pain is real. "Each period of stress, especially if it results from frustrating, unsuccessful struggles, leaves some irreversible chemical scars which accumulate to constitute the signs of tissue aging," explains Selye.[4]

Selye's research appears to indicate that humans have only a limited supply of deep adaptive energy. Most of the energy expended in the stress response can be recovered through rest. But a certain amount of this energy resource may be irretrievably lost. For this reason, it is important to reserve this adaptive energy for those occasions where the issues are significant and not to squander it on trivial conflicts.[5]

Let me illustrate further. At the risk of being overly simplistic, perhaps we can make a comparison between stress and driving an automobile. Every time we enter into a stress response, we are taking our car for a ride. When the gas tank runs out, we can always fill it up again (replenishing our supply of superficial adaptive energy). Yet each trip also puts wear and tear on the vehicle that is irreversible (depleting our supply of deep adaptive energy). This is not a reason to never drive. But it is a caution to beware what kind of trips we take.

IS IT WORSE TODAY?

Stress has been called a national epidemic. Is it a modern disease? Haven't people always had stresses? The answer to both questions is yes. Humankind has always had problems, and many of them were caused by stress or resulted in distress. Yet our current stress plague differs both quantitatively and qualitatively from the experience of our ancestors. Conditions of our modern age tend to overstimulate our stress-response system more than in previous times, and many of the issues are too complex for successful resolution.

"But look at the statistics," you protest. "Infant mortality is down and life expectancy is up. We have one of the highest standards of living in the world. The elderly have Social Security and Medicare, while the poor have food stamps and Medicaid." Yes, and we all have stress. It is woven as tightly into the fabric of modern life as is television.

No one in the history of humankind has ever had to live with the stressors we have acting upon us today. They are unprecedented. The human spirit is called upon to withstand pressures that have never before been encountered.

Our stress levels are unprecedented for many reasons. Some have already been discussed in the previous chapters, and more will be discussed throughout the book. Exponential change is one stressor we dare not underestimate. Universal indebtedness is a relatively new stressful phenomenon. Hurry and noise contribute their share to our stress load. Complexity and overload remain hidden to most people's understanding but are crushing stressors. Both parents working stresses the parents, the family unit, and the children. Child-development experts repeatedly warn that children are pressed to grow up too soon.

Child psychologist David Elkind believes there are at least three contemporary sources of stress that mark our age as a difficult one. First, due to the alarming increase in violence and crime, we are more *afraid*. Second, due to rapidly changing job markets, technology, and economic factors, we are more professionally *insecure*. Finally, due to widespread separation and divorce, we are more *alone*.[6]

Such "aloneness" is a more important factor in stress disease than most realize. Social supports have been bowled over by progress. Although affirming relationships are probably the single best protector against stress-induced damage, we live in an impersonal world. *Study after study* confirms that a healthy marriage, family, or community support structure yields better health and increased longevity—a kind of buffering system against the pain of distress.

One of the largest surveys followed five thousand residents of Alameda County, California, for nine years. The conclusion? After correcting for all other variables: "Those who were unmarried, had few friends or relatives and shunned community organizations were more than twice as likely to die during that time than people who had these social relationships."[7]

Understanding the linkage between supports and stress helps us to define a contemporary trend: Over the last several decades, stresses, expectations, and pressures have increased, while social and emotional support systems have decreased. It is little wonder, then, that stress disorders are experienced in nearly every household.

PHYSICAL STRESS, MENTAL STRESS

An additional contribution to our stress problem is revealed by examining the difference between physical and mental pressures. Our bodies distinguish between stressors that are mental in nature and those that are physical. Physical hard work, for example, is not really a stressor at all, as long as one has some control over it. One can work twelve hours a day, six days a week for an entire life at hard physical labor and suffer no ill effects—as long as the person has decision-control over the work schedule. As a matter of fact, such hard physical labor would almost certainly have salutary health benefits. But if the strain is mental and a person is constantly being frustrated and thwarted, the negative health effects can be catastrophic.

"Even the greatest experts in the field do not know why the stress of frustration is so much more likely than that of excessive muscular work to produce disease (peptic ulcers, migraine, high blood pressure, or even a simple 'pain in the neck')," admits Dr. Selye. "In fact, physical exercise can even relax and help us withstand mental frustration. . . . Certain emotional factors, such as frustration, are particularly likely to turn stress into distress, whereas in most instances, physical exercise has an opposite effect."[8]

In one study, a patient was first given a cardiac treadmill exam. Despite vigorous physical exercise, the patient's cardiovascular status remained normal throughout. He then was asked to subtract seven from 777 serially for three-and-one-half minutes. His blood pressure went up forty points. Similar results have been achieved in other studies. Certain biochemical stress parameters, such as plasma cortisol levels, are more affected by psychological stressors than by physical stressors. Chronic uncertainty, sustained levels of increased vigilance, or struggling with a mental task are more stressful than chopping wood.

"The widespread substitution of mental strain for physical strain is no advantage from our point of view," maintained E. F. Schumacher. "Proper physical work, even if strenuous, does not absorb a great deal of the power of attention, but mental work does; so that there is no attention left over for the spiritual things that really matter. It is obviously much easier for a hard-working peasant to keep his mind attuned to the divine than for a strained office worker."9

SPICE OF LIFE, KISS OF DEATH

Individuals differ significantly regarding how much stress is desirable or what types of events are stressful. What strains some does not bother others. I, for example, do not mind waiting in lines but do not enjoy going to formal parties. Another person might react the opposite—despising lines but loving parties. A stressor that for one might be pleasure, for another might be pain. For one, the spice of life; for another, the kiss of death.

Some people desire a low level of stress to feel comfortable. Our modern pace was not particularly designed with them in mind. Others seek a high, almost frenzied level of stress and seem to thrive on it. Different stressors, different personalities, different results. Let's look at some of these.

Type A

The type A personality, usually male, is commonly characterized as "driven." Their most common traits are a sense of time urgency and free-floating hostility. Type As have a drive to control others, an aggressiveness and competitiveness characterized by a need to win, and a tendency toward self-destruction. They think multiple thoughts and do multiple actions at the same time. Margin is not a priority to preserve but a gap to be filled.

These hardworking, time-pressured individuals are more prone to cardiovascular disease. (Of the thirty-one traits identified, hostility is the most pathogenic.)10 Their carburetors are set on high, and they surge into overdrive at the slightest provocation. One physician describes "a distinct profile of the vigilant male beset with internal fury and living in a state of relentless, joyless striving."11

Most people find a vacation relaxing, but type As often do not. Relaxing is one of the most stressful things on their agenda, which is why they seldom do it. Progress and type As feed on each other. They are very productive people and usually the leaders of companies, programs, or institutions. They live on a high level of stress, however, and have significant health problems because of it.

The Extrovert or Introvert

The introvert is a personality type vulnerable to the stresses of the crowd. Introverts like to be alone. They appreciate quiet, solitude, and time to think and feel in their own internal world. They generally do not like having a large number of social interactions, going to parties, or meeting new people.

The majority of Americans (by a three-to-one margin), however, are extroverts, and extroverts are energized by such social exchange. Extroverts usually don't understand introverts and try to push them into situations where they simply don't wish to be.

The Depressed or Anxious

Another group of people in a special stress category are those who have generalized depression or anxiety. According to psychologist Judy Eidelson and psychiatrist David Burns, "depression is the certainty that things *are* horrible and hopeless; anxiety is the belief that at any moment things *will become* horrible and hopeless."[12] Whether depressed, anxious, or both, these people feel pressure from stressors that are inflated or sometimes not even there at all.

Some, for example, are always stressed when they ride in a car. They have never been in an accident but are fearful that today will be the day. Every car they pass along the route, therefore, becomes a stressor. These anxious and/or depressed people will be burdened much of their lives simply because they perceive stressors as more of a threat than they really are. One important lesson emerges from such an illustration: Often our *perception* of the stressor damages us more than the stressor itself.

The Elderly

Some evidence indicates that mental stressors induce more tension in the elderly than in the young. Performing serial seven subtraction is only mildly stressful for those in their twenties. Many elderly, however, are hyperresponsive to such stimuli and become agitated in performing the task.

Children

Pediatricians, child psychologists, and developmental experts all believe that our current age is more stressful for children. According to one Harris poll, three of every four adults agree. Social change is too rapid, competition is too stiff, and expectations have risen too high. Added to the host of already oppressive burdens are children's insecurities about family stability. Children have a great stake in whether their parents stay together or not, but virtually no control over the issue.

CONTEMPORARY STRESSORS

Life is full of the daily *minor struggles*: ringing telephones, fighting children, traffic jams, and overdue bills. These chip away at our lightheartedness and erode our joy. Then there are the *major struggles*, such as the infirmities of aging, the loss of a job, or the divorce of your closest friends. These stressors don't chip, they detonate. We reel under the impact, and the pain is often palpable.

Our lives are riddled with stressors that intersect and cross-connect in a hundred different ways. It is often hard to separate them, to discern patterns. We feel ourselves being hit but cannot pin down the enemy. Yet identifying the stressors *is* an important task. Without correct isolation of the culprit, we will be ill-equipped to defend ourselves.

Our stress diet selects from a diverse menu. The following are some of the most prominent items.

Change—Do not underestimate it. We pay a price for each change we must adapt to. The Life Change Index is one scale that quantifies change and assigns a corresponding health risk: The greater the change, the higher the risk. Yet how to control the pace of change has so far eluded us.

Mobility—Mobility is a subset of change. People move, for the most part, because of perceived advantages. Each move, however, entails an adaptation to the new environment (which is stressful) plus a severing of old ties (oftentimes even more stressful).

Expectations—Modernity has increased our expectations but has not permitted a commensurate ability to meet them. Frustration results. This might occur in athletic skill, academic performance, physical attractiveness, occupational prestige, family functioning, or fulfillment of "the good life."

Time pressure—The clock dominates our schedule as never before in history. We have more activities to arrive at and more deadlines to meet. Most of us are all too familiar with the feeling of panic as an appointed hour nears with work yet undone.

We are ruled not by the week or day but by the minute. Margin would like to help free us from the reign of the clock but so far has had little cooperation from us.

Work—For many, distress and work are the same word. There is, for example, the Boston obstetrician who left his practice and opened a laundromat instead. Or the commercial airline pilot who, after waiting in line to take off, taxied back to the terminal, walked off the plane, and quit. Or the advertising salesman who shouted so loudly at his boss that he punctured a lung.

We change jobs more frequently, and we rotate more shifts. We have more deadlines yet less control. "The pressured job pace has caused thousands of males to 'outrun their hearts,'" comments sociologist Jon Johnston.[13]

Control—Stress can be successfully managed if we have control over what is happening. If the situation is beyond our influence, however, frustration leads to psychic or physical damage.

Fear—Some researchers believe fear to be the root cause of all stress reaction. We have many reasons for our insecurities: pressured deadlines, fragile job futures, economic vulnerability, loss of control, conditional relationships, overloaded lives.

Relationships—The intact, supportive relationships we all require for healthy living have dissipated under the tutelage of progress. The family has been systematically dismantled, and at the same time, long-term friendships are increasingly rare. Too often, "negative people" appear, unbidden, to take their place. "Negative people are the worst energy drains of all because they take away your enthusiasm, shoot down your ideas, chip away at your self-confidence and leave you feeling weak and drained," notes wellness expert Dr. Ann Tyndall.[14]

Competition—Our modern world is an overly competitive place in which to live and work. When we couple a win-lose format with a pyramidal system, the winner gloats while the multitude of losers try to deal with the stress of not measuring up.

Overload—Overloading is a widespread stressor as yet invisible to most. The entity of concern is not *what* we are overloaded with, but *overload* itself. More on this in the next chapter.

Illness and death—As we live to increasingly older ages, we are susceptible to more illness. These are often chronic diseases, causing disability and pain while straining financial resources. Many fear being old and sickly more than they fear death—not only for their own sake but also for the sake of their families.

The death of a family member is another profound stressor. Studies of the surviving spouse have consistently revealed prolonged depression of not only the emotions but also the immune system. In days past, sickness and death were often accepted as "the will of God" and as such directed us to His comfort. Today, our expectations point us in other directions, and profound stress often results.

Frustration, anger—Perhaps the greatest emotional stressors are frustration and anger. These block our ability to use stress in a positive manner and virtually assure painful and destructive results at some level. It is therefore wise to scout society's landscape for their presence.

While it is important to identify these stressors for the purposes of understanding, it is equally important to reintegrate them into life and then analyze the effect of combined stressors. The whole is greater than the sum of the parts. We might be able to adapt successfully to one or two assaults on our internal response mechanism. When six or eight major stressors compound the challenge, however, our chances of success are diminished. Yet multiple stressors all at once are what our culture throws at us. Little wonder we see dysfunction all around.

CHARRED BACON

Stressors not successfully handled can have serious consequences, with effects persisting long after the stressor has ceased to act. Such symptoms often result in a visit to the doctor's office.

The effects of stress disorders are noticed in three spheres: psychological, physical, and behavioral. Burnout is a pervasive disturbance in all three areas.

Psychological Symptoms

Most people are aware of the link between stress and our emotional response. The other secondary physical and behavioral effects are somewhat more obscure and need to be taught, but the emotional/psychological effects are self-evident. The psyche, it seems, is the point of entry for the stress virus, with symptoms including:

▶ Depression, withdrawal
▶ Mental fatigue
▶ Chronic anxiety

- Feeling that things are slipping out of control
- Negative thinking
- Difficulty making decisions
- Exaggerated worrying
- Paranoia
- Impatience
- Forgetfulness
- Apathy
- Confusion
- Anger and hostility

Physical Symptoms

Our response to stressors takes place not only at the thought level but also at the organ and even the cellular level. "The brain writes prescriptions for the body," explains Dr. Eliot. Driven by the alerted nervous system and a host of biochemical messengers, our body is charged for the assault but has no foe to fight. Symptoms we might experience include:

- Stimulation of the cardiovascular system—rapid pulse, palpitations, increased blood pressure, chest pain, arrhythmias (can be fatal)
- Gastrointestinal overactivity—hyperacidity, ulcers, irritable bowel, diarrhea
- Tightening of the muscles—especially of the head and neck or low back
- Headaches
- Weight changes—food used as a tranquilizer
- Increase in infections and cancer—compromised immune system
- Rashes, itching
- Insomnia
- Unexplained fatigue
- Shortness of breath
- Perspiration or cold, clammy hands
- Nervous tics, tremors
- Teeth and jaw-clenching

Behavioral Symptoms

What our mind and body experience, our behaviors often express. If, for example, we are psychologically depressed and physically exhausted, we will begin to act in a manner consistent with these symptoms. These behaviors include:

▶ Irritation with friends, colleagues
▶ Bossiness
▶ Outbursts of temper
▶ Withdrawal, detachment
▶ Change in sleep pattern
▶ Change in eating pattern
▶ Change in sexual drive
▶ Accident proneness
▶ Reckless driving
▶ Inappropriate laughing
▶ Reversals in usual behavior
▶ Compulsive shopping
▶ Increased use of tranquilizers, alcohol, cigarettes

Burnout

Next time you fry bacon, leave one strip in the pan for an extra fifteen minutes. Then pick it up and look it over. This shriveled, charred, stiffened strip is analogous to what a person experiences in burnout. Some of the symptoms and attitudes of burnout include:

▶ Exhaustion
▶ Depression
▶ Irritability, hostility
▶ Paranoia, suspiciousness
▶ Withdrawal, noninvolvement
▶ Multiple psychosomatic illnesses
▶ "I can't stand this any more."
▶ "I dread going to work."
▶ "I'd rather be alone."
▶ "I don't care."
▶ *"I hate it!"*

STRESS REDUCTION, STRESS MANAGEMENT

Avoiding all stress is not an alternative to our overloaded condition. Those who have *no* stress in their lives—no novelty, no challenge, no change—are as miserable as those who have too much. "The majority equally dislike a lack of stress and an excess of it," points out Selye. "Hence each of us must carefully analyze himself and try to find the particular stress level at which he feels most comfortable, whatever occupation he selects. Those who do not succeed in this analysis will either suffer the distress of having nothing worthwhile to do or of being constantly overtaxed by excessive activity."[15]

There are two broad recommendations for the overly stressed:

▶ Stress reduction—decrease your stress load.
▶ Stress management—learn how to control your stress response.

Although most books dwell on stress management, I strongly feel both approaches are important. Margin can assist with either approach but is much more closely related to reduction.

Stress reduction often requires courage. It may mean rearranging life: getting a different job, living with less income, establishing boundaries (saying no), creating some margin. Once you have identified the stress dynamics in your life, it is important to remedy the destruction, even though at times the remedy might require radical change.

Stress management is accomplished by realizing we do have some control in our response to stressors. We can learn how to relax in the midst of strife, to slow our heart rate, to talk to ourselves positively, to behave rationally. It is not always easy, but it is possible.

Below are suggestions for decompressing stress-filled lives. These are not dreamed-up platitudes but the recommendations of researchers and experts in the field.

▶ Practice gratitude.
▶ Generate goodwill.
▶ Do volunteer work.
▶ Set realistic expectations.
▶ Laugh ("inner jogging").
▶ Play.
▶ Meditate.
▶ Pray.
▶ Accept what cannot be changed.
▶ Avoid frustration.
▶ Exercise ("sweat to forget").

▶ Learn to relax ("behavioral aspirin").
▶ Put more control in your life.
▶ Reconcile conflict in personal relationships (confession/forgiveness).
▶ Above all, avoid anger and the desire for revenge.

A DOSE OF MARGIN

Some in our midst (usually our leaders) quickly grow impatient with all this stress talk and would instead challenge the weak to quit all the whining and get with the program. They love stress and seem to thrive on marginless living. The driven live on the edge and wouldn't have it any other way. They eat, breathe, and sleep adrenaline. Productivity is the goal, not living. Margin is a hole to be plugged as quickly as possible.

Yet even these racehorses have their limits, as they will eventually learn. And when they do, I hope they will not underestimate the stress-reducing value of taking a dose of margin against the pain.

The Pain of Overload

"It hurts," said David Tate.

As a mere 180-pound member of the Chicago Bears' defensive secondary, one would think he was discussing taking a hit on the playing field. Instead, the pain comes from being "splashed" in the 1990 Bears' "Locker Room Wars."

The Bears' huge defensive linemen and the smaller defensive backs have a good-natured but weighty battle of intimidation going on. Following an exchange of verbal assaults, the big guys start moving, trying to circle and isolate one of the "Brat Pack." On most occasions, the smaller, faster defensive backs are able to strike and quickly escape. But if captured, they pay a huge price. Tate was dropped to the ground and the 320-pound William "Refrigerator" Perry collapsed on top of him. Then 270-pound Richard Dent, 275-pound Dan Hampton, and 270-pound Steve McMichael jumped on top—1,135 pounds of pain.

"I don't think they know how heavy they are," said Tate. "Once you've gotten splashed, you avoid it at all costs—even if it means backing down."[1] "Splashing" is perhaps the consummate picture of overload.

Overloading is a painful occurrence. Yet, in one form or another, it happens daily to nearly every one of us.

A MATTER OF THRESHOLDS

The spontaneous tendency of our culture is to inexorably add detail to our lives: one more option, one more problem, one more commitment, one more expectation, one more purchase, one more debt, one more change, one more job, one more decision. We must now deal with more "things per person" than at any other time in history. Yet one can comfortably handle only so many details in his or her life. *Exceeding this threshold will result in disorganization or frustration.* It is important to note here that the problem is not in the "details." The problem is in the "exceeding." This is called overloading.

Overloading occurs whenever the requirements upon us exceed that which we are able to bear. For example, camels are able to carry great loads. If, however, a mere straw is placed on a camel maximally loaded down, its back will be broken. The back is not broken by the proverbial straw. It is broken by overload.

Breathing and hyperventilation serve as another example. Necessary to sustain life, breathing is obviously good for us. If, however, we start breathing thirty times a minute instead of sixteen, we hyperventilate and become sick. Air and breathing are not the villains here. Too much, however, causes overloading. A threshold is exceeded.

THE LAW OF LIMITS

As we have already discussed, all systems have limits. Human beings are systems, and as such have physical, performance, emotional, and mental limits. To understand the concept of overloading, it is helpful to understand the law of limits, for overloading is a phenomenon of limits. "Researchers," according to sociologist Alvin Toffler, "strongly agree on two basic principles: first, that man has limited capacity; and second, that overloading the system leads to serious breakdown of performance."[2]

Physical Limits are easiest to recognize. A room of a given size can hold only so much furniture. We might comfortably put ten pieces of furniture in the room and possibly even thirty. But we would not try to put one thousand tables and chairs in a room too small to hold them.

This would overload the room in a visibly foolish way.

To cite another example, engineers study stress loads when designing bridges, and we often see "Load Limit Ahead" signs as we approach such a bridge. A forty-ton truck would not attempt to cross a bridge limited to twenty-ton vehicles. Because such physical limits are visible and measurable, humans do not commonly overload in these areas. Few attempt to swim the Pacific Ocean or to climb the stairs of the Sears Tower.

Performance limits are related to physical limits but also introduce the factor of will. The endpoint is not as objectively defined, and we often are not quite as willing to accept the fact that there are limits. This is where stress fractures come from—people want to push themselves just beyond the limit of breakdown.

Figure 5.1 - Human Function Curve

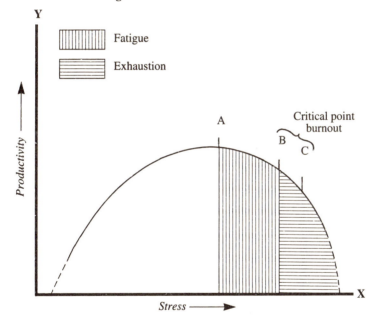

Sleep might serve as another example. We all need sleep. But how much? Those who regard the need for sleep as a sign of weakness might try to push the limit and see how few hours they can get along on. Four hours a night? Three? Yes, you can sleep three hours a night, but you are impinging on a limit, and there will be painful consequences.

The human function curve (figure 5.1) illustrates the principle well.[3] Our performance increases with increasing demand and increasing effort—but only up to a point. Once we reach our limit, fatigue sets in, followed quickly by exhaustion and collapse.

Emotional limits are even more vague. How much straining can the psyche withstand before being overloaded? Physically, most of us could carry a one-hundred-pound person on our back. But we could not carry ten. We would not even try. Our refusal would not be viewed as a statement against carrying people but rather as a statement about physical limits, about overload and pain.

What is clear to us in the context of physical limits is less clear regarding emotional limits. To extend the analogy of carrying people into the emotional context, you might be able to emotionally "carry" one person. But what about five? ten? one hundred? Where should we draw the line? What boundaries should we establish? One of the most serious causes of emotional and spiritual struggles experienced by Christians today, according to psychologist Dr. John Townsend, is the "problem of unclear boundaries."[4]

The limits of emotional overloading are hard to define, and helping people is one of the easiest places where emotional overload is manifested. "In a culture where whirl is king, we must understand our emotional limits," asserts Richard Foster. "Ulcers, migraines, nervous tension, and a dozen other symptoms mark our psychic overload. We are concerned not to live beyond our means financially; why do it emotionally?"[5]

Mental limits are as difficult to define as emotional limits, but the existence of such limits is indisputable. "Could it be that by information overload and complexity, or by mechanical actions whose speed outpaces human response time, technologies are 'stretching the mind beyond the end of its tether'?" asks science policy analyst Edward Wenk, Jr.[6]

Information overload soon results in mental short-circuiting. The memory banks are full, and the mind shuts down for a rest. Air-traffic controllers are a prime example of too much mental stress too fast, and burnout on this job is routine. "Man has committed himself so deeply to constructing ever larger and more complex artificial systems," explains Aurelio Peccei, founder of the Club of Rome, "that it has become difficult for him to control them." Peccei continues by emphasizing, "No one can say with certainty; but psychic and social damage . . . warn us that inner limits have perhaps been surpassed, that our minds and our nervous systems cannot take much more overloading."[7]

"I CAN DO ALL THINGS . . ."?

In running and swimming, we continue to break old records nearly every year. Runners keep running faster, and swimmers keep swimming faster. But there must be an end to this, true? We cannot run the mile in one second. Neither will it ever be possible for anyone to run it in one minute. There is a built-in physiological limit beyond which records will rarely be broken.

So it is in life. We are not infinite. The day does not have more than twenty-four hours. We do not have an inexhaustible source of human energy. We cannot keep running on empty. Limits are real, and despite what some stoics might think, limits are not even an enemy. Overloading is the enemy.

Some will respond: "I can do all things through Christ who strengthens me."[8] Can you? Can you fly? Can you go six months without eating? Neither can you live a healthy life chronically overloaded. God did not intend this verse to represent a negation of life-balance. Jesus did not heal all, He did not minister to all, He did not visit all, and He did not teach all. He did not work twenty-hour ministry days.

It is God the Creator who made limits, and it is the same God who placed them within us for our protection. We exceed them at our peril.

LIMITS AND THE SATURATION POINT

Often we do not feel overload sneaking up on us. We instead feel energized by the rapidity of events and the challenge of our full days. Then one day we find it difficult to get out of bed. Life has become a weight. Perhaps it is in our parenting that we feel exhausted. Perhaps it is that second job we took to pay for the new car. Or perhaps we can't bear to hear of yet one more people problem.

What happened to change our enthusiasm to pain, and why did the change come upon us so unexpectedly? Not all threshold limits are appreciated as we near them, and it is only in exceeding them that we suddenly feel the breakdown.

According to electronic systems expert Roberto Vacca, the development of many modern systems exhibits, "the character of continuous and exponential growth, and their variation obeys a well-known mathematical law, the law of the phenomenon of growth in the presence of limiting factors. At first the effect of these limiting factors is hardly noticeable, but there comes a time when they begin to predominate and to produce the phenomenon known as 'saturation.' . . . Often the effect of the limiting factors is not felt gradually: it may be felt all of a sudden."[9]

Returning to the high school chemistry lab may help us better understand the principle of saturation. Let's begin with a flask of hot water. Next, let's dissolve as much of a chemical salt into the hot water as we possibly can. Spoonful after spoonful disappears easily into solution. Then, perhaps with the fiftieth spoonful, all of a sudden no more dissolves. Instead, the added salt just sinks to the bottom of the flask. At the "saturation point," the water was unable to make any more salt go into solution. The tenth spoonful dissolved nicely, as did the twentieth, as did the forty-ninth. Then, bump, we hit a limit.

Next, let's take the experiment one step further. Add a little more hot water to the flask until all the salt is completely dissolved. Now let it cool. As we cool the salt water down, the solution finds itself in a dilemma. Cold water can't hold as much dissolved salt in solution as hot water can. But neither can the salt find a way to precipitate out. The cold water is stuck, holding more dissolved salt than it is supposed to be able to. It is "supersaturated."

A very interesting thing happens if we introduce a salt crystal into this supersaturated solution. Suddenly, all kinds of crystals precipitate out. The solution knew it was overloaded, and the added salt crystal allowed it the opportunity to dump its overload.

Now let's apply these principles to our own experience. We keep adding more and more to our lives—details, activities, decisions, debt, etc. At first, they all "dissolve" into the flow. But then we reach a limit and nothing more seems to dissolve. We are "saturated."

Some, however, won't accept saturation. In order to force more in they turn up the heat. By working harder, talking quicker, and running faster they are able to dissolve a little more. But when they slow down again, they find themselves "supersaturated."

When our lives are saturated, we dare not take on anymore. Have you ever been there? And when our lives are *super*saturated, we dare not stop to even think about it. Otherwise one piece of well-timed salt falling into the wound might cause us to precipitate out all over the place.

Most of us can identify with one of these two conditions: saturated or supersaturated. We have dissolved as much into our lives as they can possibly hold—and, in some instances, even more than they can hold. At first we didn't realize this was happening because each new thing seemed to dissolve so nicely. But then we came to the fiftieth spoonful—and bump—we hit our limit.

It is similar to the straw that broke the camel's back. The camel was doing fine until. . . . Most times we seem to be bearing up fine under the heavy load, but then something snaps. When you feel such a snap, understand it for what it is. Don't blame your work, your friends, or your children. Blame overload.

EVERYWHERE AND INESCAPABLE

While working at a hospital in central India I observed that poverty was omnipresent and inescapable. The poor were at the train station, alongside the road, and on every city street. Even the wealthiest people could not isolate themselves from the presence of poverty.

Overload in the United States is similar to poverty in India. It is everywhere and it is inescapable. Everyone I know suffers from overload in at least some form. For one person it might be traffic overload, for another change overload, and for a third it might be expectation overload. For most of us, it is a combination of multiple overloads, configured according to the context of our individual lives. Wherever we go, the syndrome has gone before us. It is not chosen. It is simply a part of living, compliments of progress.

THE VARIED WAYS WE HURT

Despite its universality, the syndrome manifests itself differently in each person. Everyone is overloaded, but the degrees vary. Also, each person has a different tolerance. The threshold point where breakdown begins to occur varies from person to person. But I have not yet met a person who could tolerate ever-escalating overload without eventually feeling its painful weight. We are all camels awaiting the straw.

If the overloaded seek professional help, what kinds of manifestations of the disorder might the counselors discover? Some victims of overload experience *anxiety*. The load is simply too much to manage, and tranquilizers are a hoped-for solution. If the load is not lightened soon, however, *breakdown* can occur. "When [our bodies and feelings] can't cope any longer with the demands made upon them, when the overload becomes too great, their only course of action is to shut everything down," explains Robert Banks. "For many people, physical or nervous breakdown is the only way out of the impasse."[10]

Others manifest *hostility*, blaming their overload on those around them. The nightly news details the results: shootings on the freeway due to traffic overload; rudeness in big cities blamed on people overload; brawls in the NBA because of competition overload.

Some personality types lapse into *depression* when overloaded. They might feel hostile, but the hostility is directed inward. Having failed their own expectations and the expectations of others, they withdraw into a fog of gloom.

Many develop *resentment*, often toward their jobs. I love medicine, but the one thing that takes away the love faster than anything else is overloading. Then work becomes an enemy. A physician friend was recently lamenting his continual twelve-hour days. "No, your ulcer isn't bleeding," he moaned silently while listening to the patient describe his stomach pain. "It can't be. It just can't be!"

EASILY MISDIAGNOSED

Because the overload syndrome expresses itself differently in different people, we must be careful with our judgments. Misdiagnosis is common. As a matter of fact, I would say that misdiagnosis is the rule. The overload syndrome is often inaccurately labeled weakness, apathy, or lack of commitment.

For example, I recently read an article very critical of the phrase, "I'm too busy." The author, a nationally known spiritual leader (whom, incidentally, I greatly respect), was quite upset at hearing this excuse so frequently. Saying you're too busy is the perfect cover, he wrote, because the pretense of busyness is very difficult to counter. After all, how can someone tell you, "No, you *aren't* too busy. You're just using that as an excuse"? The excuse of busyness, he concluded, should be recognized for what it is—the problem of not caring enough.

There is obvious frustration in these accusations. But in many cases his clinical opinion will have missed the diagnosis. The problem is indeed busyness, not apathy. The problem is overload. It is real, and it is here to stay. Let's blame it, not each other.

Each of us needs to seek his or her own level of involvement and not let the standard be mandated by the often exorbitant expectations of others. Some around us who are much more involved than we are may not understand why we choose to hold back. Others might be much less involved than we are—we assume they don't care. We must understand that everyone has a different tolerance for overload and a different threshold level when breakdown begins to occur. It is important for us to set people free to seek their own level.

When given this freedom, some unfortunately will still use the overload principle as an excuse for laziness. Here we return to the accusations of apathy leveled by the frustrated leader. This will inevitably happen. Exploitation will occur by some who claim to be overloaded but instead are simply undisciplined. In this case I may wish to employ a large measure of grace as I talk to them about their level of involvement. But as soon as I condemn them, judge them, or try to control them, I violate who they are before God. Making them accountable to Him does not mean that they must then do as *I* wish them to do, to live their lives as *I* think their lives should be lived. My own spiritual walk in the midst of my own overload is enough of a burden to keep me fully occupied.

In my experience, the greater problem in our society, including the Christian community, is not the lack of accountability but the desire to control other people's lives. It is better to not judge the sluggard than it is to mistakenly judge the already overloaded. When people are overloaded, the last thing they need is the additional burden of our reproof. So if we err, at least let us err on the side of grace.

UNPRECEDENTED

Hasn't overload always been with us? No.

An important thesis of this book is that we live in an unprecedented age. Our modern day is not only qualitatively different from any other but also quantitatively different. Future history books will need to use a different vocabulary to describe contemporary phenomena, and prominent among these words will be "exponential," "limits," "thresholds," and "overload."

Overload is a matter of mathematics, and as already shown in chapter 3, today's math computes differently. If in 1960 you dumped one tablespoon of gasoline on my front yard, chances are I would not be upset. I probably would not have even noticed the spot. If you returned every year and doubled your dumping, by 1968 the tablespoon would have grown to a gallon. At that point I would be asking you questions. When you showed up in 1990 with a tank truck and dumped four million gallons, I would probably have become hostile.

This example once again illustrates the dramatic principle of exponentiality. Under the power of exponential influence, matters erupt—they explode. But let's look at this same illustration taken linearly. If the amount of gasoline was only increased by one tablespoon per year instead of doubled, then by 1990 the amount dumped would only be two cups. I would still have a lawn, and we would probably still be friends.

Life, change, history—all are unfolding exponentially. We are not dealing with two cups but rather with four million gallons. Threshold limits are being reached with frightening suddenness. Overload is happening overnight.

Many people, however, are trapped in a linear paradigm, a mindset that can only see straight ahead. While they understand our qualitative changes, they have failed to comprehend the quantitative nature of "future shock." As long as this is the case, the reasons for our contemporary problems will remain invisible to them.

INVISIBLE KILLERS

Ignaz Philipp Semmelweiss, a nineteenth-century surgeon, is one of my heroes. Many of his obstetrical patients in Vienna were dying of postpartum infections, and Semmelweiss was not only puzzled but deeply disturbed. Finally an observation struck him. The mothers who developed the fever and died were the same ones being examined by physicians just returning from performing autopsies on recently deceased victims. It appeared something was being carried from the morgue to the postpartum ward and was killing patients. He had all the doctors under his authority begin washing their hands in a solution of chlorinated lime after performing autopsies. The infections stopped.

What an exciting discovery! The beginnings of a secret had been unlocked, and lives were saved. Semmelweiss told his other colleagues and suggested they also wash their hands following autopsies.

The response was brutal. How could physicians' hands carry invisible agents of death? Semmelweiss was scorned and rejected, and he ended his days prematurely in an insane asylum. Meanwhile, mothers continued to die. Shortly thereafter, Pasteur and Lister proved the existence and contagiousness of microbes, and only then was the Austrian surgeon vindicated.

Overload, limits, exponentiality—these too are invisible killers. I see the carnage in my friends, in my community, in my church, in my work, and, yes, in my own life. I see the damage in our nation and in the world. Yet we have no shortage of scorners who say, "Life is no different. We have always had troubles." Trapped in a paradigm that wears blinders, we continue to strain under the load. Finally, inevitably, someday we will understand. But in the meantime, what needless pain we bear.

SPECIFICS OF THE SYNDROME

The following are abbreviated discussions of the overload syndrome in its varied manifestations. Perhaps some of the distresses in your life will be clarified as you read. Yet as relevant as the specifics are, the overarching theme of this chapter focuses not on those specifics but on the *parent pain*: overload.

Activity overload—Booked up weeks in advance, we are a busy people. In an attempt to squeeze more things in, we try to do two or three at the same time. Activity overload takes away the pleasure of anticipation and the delight of reminiscence.

Change overload—"Nothing defines our age more than the furious and relentless increase in the rate of change," summarizes historian Arthur M. Schlesinger, Jr.[11] For millennia upon millennia, change was slow, controlled, assessable; now it convulses at warp speed.

Choice overload—In 1978, there were 11,767 items in the average supermarket; today the number is 24,531—including the 186 different choices of breakfast cereal we found in our local grocery store. Purchase a satellite dish and choose from 1,500 movies every month. But realize, warns Toffler, "We are, in fact, racing toward 'overchoice.'"[12]

Commitment overload—Most of us have more commitments than time. "Some people can't say no," observes Dr. J. Grant Howard. "They take on too many relationships and too many responsibilities. They enroll in too many courses, hold down too many jobs, volunteer for too many tasks, make too many appointments, serve on too many committees, have too many friends. They are trying to be all things to all men all at once all by themselves."[13]

Competition overload—Few things have been as consistently emphasized in the "American dream" as the virtues of competition. Though its effects are widely evident in business, in academia, and in politics, this mania is perhaps best illustrated in athletics. One boy had a wrestling record of 30-1 and won the state tournament. In the first grade.

Debt overload—Currently every sector of society is awash in red ink. Concerning our national debt, "We're institutionally incapable of saying 'No,'" complains Senator Alan Simpson. In our foreign trade deficit, we are now the world's largest debtor nation. Corporate and personal consumer debt levels are functioning more like anchors than catalysts.

Decision overload—Every year we have more decisions to make and less time to make them. The small decisions don't cost us much but are objectionable by virtue of sheer numbers: Which soda? Which pizza toppings? Mint toothpaste or tartar control gel?

Along with these trivial decisions have come a myriad of relatively new choices that are not at all easy: whether or not to have children and how many; whether to move or change jobs; whether both spouses should work outside the home; whether to put Grandma into the nursing home. Trivial or tough, having too many decisions to make in too short a time is vintage overload.

Education overload—Each decade the educational level of the general populace rises. While agreeing that education is important, I must ask the heretical question: How much education is enough? Information proliferates far faster than our ability to assimilate it. So, although we study more and more, we are always falling farther behind.

Expectation overload—Expectation overload is one of the most difficult to control—and one of the most dangerous. Nevertheless, a clear result of our affluent communications age is the steady rising of expectations. "Your world should know no boundaries," advertises one investment firm. "If you can dream it, you can do it. Now there's no limit to your ability," claims an insurance company.

Fatigue overload—We are a tired society. Even our leisure is often exhausting. With generator indicators continuously pointing to "discharge," it is little wonder our batteries are drained. Our weary, withered state is not God's plan. Fatigue overload attacks our emotions, leaving us self-protective; it attacks our bodies, leaving us weak; and it attacks our relationships, leaving us isolated. That we are fatigued is not the fault of activities or friends—it is the fault of overload.

Hurry overload—Haste is a modern ailment. It also is fashionably

American. Our lives are nonstop, lived at a breathless pace. We walk fast, talk fast, eat fast, and then excuse ourselves by saying, "I must run." Time urgency is a national emblem. "Hastiness and superficiality—these are the psychic diseases of the twentieth century," accuses Aleksandr Solzhenitsyn.[14] But, as the Finnish proverb teaches, God did not create hurry.

Information overload—A single edition of the *New York Times* contains more information than a seventeenth-century Britisher would encounter in a lifetime. In the field of health, I would have to read 250 articles every day to stay current. If you add the 30,000 scientific journals in the world to the 22 million books in the Library of Congress, it is little wonder one observer advised, "'Print control' is probably more urgent than birth control."[15]

Media overload—Ninety-eight percent of American homes have television, with the average family having two sets turned on seven hours a day. We buy more books per capita than ever before and can choose from forty-five thousand new titles every year. Seventeen hundred daily newspapers keep us informed. But how does one read a three-and-one-half-inch thick Sunday paper?

Ministry overload—"Christians will run you into the ground," someone once commented. Seeing the great number of needs, pastors and laypeople often place unbearable demands upon themselves—and others. "I think churches may tear a family apart by overloading and overburdening," observes one family-ministry pastor.[16]

Pastors, too, are at risk: "Many ministers today are headed toward the mental, physical, and spiritual salvage yard because they expect too much of themselves," says one physician who counsels pastors. "And most do not have a clear idea of the forces driving them to that tragic end."[17]

Noise overload—Noise "is perhaps the most pervasive and insidious pollution in our industrial world," declares Theodore Berland, author of *The Fight for Quiet*.[18] "Fifty percent of the U.S. population is exposed every day to noise that interferes with speech or sleep," according to Rutgers University's Noise Technical Assistance Center.[19]

People overload—"I would rather sit on a pumpkin and have it all to myself, than be crowded on a velvet cushion," confessed Thoreau. Personally, as a fellow introvert, I agree with him. But such is not the world we live in. God has given us people to love and appreciate.

Many people. *Billions* of people. Now every time the world turns, two hundred fifty thousand more people are added. Each of us is exposed to a greater number of people than ever before. Socialization and community are wonderful. Unfortunately, such crowding often leads to depersonalization, rudeness, and violence.

Pollution overload—Billions of tons of sulfur dioxide, nitrogen oxide, carbon monoxide, smog, smoke, ozone, soot, dusts, carbon dioxide, pesticides, fertilizers, lead, PCBs, asbestos, and thousands of assorted chemicals all complicate our air, soil, and water. A little pollution will not hurt us, as the earth, like its Creator, is willing to forgive. Pollution overload is another matter.

Possession overload—We have more "things per person" than any other nation in history. Closets are full, storage space is used up, and cars can't fit into garages. Having first imprisoned us with debt, possessions then take over our houses and occupy our time. This begins to sound like an invasion. Everything I own owns me. Why would I want more?

Problem overload—The process of evolving civilization has not succeeded in diminishing our problem load. As we have already seen, we solve one problem only to create another one—or two or three. A problem pile can be worked on. But overloading has turned the pile into a mountain.

Technology overload—It has been estimated that the average person must learn to operate twenty thousand pieces of equipment. Some elicit our gratitude, others our exasperation. Engineer Donald A. Norman criticizes gadgets which are "infuriating by design": "'You would need an engineering degree from MIT to work this,' someone once told me, shaking his head in puzzlement over his brand-new digital watch. Well, I have an engineering degree from MIT. Give me a few hours and I can figure out the watch. But why should it take hours?"[20]

Traffic overload—Roadways are called "clogways," our national flower has become the cloverleaf, and rush hour is neither rush nor an hour. Cars are multiplying twice as fast as people. Americans drive nearly two trillion miles a year. The word *travel* comes originally from *travail*, and we are rediscovering its true meaning.

Waste overload—"Without further action, New Jersey could actually choke on its own garbage," proclaimed Governor Thomas Kean in 1987. The nation's fourteen thousand landfills are rapidly filling up. It seems most people again assume that the world is flat and that we can dispose of our waste by pushing it over the edge.

Small amounts we could bury in the backyard. But garbage piled this high can't be dumped anywhere without interfering with flight patterns.

Work overload—Work is God-ordained. Work overload, however, was not part of the original plan. Yet every morning millions of Americans head drudgingly to an exhausting work schedule that leaves them stressed and worn-out. Because there are more things to buy at higher prices, people work longer. Yet somehow they manage to get deeper into debt. Now Mom and Dad both work outside the home. Total family work-hours often exceed eighty a week, and we find yet another family "over-working and under-relating."[21]

WHY DO WE DO IT?

If overloading causes such widespread social and personal dysfunction, why do we do it?

One reason we so casually overload is lack of understanding. Because it is a relatively new phenomenon, we don't see it even when it has us by the throat.

Second, some accept overload uncritically because of conscientiousness. "It is our duty to do all that we can," they reason. But how does one define "all that we can"? A line must be drawn this side of overload if we are to stay healthy. Drawing such a line causes the overly conscientious to feel guilt. I appreciate those who have this sense of duty. Nevertheless, chronic overloading is not God's will. It is okay to draw a line.

Yet a third dynamic that inflicts overload on many unwilling victims is "follow the leader." Our economy and our society are run by the driven. They climb to positions of power by force and then demand the same overcommitment from those under them. That our leaders should require of us an honest hard day's work is not disputed. But when they require overloading that destroys the worker, then they have exceeded the moral mandate for leadership.

In all that precedes, I *am not* suggesting that we should strive to have a pain-free, stress-free life. The Christian walk will always be full of problems and work. Many times we must be prepared to suffer willingly. What I *am* suggesting, however, is that given the ubiquity of overload, we need to choose carefully *where* our involvement should come. We must not allow ourselves to be hammered by distress in the many areas of life that have absolutely no *transcendent importance*. It is not the will of the Father for us to be so battered by the torment of our age. There must be a different way—a way that reserves our strength for higher battles. And indeed there is.

SETTING LIMITS

To date, people do not operate on the principle of overloading. Instead, they operate on the basis of "one more thing won't hurt." Yet this is only true if it is true. Once we are maximally loaded down, adding one more thing *will* hurt. The pain of overload is real pain.

Chronic overloading also has a negative effect on our spiritual lives. We have less time for prayer and meditation, less energy for service, and less interest in relationship.

If we don't move to establish effective priorities, overloading will continue to fill up our schedules and keep us captive. We must learn the art of setting limits. We must learn to accept the finality and nonnegotiability of the twenty-four-hour day. We must learn not to overdraw on our account of emotional energy. And we must learn to respect such limits in others.

Margin can teach us these things. Margin can restore to us that which has been taken away. It is an idea whose time has come.

PART TWO

THE PRESCRIPTION: MARGIN

Margin

Despite its timeliness, few people are aware of the concept of margin. Not that the concept is inconsequential. Indeed, it is compellingly important. Nor is the concept difficult to understand. Quite the opposite, it is elementary. Rather, the reason margin has not become a household word is simply because it has not yet been properly introduced.

It is now time. For if today margin is useful, tomorrow it will be urgent. If today it is valuable, tomorrow it will be essential.

Although some people seem capable of thriving without margin, most of us find it a prerequisite for well-being. Margin grants freedom and permits rest. It nourishes both relationship and service. Spiritually, it allows availability for the purposes of God. From a medical point of view, it is health-enhancing. It is a welcome addition to our health formulary: Add a dose of margin and see if life doesn't come alive once again.

THE OPPOSITE OF OVERLOAD

Margin is the amount allowed beyond that which is needed. It is something held in reserve for contingencies or unanticipated situations.

Margin is the gap between rest and exhaustion, the space between breathing freely and suffocating. *It is the leeway we once had between ourselves and our limits.*

Margin is the opposite of overload. If we are overloaded we have no margin, or we have negative margin. If, however, we are careful to avoid overloading, margin reappears. Most people are not quite sure when they pass from margin to overload. Threshold points are not easily measurable and are also different for different people in different circumstances. We don't want to be underachievers (Heaven forbid!), so we fill our schedules uncritically. Options are as attractive as they are numerous, and we overbook.

If we were equipped with a flashing light to indicate "100 percent full," we could better gauge our capacities. But we don't have such an indicator light, and we don't know when we have overextended until we feel the pain. As a result, many people commit to a 120-percent life and wonder why the burden feels so heavy. It is rare to see a life prescheduled to only 80 percent, leaving a margin for responding to the unexpected that God sends our way.

POWER MINUS LOAD

One reason margin is easy to define is because the math involved is straightforward:

> ### Power – Load = Margin
> *Power* is made up of factors such as skills, time, emotional strength, physical strength, spiritual vitality, finances, social supports, and education.
> *Load* combines internal factors (such as personal expectations and emotional disabilities) and external factors (such as work, relational problems and responsibilities, financial obligations, and civic involvement).[1]

When our load is greater than our power, we enter into negative margin status, that is, we are overloaded. Endured long-term, this is not a healthy state. Severe negative margin for an extended period of time is another name for burnout.

When our power is greater than the load, however, we have margin. Even a cursory examination of this formula reveals that to increase margin one need simply increase power or decrease load—or both.

Given that the formula is simple and the consequences of living without margin are painful, why is the concept not universally understood? The answer reveals a principle: not all societal pathogens are equally opaque. Or, in other words, the causes of some pains are more readily apparent than others.

THE SEMIVISIBLE

If starving, we need not be told that food is what we lack. If thirsty, we need not be told that water is what we desire. If sleep-deprived, we need not be told that sleep is what we yearn for. If exhausted from a thirty-mile walk, we need not be told that rest is what our body craves. If bankrupt, we need not be told that money is what we require.

Why, then, when we so desperately need margin in our lives, is it necessary to *explain* our need for it? Why don't we understand it by instinct?

In answering this question, it is helpful to note that some burdens and pains in life are visible while others are not. "Visible" means that they can be perceived with one of the five senses or they can be quantified, measured, or weighed. For example, if you smash your finger with a hammer, you do not have to guess about what hurts or why. Physical pains are obvious and visible. In much the same way, financial pains are usually visible. If the credit-card statement reveals a three-thousand-dollar debt, the source of your distress is not obscure.

Other pains, however, cannot be perceived by the senses in quite the same way; neither can they be weighed, measured, or quantified. They are invisible or, perhaps more accurately, semivisible. Emotional, psychological, social, relational, and spiritual pains often fit this description. The pain is real, to be sure. But the details of cause and effect are hard to sort out. It often requires months of introspection or counseling to clarify wounds in these areas.

In this same way, margin is semivisible. Living without it does not cause a sensory pain, but instead a deep-seated subjective ache. Because the ache and heaviness are only semivisible, the pain of marginless living is hard for us to talk about. We feel guilty and weak if we complain. We feel vulnerable to the slings and arrows of the contemptuously stoical. It is hard to justify our inner pains when we don't even know who the enemy is. How do we talk about our anguish when we don't have a vocabulary to use?

Living without margin has, to date, been unseen and unexplained—but not unfelt. Yet it is not buried so deeply that we must send the philosophers out to find it. Instead, it is common and universal enough that even a simple family doctor can explain the concept. And once explained, the fog lifts.

Very seldom do people attempt to refute the diagnosis. Instead, most say, "So *that's* the problem!" It is as if a switch is tripped in their understanding. Instantly, they have hope that their burden is finally being understood.

A MATTER OF THRESHOLDS

To further illustrate how this historical process of discovery happens, let's look briefly at the beginnings of stress research. Stress is similar to margin; both are threshold phenomena (a certain overloading limit must be reached before the consequences are felt) and both are semivisible (the causes are not readily apparent). Understanding how the awareness of stress was brought to light will help us to understand how this same process is now happening to margin.

Our great-grandparents did not go around complaining about how "stressed" they were. As a matter of fact, no one talked about stress until at least the 1950s. As noted in chapter 4, it was not until then that the concept was discovered and published by Dr. Selye. Now, however, every American knows about stress. People throw around the term as if it has always been a given, as if our widespread use of therapeutic language (now taken for granted) dated back to the crossing of the *Mayflower*. Most of us still do not know how to quantify stress—it is semivisible. But no one tries to refute it any more.

Stress is a threshold phenomenon. Until a certain level of change and adaptational demand was reached, no one was aware of it. Once that threshold was exceeded, however, stress was explained, understood, applied, and then canonized.

Margin is also a threshold phenomenon. It is so simple a concept that one wonders why we didn't see it before. But it did not appear on our pain agenda until a certain threshold was reached, namely, until progress overburdened us to such a degree that margin disappeared. At that point, the problem evolved rapidly from latency to anguish.

It is not that we need margin today but never had need of it before.

We have *always* had need of it. It is as basic a necessity as rest. It's just that the threshold had never been reached before, allowing us to discover our need.

Margin is simply an idea whose time has come—nothing more and nothing less. It is simple, fundamental, and easily accessible. And it is a friend whose company we would be wise to cultivate.

MARGIN: YESTERYEAR'S CHARM?

Margin was an unrecognized possession of the peoples of the past. Throughout most of the history of the world, margin existed in the lives of individuals as well as societies. There were no televisions to watch or phones to answer. There were no cars, and travel was seldom undertaken. Daily newspapers were unknown. The media could not broadcast the cluster of events taking place in town. Churches and communities did not offer twenty simultaneous programs. With no electricity to extend daylight, few suffered sleep deprivation. Time urgency, daily planners, and to-do lists had not yet been adopted by the masses.

Instead, by default rather than choice, people lived slower, more deliberate lives. They had time to help a neighbor. Their church and social activities more often drew them together than pulled them apart. The past might have been poor and deprived in many respects, but its people had margin.

Perhaps this is a key to understanding why the past often holds such charm. Surely we overrate its positives and, at the same time, overlook the hardships. Yet, one suspects there must be at least *some* substance to our widespread nostalgia. Those who dismiss the feelings of fondness we have for the past with a haughty sweep of the hand are not being careful enough.

It is intriguing to postulate that margin might be the unsuspected link. Without even knowing exactly what it is that we miss, we miss margin. As progress arrives, margin dissipates. Progress devours margin, and we yearn to have it back.

THE THIRD WORLD'S REMAINING TREASURE

To corroborate this hypothesis, we might compare life as it was lived in our past and the lifestyle we observe in developing countries today.

Conditions in Third-World countries are sad in many respects and some-times even heart-rending. But after working in several of these coun-tries, I am struck by the recurring impression that the people have margin. They sit and talk, they watch children play, they walk without hurry, and they sleep full nights.

Talk to those who have spent time in the Third World and see what they report. True, life there is often frustrating—and sometimes completely exasperating. Many of the modern conveniences are dis-tressingly absent. But the slower pace is consistently commented upon, and almost always with affection.

Good friends of ours recently returned to the States after doing medical work in Mali, West Africa. They don't miss the sand and the heat. They don't miss the scorpions and the insects. They don't miss hepatitis and malaria. But they *do* miss Mali. Why? They miss their friends, both Malian and Western, and they miss the work there. But they also miss their margin. Take, for example, the evening ritual. Fol-lowing dinner, the family retired to the courtyard of their home. There Mom pitched, Dad fielded, and the boys ran the bases. When this family returned to the States, their margin vanished about ten milliseconds after the plane touched down. And with it their evening courtyard base-ball game.

Do you think they miss it?

Another friend from West Africa recently visited her ailing grand-mother in the States. After the return flight to Burkina Faso, she wrote, "I loved going back to Georgia but was really struck by the fast pace that was everywhere. America is years ahead on progress but also on stress. The lifestyle here is slow and relaxing."

Do you think she missed it?

From across the continent comes a similar story: "I think back to the nine years our family enjoyed on the lower slopes of the Kiliman-jaro in East Africa. There, while our work was sometimes tense, the pace surely resembled more a walk than a run. There were plenty of green trees to sit under and a conscience that allowed us to sit down under them," comments former missionary Mildred Tengbom. "We weren't constantly being told that our value depended on how 'active' or 'involved' we were."[2]

Now back in the States, do you think they miss it?

Africa, it seems, is wealthy in margin. More evidence comes from a surgeon who spent one year there.

All things considered I would have to say that it was much healthier for me living overseas. There are stresses, of course, but of a much different type and magnitude. . . .

Although I do not consider myself a "workaholic," I do find it difficult to control the time I spend in my practice. Still, I thought I was reasonably happy until I found out how beneficial a "sabbatical" in Africa can be. . . . I wasn't exactly loafing, since I did nearly five hundred operations in that year, but I still had large amounts of free time to read, rest and play. . . .

In the absence of television, telephones and shopping centers, the inner life gets some long-needed attention. . . . I often had time for a midday nap, to eat almost all meals with my family, and to enjoy having evenings and weekends relatively free as well. With a swimming hole nearby, complete with vine swing, and surrounded by a gorgeous tropical rain forest, we could always find fun things to do. . . . We played table games, assembled puzzles together, read nearly thirty books aloud, and did creative things such as handcrafts and art. . . . The leisure time also afforded the opportunity to meditate, listen to God more, and reflect on priorities and the direction my life should take.[3]

Do you think he misses it?

ISLAND LIVING

Several years ago, after the American intervention of 1983, our family went to the small Grenadian island of Carriacou to help Project Hope and the U.S. Agency for International Development bring medical care to its seven thousand people. One observer characterized the sleepy life on Carriacou and its capital city Hillsborough as follows: "Very little happens on Carriacou, and what does happen, happens slowly. Hillsborough bustles on Monday, when produce arrives, and on Saturday, mail day. Otherwise, this little town just gazes out to sea."

The clinics were often full, but expectations were low, paperwork was humorously minimal, and complexity was nonexistent. We could perform no laboratory tests, order no X-rays or EKGs, and do no surgery. Yet, surprisingly, as the Carriacouans often observed: "Nothing works, but everything works out."

Although our stay there was relatively brief, as a family it was one of the most memorable experiences of our lives. We got up together, ate all our meals together, and often went swimming together. We captured tarantulas together and had crab races on our living room floor together. Perhaps most notably, it was the only time in our parenting when *both* Linda and I were able to tuck in and pray with our boys *every night* we were there.

Do you think we miss it?

In a *Journal of the American Medical Association* editorial, one physician fantasized about having the ability to prescribe such an island experience for his many frazzled patients:

> I have a fantasy about a deserted island. This island is temperate, is well provisioned with water, fruits, and vegetables, and perhaps has good fishing. A safe place but no communications, no people, maybe a dog or a goat, and no way off save by a visiting ship once a twelvemonth. . . .
>
> I can write the prescription, which reads:
>
> Rx: One deserted island
>   One year
> Sig: As directed
>   No refills
>
> Such a prescription could be life-giving, even lifesaving. A kind of Statue of Liberty for the weak, tired, and dizzy, for the yearning souls eager to be cocooned lest they break or dissolve, for those certain that life cannot be lived absent pills, lotions, potions, or salves.[4]

Margin as medicine. A prescription against the pain.

There are few claims the Third World can make of superiority in lifestyle to ours. Having margin, however, is one of them.

IMPORTATION CUSTOMS AND DUTY

To be sure, Third-World living does not assure margin. Missionaries, for example, are sometimes the most exhausted people you would ever want to meet. Rather than constituting evidence against the theory of margin, however, their experience only proves its validity and importance.

Oftentimes the reason these strong and highly motivated people wither under the immense load is not because the developing culture killed their altruism, but rather because they became victims of well-intended twentieth-century self-destruction. Sometimes we take our marginless living with us. When you combine missionary conscientiousness with imported Americanized schedules, and home-office expectations with Third-World need, climate, and disease, burnout is an ever-present risk.

The nationals down the street aren't plagued by the same dangerous busyness we see in some missionaries. It only occurs in the lives of those who have been culturally caught up in the idea that to honor God they have to be "all things to all men all at once all by themselves," to revisit Grant Howard's phrase. A national would never try to administer three different programs in three different locations on three different days in three different languages using three different pieces of technology that break down on three different voltages. (By the way, neither did the missionaries of fifty years ago.)

Nobody can keep running on empty. Let's stay busy to be sure. But together let's also develop the necessary theological underpinnings for margin that will allow us to accept its importance without guilt. For just as we need to eat and sleep, so we also need to breathe.

AVAILABILITY

Avid supporters of progress would probably be quite upset at any suggestion that Third-World cultures have some superior claims to ours. I can hear the rebuttal forming: "What an incredibly regressive idea! If you want to sit on a log all day and watch your children die of disease and your society penalized by ignorance, then go ahead. I'll stick with progress."

But to defend progress and its absence of margin is to presume that all that is good in life and all that God wants us to accomplish is possible only in a booked-up, highly efficient, often exhausted way of life. I do not believe this is true. His asking us to walk the second mile, to carry others' burdens, to witness to the Truth at any opportunity, and to teach our children when we sit, walk, lie, and stand all presuppose we have margin and that we make it available for His purposes. *Obedience to these commands is often not schedulable.*

Actually, margin is not a spiritual necessity. But availability is. God expects us to be available for the needs of others. And without margin, each of us would have great difficulty guaranteeing availability. Instead, when God calls, He gets the busy signal.

EFFECTS OF NO MARGIN

What would you think if this page had no margins? What would be your opinion of the publishers if they tried to cram the print top to bottom and side to side so that every blank space was filled up? The result would be aesthetically displeasing, hard to comprehend, and probably even chaotic. Like some of our lives.

Yet even if we agree that margin is a good idea, for most of us it seems an unaffordable luxury. We don't really desire to be overdrawn on our personal reserves. It's just that we can't seem to keep it from happening. Overbooking overpowers. There is so much to do and so much to buy. Troublingly, each succeeding year the problem only gets worse.

The effects of no margin are familiar to us all: people who are harried, more concerned with personal sanity than with service to the needs of others; people who have no financial margin, painfully uninterested in hearing of yet another "opportunity" to give. Such people are no longer concerned with building a better world. Instead, they simply want to survive another day. Such people are no longer motivated to meet the needs of others. Instead, they simply want to escape their suffocating schedules. Overworked and overwhelmed victims occupy our no-margined world.

Despite these obvious drawbacks to living without margin, our age consistently deprives us of it. We work hard to gain a foothold of freedom but are quickly pushed back into the quicksand. Overload just happens. Margin, in contrast, requires great effort. Positive margin status is what we call in science an "unstable state," one which spontaneously decays. Margin flows toward overload, but overload does not revert to margin unless forced.

Progress has had many overpriced ideas, but trading us burnout for margin was one of its most uncharitable.

FOUR MARGINS

To be healthy, we require margin in at least four areas: emotional energy, physical energy, time, and finances. Conditions of modern living, however, have drained these margins rather than sustaining them. In emotional energy, seldom have we been so stressed, so alone, and so exhausted in spirit. In physical energy, we are overfed, underactive, and sleep-deprived. In time, our clock-dominated nano-second culture leaves us wheezing and worn out. And in finances, universal indebtedness makes our societal landscape look like a fiscal Gettysburg.

An easy way to test if you have margin in one of these areas is to increase the demands on the system 10 or 20 percent. Then see what happens. If you thrive, you had sufficient margin. If you wilt, you didn't.

Let's take, for example, medical residency programs. These programs are so overloaded and tightly coupled that if we introduce added demands, the systems have no way of compensating. If, for example, influenza season hits and the patient load suddenly surges (which, by the way, is happening even as I write), there is no margin to put these patients in. Or, if residents become too ill to take call, other already-exhausted eighty-hour-a-week residents cannot take their place. Thus, you see residents with 102 degree fevers working twenty-four-hour shifts (which, by the way, happened last week). I used to do it, too, until I developed a better understanding of health.

GROWN ACCUSTOMED TO ITS PACE

My decision to be involved in medicine only half-time was not an easy one. I practiced in a wonderful community with an exceptional and compassionate group of medical colleagues and at a pleasant new hospital. My patients respected my judgments and appreciated my care. I traveled around the country attending medical meetings: Boston, Orlando, Phoenix. My income was more than comfortable. I had everything a person could desire: a loving family, a prestigious profession, grateful patients, and a life free from need or want. About the only thing I didn't have was margin.

The decision required two years of agonizing internal deliberations and, in the end, was a strongly countercultural thing to do. Yet, when coupled with other lifestyle choices, that decision has given me the margin I have been writing about. Also, Linda has not worked outside the home since our first child was born. Though we have both spent thousands of hours working on writing projects, it could nevertheless be said that our husband-wife unit works one-fourth as much outside the home as the average marital unit in the United States. Despite this level of freedom and availability, our margin is consistently used up. At the end of a tiring week, we fall into bed and sigh, "How do people manage who have no margin?"

I lived at least sixteen years without margin: college, medical school, residency, and practice. And, since the decision to cut back my involvement in medicine, I have lived ten years with it. I can say with certainty that if margin were taken away from me now, I would beg shamelessly to get it back.

Margin in Emotional Energy

Of the four margins—emotional energy, physical energy, time, and finances—margin in emotional energy is paramount. When we are emotionally resilient, we can confront our problems with a sense of hope and power. When our psychic reserves are depleted, however, we are seriously weakened. Emotional overload saps our strength, paralyzes our resolve, and maximizes our vulnerability, leaving the door open for even further margin erosion.

DEADLINES AND DEAD FRIENDS

Harold was in charge of organizing and teaching continuing education topics for a well-known pharmaceutical firm. He was an excellent communicator. Unfortunately, he was an even better procrastinator. Five months before each conference meeting was scheduled, Harold's employer required a detailed report of time, events, and speakers, as well as full-text handouts for the topics to be covered. All of this information was then sent to the participants.

As someone who has organized medical education conferences, I sympathized with the complexity of Harold's job. Both foresight and organization are required. Nevertheless, the demands didn't sound all that unreasonable to me.

Harold felt differently. His boss insisted that the reports be submitted on time—not one day late. Harold, however, never did anything on time. Consequently, three weeks before the approaching deadline, his collapse would begin in earnest. Telephones were ringing, printers had questions, secretaries wondered about registration information, computers were spewing out piles of only partially relevant information, and his most important notes were hiding somewhere under a mountain of paper. Harold slept little and argued much. His palms would sweat, but his mouth was dry. He lived on antacids.

Convinced his boss was out to get him, Harold complained, "You can't talk to that man! I hate my work when it gets like this. I don't even like getting up in the morning, let alone going to the office." Nor did it help that he was having trouble in his marriage or that his two teenage daughters were increasingly disrespectful.

"Could you please give me something to calm me down?" he asked. "Maybe something to help me sleep? I just can't go on like this."

After our visit, I drew some laboratory tests and sent him off to the pharmacy. Later, I called to check how things were going. "Aside from a mildly elevated cholesterol," I said, "your tests all look fine. How are you doing?"

"Much better, Doc. I'm sleeping better now that the deadline has passed. I *almost* got everything in on time. I'm definitely not as anxious as I was, and I don't feel as depressed."

"How is it going at home?" I inquired.

"Better there, too," he said. "Well, that's not exactly true. My daughter's boyfriend shot and killed himself three days ago. So we've had a lot of things to work through. It's been tough on her."

WOUNDS OF THE SPIRIT

When Harold comes in to talk, I hurt with him. I wish I could do more. But there are no quick fixes. His anguish causes me to look progress in the eye and ask, "What is going on here?" Why do so many workers have so much stress? Why do so many marriages have so little vitality? Why do so many adolescents take their own lives? Aren't these fair questions to ask of progress?

Despite the importance of emotional margin, our contemporary level of emotional stamina is not high. Those who predicted the human race would evolve out of emotional problems were mistaken. Such troubles, far from being rarities, rage throughout our society. I am constantly impressed with how drained we seem to be. Broken relationships, financial insecurities, and overburdened schedules rip through us like a chain saw. The wounds we care for in medicine today are more often wounds of the spirit than wounds of the soma.

What happens when our emotional energy reserves are chronically depleted? "If we string ourselves out, expending 100 percent of our time and energy, there is no way in which we can adjust to the unexpected emergency," concludes Pastor Louis H. Evans, Jr. "We become defensive about our expended energies because there isn't anything left to give. Having nothing in reserve, we tune out the need."[1] Stuck in survival mode, there never seems to be enough strength for service.

EMOTIONAL SKIN

Skin is a wondrous organ, and as a matter of fact, is the largest organ of the human body. It keeps out bacteria, chemicals, and the sun's rays. As importantly, it keeps out water. If we jump into a swimming pool or soak in the tub, water is not allowed to penetrate the skin and enter the body.

Simultaneously, the skin has the job of keeping our own body fluids in. Humans are 60 percent water, and if the skin did not do its job correctly, in no time at all we would be puddles on the floor.

This fascinating organ, however, does not forbid *all* exchanges between our inside and outside environments. In fact, if it did we would die. There are times when the skin must allow exchange, usually in the form of water, salts, and heat, to help us equilibrate our temperature.

Some people are referred to as "thick skinned." This does not literally mean that they have hyperkeratosis, but instead that not much penetrates through to their feelings. Not much is allowed to seep in, and not much is allowed to leak out.

Most of us, however, have an emotional skin that permits an exchange with our environment. Of course we want to feel! But not too much. And not too little. Our emotional skin must allow feelings; it must not allow the excessive depletion of our emotional reserves, however.

A QUANTUM OF EMOTIONAL ENERGY

Each morning we rise to meet the day with a certain measure of emotional energy, a quantum of stamina. For some, this energy reservoir is huge, while for others it is nearly drained empty. Some are buoyant and resilient, filled with a zest and vitality that never seems to change. Others have had their emotional chins on the ground for most of their lives and can't remember what it feels like to smile.

This quantum of emotional energy is not fixed but instead is in constant flux with the environment. We are always losing energy into the environment and receiving energy back again. Sometimes the reservoir is being drained, as when we are sad or angry. Other times the reservoir is being filled, perhaps by expressions of encouragement or activities successfully completed.

No matter how large or small the quantum of emotional energy is at the start of the day, and no matter how fast or slow it is exchanging with the environment, one thing is certain: *The amount within us is finite*. No one has an infinite capacity for emotional discharge. When our reserves are depleted, they are depleted. If we make further withdrawals, we will enter debit status. With our margin exhausted, pain will be felt, sometimes—often in our culture—at dangerous levels.

It is important to understand our emotional reserves. It is important to understand how much we have at the beginning of each day and which influences drain our emotions dry or recharge our batteries. It is important to learn what our limits are, and not to make further withdrawals if we are already maximally depleted. And it is important to respect these limits in others.

We often have trouble accepting the idea of rationing our emotional energy. It is simply too difficult to quantify feelings. We feel ashamed admitting that our spirit is exhausted and collapsing within us. But our hesitancy in no way constitutes proof that such limits are only a convenient fiction for the weak and the lazy. Instead, our hesitancy is an obstacle to overcome. Margin gives us permission.

LIKE WEEDS IN A GARDEN

One would have hoped that the process of progress would have been kind to our emotional life, making it ever easier to replenish our reserves. It might have seemed reasonable to speculate that as our society improved in the areas of education, affluence, and entertainment, we would see a commensurate improvement in overall emotional well-being. Yet such has not been the case. These advancements have not resulted in unburdened emotions and liberated psyches. But why not? Our babies seldom die anymore, and famine is virtually unknown to us. We have telephones when we get lonely, air conditioners when we get hot, aspirin when we have a toothache, and television when we get bored. Why then do so many remain so emotionally drained?

I am not suggesting that emotional turmoil and emptiness is an invention of the late twentieth century, for this type of pain has been with us since the beginning of humankind. Yet as our survival needs were secured by civilizational improvements, might we not have expected that emotional disorders would increasingly disappear? Anxiety, depression, suicide and suicide gesturing, personality disorders, obsessive behaviors, eating disorders, panic attacks, alcohol and other drug abuse, phobias, psychoses—these are not diagnoses on the verge of extinction. Instead, these maladies seem to thrive in our society like weeds in a garden. And they all drain us dry emotionally.

Is it possible we are "living in a deteriorating 'psychic environment'"? Over the last decade, the number of therapists has risen tenfold. We have more mental health workers in the United States than police. The mental health beds are the only ones in our troubled healthcare system that are filled all the time. Spending for mental health is escalating more rapidly than all other health categories, increasing 100 percent in the last five years. A study by the National Institute of Mental Health revealed that nearly one-third of all Americans have experienced at least one psychiatric illness during their lifetime. It has been estimated that 40 percent of us will be in psychotherapy at some point. Another study by the Institute reported that in just six years psychiatric hospitalizations for adolescents tripled. Twenty-seven percent of high school students "reported that they had thought seriously about attempting suicide," according to a 1991 Center for Disease Control survey of over eleven thousand students in all fifty states.[2] "If we look around us we find widespread evidence of psychological breakdown," observes Toffler. "It is as though a bomb had gone off in our communal 'psycho-sphere.'"[3]

Many of those trapped in this incredible web of psychic pain are victims, and they are to be commended for seeking help. If you develop typhoid in Bangladesh, it is not the fault of a weak constitution but instead the problem of a highly infectious environment. To seek effective treatment is the appropriate response.

ESCAPING OUR AGE

To our modern era social critics have attached labels that speak of this threatened emotional meltdown. It is not uncommon to hear entire decades characterized as the "age of anxiety," the "age of depression," the "age of melancholia," and even the "age of depressed anxiety." Over the course of a lifetime, one out of seven will experience a psychiatrically significant problem with anxiety. The use of tranquilizers has become so prevalent that for decades they have been near the top of the list of most widely prescribed drugs—at a cost of nearly one billion dollars annually. All of which prompted one observer to comment, "Millions of suburbanites seem to find that 'the good life' is only endurable under sedation."[4]

When the minor tranquilizers appeared on the scene in 1960, there was great hope. Finally, something to control anxiety and to soothe frazzled nerves! The disillusionment came when we realized that while these drugs did assist in controlling symptoms, they did not cure the underlying problems. People's pain continued, now compounded by tranquilizer addiction.

The widespread use of illicit drugs in our country is evidence that many perceive their personal lot not as a blessing to celebrate but, instead, as a burden to escape from. Why would America's fifteen million problem drinkers risk their bodies, their families, their jobs, and their future for a few hours of drunken stupor? Is it not because they believe the world they enter through alcohol is preferable to the reality they leave behind?

AGENT BLUE

Norman was a patient in his early sixties, hospitalized the day before. I knew him fairly well, enough to say that we were friends. Yet when I entered his room and approached him with a greeting, he just sat there on the edge of his bed, face drawn, shoulders slumped, looking weakly at his hard-boiled egg.

There was no anger or even distance in his silence. I was not offended. I knew that his paralysis came from the malignant darkness of depression. After a minute or so, Norman mumbled in a barely audible voice, "Could you . . . peel my egg? I just . . . can't . . . seem . . ."

The suffering of depression is often unbearable. If you look, you can see it in the eyes: privately tortured eyes reflecting a sea of pain, always misty, ready to overflow at the slightest provocation. When I sit next to such a patient in the examination room, I ask a gently probing question and pass him or her the tissue box at the same time. As the pain surfaces, the tears spill over. It happens 100 percent of the time.

"It is almost impossible to convey to a person who has not had a depression what one is like," explains Jack Dreyfus, founder of the Dreyfus Fund.

> It's not obvious like a broken arm, or a fever, or a cough;
> it's beneath the surface. A depressed person suffers a type of
> anguish which in its own way can be as painful as anything that
> can happen to a human being. He has varying degrees of fear
> throughout the day, and a brain that permits him no rest and
> races with agitated and frightening thoughts. His mood is low,
> he has little energy, and he can hardly remember what pleasure
> means.[5]

Yet in medical practice, depression is a daily finding. It is not limited to a certain socioeconomic group, nor to a certain educational level. No one is immune. Like a flu virus, it strikes any age, any race, any occupation, at any time. Unemployment does heighten the risk, but even successful business executives, such as Jack Dreyfus, suffer from it. High school dropouts might have it, but so do many Harvard graduates. Nihilistic unbelievers feel its pain, but so have some of the greatest preachers in the history of the Church. An increasing number of children and adolescents are being diagnosed with it, and on the other end of the spectrum, many elderly spend their last days caught in its grip.

Researchers at the National Institute of Mental Health are attempting to identify Agent Blue, the unknown factor(s) that causes such a high rate of depression in our society. The Institute's Dr. Eliot Gershon calls the increase in depression and suicide "ominous because we haven't seen where it's going to stop." He goes on to explain that "the high rates among people born since 1940 cannot be explained by genetics or the increased reporting of depressive illnesses."[6]

A disturbing 1989 report in *The Journal of the American Medical*

Association examined several large epidemiologic studies concerning the incidence of depression. Ten studies from the United States, Sweden, Germany, New Zealand, and Canada revealed an increase in lifetime rates of depression for those born after 1940. (Interestingly, the article also reported that comparable studies in Korea, Puerto Rico, and of Mexican-Americans living in the United States revealed no such increase in rates of depression among these groups.) The authors summarized the findings as follows:

> The cohorts born since World War II have been among the healthiest physically and were raised during a period of economic prosperity in the United States and Western Europe. Nevertheless, they show high rates of alcoholism, substance abuse, depression, and suicide. . . . Clinically, the data suggest that physicians from all specialties can expect to see more and younger patients presenting with major depression.[7]

But where is this "dark undertow" coming from? Why, in one recent morning in the clinic, were nine of my eleven patients on antidepressants? Where is emotional resilience hiding these days?

CONTEMPORARY LEECHES

The answer lies in the fact that we have been ambushed by a load of psychic trauma unparalleled in human history. This is not to say that other people in other times haven't had it rough. Many have had it much rougher than we do. *But never before have people faced the particular constellation of factors which today are plotting together for our misery.*

We have already noted how the unprecedented pathogens of stress and overload often wage war on our emotions. Add the assault of speed, the kind whose sheer velocity precludes adaptation to change. Compound the situation by fracturing families, dissipating any sense of community, and decreasing social supports of all kinds. Separate the elderly from their extended families. Add uprootedness by factoring in mobility. Add individualism to narcissism. Alienate adolescents in the direction of R-rated movies, drugs, heavy metal music, early sexuality, and suicide. Add teenage pregnancy and single parenting to welfare dependency. Add child abuse, sexual abuse, and wife abuse to pornography.

Add the crime in every city to the reports of crime on every television. Add indebtedness and bankruptcy to job insecurity and demanding bosses. Add unaffordable housing to unaffordable health care. Add traffic to noise to hurry to impossible work schedules to technology that doesn't work to ringing telephones to crying babies.

When you put it all together, there is little wonder we see anxiety and depression. Little wonder the therapists' offices are full. Loneliness, hopelessness, rejection, fear, insecurity, frustration, cynicism, hostility—these are not the things to fill one's emotional reserves with. The vampires have been busy, haven't they?

"Why is mental health such a major problem, and why is treatment so much more common and so expensive?" asks mental health expert Walter E. Afield, M.D. "There are a number of reasons: For many Americans, life is almost relentlessly stressful. The pressure to achieve, compete—even survive—takes a significant toll on emotional equilibrium. A serious erosion of traditional support systems (including extended family, neighborhoods, communities, schools, and churches) has occurred, and many people feel—and often are—alone with their problems and pressures, far from loved ones and without psychological support."[8]

And, as Dr. Afield goes on to point out, for each person suffering from a mental or emotional disorder, the lives of at least three other persons are significantly affected.

RESTORING MARGIN IN EMOTIONAL ENERGY

If we find our emotional energy gone, how can we get it back? What are the factors to emphasize in our lives that will not only protect our emotional reserves from unnecessary depletion but will replenish the supply at regular intervals? In such a hostile environment, who will be kind to our fragile psyches? Who will feed us and not swallow us?

Following are prescriptions that work; take as needed.

Rx: 1   Cultivate Social Supports

Not only common sense but now also good science, the importance of healthy social supports is irrefutable. We do not simply *think* they work; we *know* they work. The California Department of Mental Health's "Friends Can Be Good Medicine" is not simply a slogan, it is state-of-the-art therapeutics.

Whether family and friends or community and church, the existence of intact, functioning, healthy, nurturing systems of social support are as good a resource for replenishing depleted energy reserves as can be found. Love, affection, nurturing, intimacy, connectedness, bonding, attachment, empathy, community—these are "feel good" words for a reason: because they *are* good.

If you find yourself emotionally empty, go to a caring friend. If you are bruised and bleeding, the empathetic response of another will stem the hemorrhage of emotion and begin the process of healing and filling. "There is perhaps no more effective way to relieve psychic pain than to be in contact with another human being who understands what you are going through and can communicate such understanding to you," advises psychiatrist Dr. Frederic Flach.[9]

I have found that, regarding emotional margin, there are three types of people: those that fill you, those that just sit there, and those that drain you. Unfortunately, the drainers outnumber the fillers about two to one (not a scientific number). We find ourselves in the interesting but precarious situation of being dependent on the benevolent interests of the fillers yet, at the same time, vulnerable to the malevolence of the drainers.

This is a great part of our modern dilemma. So many of us have unsatisfactory relationships and are afraid to risk intimate emotional contact. So we withdraw and "hide from love," only to find that isolation is unhealthy as well. The obvious answer is not to abandon people contact but to learn how to make our relationships mutually nourishing. As we become more active and effective in nourishing families, nourishing friendships, nourishing churches, and nourishing community, we will also discover that our own emotional health is nourished.

As an added note, we can say that not only verbal expressions of caring are important, but the physical are as well. Upon entering an exam room, I make it a practice to shake the hand of my patient or, on occasion, place my hand on his or her shoulder. This, I believe, is the beginning of my therapeutic intervention. We all *need* human contact. We all need to be hugged from time to time. Have you ever noticed how, when a child climbs onto a parent's lap and snuggles in, the entire room feels caressed by the warmth of it?

Rx: 2   Pet a Surrogate

Sometimes, because of social conventions, we are not allowed to touch one another. For those caught in a void and left with a dearth of physical closeness, I would strongly suggest considering surrogates—pets. When God wrote the inviolable law that requires living things to need one another, He included the entire animal world. And it is remarkable how closely we can approximate human-human warmth and affection by substituting human-animal contact. Pets are capable of bonding, are extremely loyal, and often exhibit deep appreciation for our affections—exactly the kind of responses needed to increase our emotional reserves.

Rx: 3   Reconcile Relationships

Broken relationships are a razor across the artery of the spirit. Stemming the hemorrhage and binding the wound should be done as quickly as possible. Yet all too often, it takes months or years. And sometimes, the bleeding never stops.

True reconciliation is one of the most powerful of all human interactions. Warring individuals who have done battle for years can erase all antagonism in a matter of minutes. This is not a matter of human psychology but rather a divine gift. One of the great privileges of our adoption into God's family is the access we have to this mysterious healing power of the Spirit. If you have not seen it happen, or if you have only seen it happen rarely, then yearn for it. Pray for it. Beg for it. And know that it is one of the gifts God most enjoys giving.

Although there is no formula, there are principles. It helps to bring God close—through our brokenness.[10] And it helps to accept God's grace—through our humility.[11] Perhaps you see that this gift is mostly a matter of emptiness and yielding. In our brokenness we confess, yielding our wrongs. In our humility we forgive, yielding our rights. And when confession and forgiveness are completed, our frozen winter of pain will also yield, thawing under the warmth of the Son.

Rx: 4   Serve One Another

"I happen to know that service is empowering," states psychiatrist and bioethicist Dr. Willard Gaylin, president of the Hastings Center. "It's great. It's terrific! Given the opportunity for training toward community and service, people love it and want it."[12]

A recent University of Michigan study followed 2,700 people for over a decade to see how their social relationships affected their health and well-being. Those who performed regular volunteer work showed dramatically increased life expectancy. Men not involved in such altruistic activity had two-and-one-half times the morbidity during the period studied than those who volunteered at least once a week.

"Doing nothing for others is the undoing of one's self," observed Horace Mann. "We must be purposely kind and generous, or we miss the best part of existence. The heart that goes out of itself gets large and full of joy. This is the great secret of the inner life. We do ourselves the most good doing something for others." The service can be noble and sacrificial, or it can be small and simple. Not to worry, explains Rudyard Kipling, "for the glory of the Garden glorifieth everyone."

Ten years ago, a 110-mile-per-hour windstorm blasted across our county, leveling trees, power lines, and buildings, and causing sixty million dollars in damage. Within days, people from several eastern states began quietly arriving in town, volunteers of the Mennonite Disaster Service. Some stayed as long as a month, living in university dormitories vacated for the summer. Most of them were involved in the rebuilding of barns. I don't remember what I did those weeks after the storm, but I will never forget what they did. They served. Every time I think of the disaster, I think also of the gift. Do you see the multiplying effects of this virtue?

I recently heard of a man who, while driving on the interstate highway system, pays not only his own toll but also the toll for the car to follow. In so doing, he is making deposits in at least three emotional bank accounts: his own, the teller's, and the following driver's.

My wife, Linda, is always alert to ways of serving others. Stopping at a convenience store recently for some ice cream, she happened to mention at the counter that it was for cherry pie. "Sounds great!" responded the youthful clerk. Fifteen minutes later, Linda brought him a huge piece of fresh cherry pie à la mode. That evening, alone in the store, he was nourished by service. A simple thing; a magnificent obsession.

And the gift goes on . . .

Rx: 5   Rest

Be with people and serve them. But be sure to get away from them occasionally.

Escape. Relax. Sleep in. Take a nap. Unplug the phone. Enjoy a walk. Don't take your beeper.

Try setting aside time every day for some quiet and for rest—perhaps fifteen or thirty minutes. Or set aside some time every week, as the

Northwestern Mutual Life Insurance Company does. Every Wednesday the company practices "quiet days." The phones in the offices are turned off, and all calls are routed to a receptionist so the employees can work in quiet.

Many of us funnel all our rest needs into already jam-packed weekends and holidays. But don't fall into the trap of thinking weekends and holidays are restful. Often they are not. Sometimes they are even more draining than the week we just escaped. In one poll, although 95 percent of working mothers looked forward to weekends, 52 percent felt exhausted when the weekend was over. Holidays, especially Christmas, can turn into the same exhausting process. Weekends, Sundays, holidays, vacations—all have been modernized, and are only restful if forced to behave.

When emotionally exhausted, the first thing I do is find quiet, solitude, and a chance to do nothing. I don't feel guilty, for fallow times are just as important as productive times. I cycle quickly, and if depleted, my energy will return shortly. All I need is quiet and some time.

Rest restores.

Rx: 6 Laugh

Humor is a medicine. It tastes better than pills, it works as well, and it costs less. Why do you think children are so buoyant, so resilient, so capable of picking themselves up and going on? There are many reasons, and laughter is prominent among them.

Only a few months after birth, and the mirth has already begun. By the time babies are four months old, they are already laughing once every hour. And by the age of four years, these clowns laugh on average every four minutes![13] Try laughing every four minutes. I guarantee that something positive will happen to your emotions and that your margin will be increased.

I am not implying that life is essentially humorous—it decidedly is not. But God has given us the gift of laughter because He knew we would need it.

Rx: 7 Cry

Sometimes we laugh so hard we cry. Other times we just cry. Crying is a form of emotional diuresis. As long as it is not an indication of a deeper depression (in which case frequent weeping is a symptom that should not be ignored), crying can have salutary health benefits. According to some studies, those who cry *more often* get sick *less often*. A good cry usually lasts six or seven minutes and releases a burdensome load of emotional pollution.[14]

Laughter lifts; crying cleanses. Both are partners in the process of emotional restoration.

Rx: 8 Create Appropriate Boundaries

The need to establish boundaries that allow us to say no is a mathematical necessity. With far too many demands and expectations upon us, we could not possibly fulfill them all, even should we desire to do so. Yet it is not easy saying no. With some, every time the word exits their mouths they have a crisis of guilt. The alternative, however, is acquiescing to the demand. Then, instead of a crisis of guilt, we have a crisis of margin depletion.

It is important to understand that most people simply are not sensitive. There is *absence of malice but presence of callous*. Other people's pain is invisible to them. Therefore, when they make demands upon us, they know not what they do.

We, then, must respond with grace, with sensitivity, yet with firmness: "I'm sorry, but I can't." To be able to say no without guilt is to be freed from one of the biggest monsters in our overburdened lives. If we decline, not out of self-serving laziness but for God-honoring balance and health, then this level of control will not only protect our emotional margin but will actually increase it.

"Boundary deficits can be deeply disabling to anyone, including Christians. People with unclear boundaries can find themselves making commitments under pressure that they would never make with a clear head. They find themselves 'caving in' to others," explains psychologist Dr. John Townsend. "We need to find maturing, caring people who will love our boundaries just as much as they love our attachment. . . . Ask yourself, 'Do the people closest to me love my *no* as much as they love my *yes*?'"[15]

If we do not learn to say no, we will never regain margin. That is a contemporary sociological axiom.

Rx: 9 Envision a Better Future

Each of us must have a transcendent vision: a hopeful, spiritually valid expectation of what the future will hold. We all must have a purpose bigger than ourselves that we can live for. We must have something we can believe in, something we can give ourselves to. We must have work, and the work must have meaning. We must have direction, and the direction must have structure. A transcendent vision with purpose, work, meaning, direction, and structure.

Unfortunately, there has been a wholesale destruction of vision, transcendent or otherwise, in modern-day living, and this destruction is seen worldwide. The only vision most live by today is the hardly transcendent television. Aimlessness is like a metaphysical black hole, swallowing up everything in sight. Perhaps the most poignant description of our existential emptiness comes from the French philosopher Jean-Paul Sartre, when he speaks of "man as a bubble of consciousness in an ocean of nothingness, bobbing around until the bubble pops."[16]

So here we have a clear choice, don't we? The vision and spirit of the age—which is really a vote for despair followed by death—or the vision of the revealed Word of God. "Our vision is not something we have concocted to suit ourselves," says sociologist S. D. Gaede, "but a perspective that suits the Reality that has been communicated to us. Believing this, we have no choice but to make the vision central to the life of the Christian community."[17]

If we believe in and work for something larger than ourselves—for our families, for the community, for the common good, and for the Kingdom—then every expenditure of emotion will have meaning, and every expenditure of emotion will be reimbursable.

Rx: 10 Offer Thanks

In everyone's life there is much to be unhappy about and much to be grateful for. Realistically acknowledging both ends of the spectrum is appropriate.

When we turn to look at our problems, we assess them and make a plan—no matter how small or grand—to work on them. This plan we formulate with our *mind* and motivate with our *will*.

Then we look in the other direction to find our obligation to gratitude. Here we may fully engage our *emotions*.

Often we send our emotions to do battle with our problems, and despair results. Then we send our will to express our gratitude, lacking any confirming passion whatsoever. *Of course*, our emotions ought to be informed about our problems; *of course*, our mind and our will ought to express gratitude. But we should send out that warrior best suited for the duty. And I think there can be little debate concerning the most appropriate assignments here.

If we can adopt such a balanced approach, we will combine a realistic and objective involvement in working on problems with a simultaneous assurance that there is much good in life. We'll recognize that the world is full of beauty, that most people are worthy of our respect and trust, and that the affairs of suffering humans are replete with acts of love, kindness, nobility, and sacrifice. And we'll remember that overseeing it all is a God who knows us well, who loves us anyway, and who is very, very good.

All people have within their grasp much to be thankful for. Gratitude fills. Discontent drains. The choice is truly ours.

Rx: 11 Grant Grace

I don't think most of us realize what a weighty emotional burden it is to judge others and to be judged in return. It is a form of emotional and spiritual suicide. Like chopping a hole in the bottom of your lifeboat because you don't want the other person to be rescued.

Grace, on the other hand, treats people not as they deserve but *better* than they deserve. Grace preempts accusation, freeing both parties. When we extend grace to our enemies, they receive a shockingly unexpected glimpse of the Kingdom. And, at precisely the same time that our adversary is released, we are as well.

Why would anyone wish to go around carrying a donkey on his shoulders when he could ride instead? Why would anyone wish to be harsh when he could instead be free? "If thou knewest all the Bible . . . and also the sayings of all philosophers by heart," asks Thomas à Kempis, "what should it profit thee without grace and charity?"[18]

Grace not only revives emotional margin, it lifts it to Heaven.

Rx: 12 Be Rich in Faith

"And now these three remain: *faith*, hope and love."[19]

"Seeing isn't believing. It's only seeing," once quipped George MacDonald. Faith, however, is seeing *without* seeing. The faith of our fathers that successfully withstood dungeon, fire, and sword is the same faith that leads us safely through contemporary dangers, toils, and snares. If it can withstand anything, then can it not withstand the problems of modernity? To be sure, when all hammers are dust, the anvil will yet endure. Even when all else fails us, year after year, faith remains.

"I believe the most vital ingredient of resilience," comments Dr. Flach in his book *Resilience*, "is faith."[20]

Rx: 13 Hold Fast Hope

"And now these three remain: faith, *hope* and love."

The world does not have a strong articulation of the concept of hope, nor does it have a credible basis for developing one. "The Encyclopedia Britannica has columns on love and faith, but not a single word about hope," observed the late psychiatrist Dr. Karl Menninger.[21] Despite this conspicuous textual absence, explains Harvard psychiatrist Dr. Armand Nicholi, "Psychiatrists have long suspected that hope fosters health, both physical and emotional." With the need for hope established, where in a despairing world do we find it? "When we turn to the New Testament," explains Dr. Nicholi, "we read again and again: 'Christ Jesus, our hope.' "[22]

Although acknowledging that "the optimism of inevitable progress has become tarnished," Princeton philosopher and theologian Diogenes Allen sees great cause for hope. "The kingdom of God is at hand when it becomes harder and harder to ignore or evade God's ways. Such convictions enable Christians to continue to work for the common good, to be philanthropic, even in a deteriorating situation. Because of faith in the good God intends us to have, Christian hope can survive even the disintegration of a culture."[23]

Scripture reminds us of the hope of the promise, the hope of the gospel, and the hope of salvation. The Apostle Paul writes, "And we rejoice in the hope of the glory of God. Not only so, but we also rejoice in our sufferings, because we know that suffering produces perseverance; perseverance, character; and character, hope. And hope does not disappoint us, because God has poured out his love. . . ."[24]

Rx: 14 Above All, Love

"And now these three remain: faith, hope and *love*."

To have accepted the love of God is to be armed and disarmed at the same time. No weapon is more powerful. But in using such a weapon it is the user who is broken wide-open. This is a love that cannot rightly be kept in—it is a bursting-out love. In its spilling out, it binds to others. And when it binds to others, it heals, it knits hearts, it builds community, and it brings everything "together in perfect unity."[25] "The effort to 'love thy neighbor as thyself' probably has done more good, and more to make life pleasant, than any other guideline," observes Dr. Selye, perhaps restating the obvious.[26]

Love is the only medicine I know of which, when used according to directions, heals completely yet takes one's life away. It is dangerous; it is uncontrollable; it is "self-expenditure"; and it can never be taken on any terms but its own. Yet as a healer of the emotions, it has no equal.

"But the greatest of these is love."[27]

Margin in Physical Energy

When we dip into the tank for some physical energy, we all want the ladle to return with something in it. Unfortunately, for too many of us the tank dried up years ago.

A large percentage of Americans are sadly out of shape and have diminished physical energy reserves because of poor conditioning. Others, such as mothers of newborns and those who work two jobs, are chronically sleep-deprived. Still others suffer from chronic biscuit poisoning. These three factors—poor conditioning, sleep deprivation, and obesity—constitute a physical energy desert where no margin can grow.

Lacking margin in physical energy, we feel underrested and overwhelmed. With no strength left for our own needs, let alone the needs of others, we put our tiredness to bed hoping tomorrow will be a stronger day.

THE NEW MORBIDITY

Thanks to progress, extraordinary tools are available to assist us in living healthier, longer lives. Once again, however, we unexpectedly find a dark side to it all. Gone are the old infectious foes, but replacing them are even more frustrating and, in some ways, more frightening enemies. They are variously known as "the new morbidity," "the diseases of civilization," and "the diseases of lifestyle." These ailments come as a result of our bad habits and our poor choices. The surgeon general has bemoaned "an epidemic of poor health practices."[1] The Center for Disease Control estimates that more than 50 percent of all deaths are related to lifestyle choices,[2] while Emory University's Health Policy Project explains that "64.7% of the years of life lost before age 65 result from preventable deaths."[3]

In many ways, the practice of medicine was more rewarding when patients were victimized by external tragedies than it is now when patients so often victimize themselves. As a result of this new morbidity, the heroic nature of medical practice has all but disappeared. A romanticized past envisions doctors risking their lives by working all hours to save a community from smallpox. Today, the vision has deteriorated into business-minded physicians taking care of patients with self-induced illnesses who live self-destructive lives, who expect to get well now and who threaten to sue if they don't.

Let's look at some examples of this morbid epidemic.

Stress-induced illnesses—These afflictions are the new bread and butter of medical practice. A high percentage of patients who visit a primary-care physician have stress-related ailments—headaches, hyper-acidity/ulcers, irritable bowel, malaise and fatigue, insomnia, chronic-pain syndromes, anxiety, depression. Burnout in the workplace produces many physical manifestations. The eating disorders of anorexia nervosa and bulimia are prevalent and increasing.

The "worried well"—Our society has also spawned an epidemic number of the "worried well." According to Harvard psychiatrist Arthur J. Barsky, M.D., "The substantial improvements in health status have not been accompanied by improvements in the subjective feeling of healthiness and physical well-being. Instead, people now report higher rates of disability, symptoms, and general dissatisfaction with their health."[4] Such patients are anxious about their health and refuse consolation, even though they have no demonstrable disease.

Pollution-related diseases—The pathologies induced by pollution are another malady of civilization. Where you find industrialization, high energy utilization, and high population density, you will find pollution-related diseases not far behind. A majority of cancers result from environmental causes (things we smoke, eat, drink, or breathe).

The incidence of bronchospastic diseases, such as asthma, is increasing, with air pollution a major culprit. Sick-building syndrome from artificially ventilated offices causes headaches and lethargy.

Lack of sexual restraint—The diseases resulting from sexual permissiveness are seen daily. Twenty-two possible infections can be caught through a single act of intercourse, giving abundant validation to the quip "You, me, and the microbe makes three." Tens of millions of cases of sexually transmitted diseases annually are followed by cervical abnormalities and cancer, pelvic inflammatory disease, infertility, ectopic pregnancies, teenage pregnancies, abortions, and AIDS.

Illicit drug use—The scourge of drug abuse has become an equal-opportunity destroyer, affecting nearly every segment of our society. The National Institute on Drug Abuse has estimated that "during the 1960s only 5% of the U.S. population had had any experience with illicit drug use. By the early 1970s . . . [this rose] to 10%." By 1980, 37 percent of the population over the age of twelve had used illicit drugs.[5] As a result, through at least portions of the 1980s, the United States owned the highest per capita illicit drug use of any industrialized country.[6] It is estimated that between fifty and one hundred billion dollars annually is spent purchasing illegal drugs. What makes people feed at a poisoned trough? According to Harvard psychiatrist Dr. Armand Nicholi, "People take these drugs to alter or to escape from a less than tolerable reality, and to meet intense emotional needs."[7]

Cigarette-related disease—Tobacco kills 350,000 Americans every year, making it the leading cause of premature death in the United States. In 1915, Americans smoked 18 billion cigarettes; the number now is 575 billion. Nearly thirty years after the surgeon general announced that cigarettes can be fatal, we still have 50 million smokers. Smoking kills more people every year than do "cocaine, heroin, [AIDS], traffic accidents, murder, and terrorist attacks *combined*."[8] One in six Americans dies from the effects of tobacco. Jimmy Carter convened a consultation on national health policy at Emory University's Carter Center by claiming, "If physicians listed tobacco as an underlying cause of death when appropriate, it would be apparent that tobacco kills more Americans every 18 months than were killed in all of the wars of the 20th century."[9]

Alcohol abuse—The second leading cause of premature death in the United States, with nine million alcoholics and another six million problem drinkers, alcohol abuse is implicated in half of all homicides, suicides, and automobile fatalities. The Bureau of Justice Statistics reports that drunk-driving arrests more than tripled over a recent fifteen-year period. Yet, by some estimates, only one out of two thousand drunk drivers is caught. The average age of first use for alcohol is 12.3 years. The American Academy of Pediatrics maintains that, of fourth graders, one in three believes drinking is a "big problem" in their age group.

THE PATHOLOGIES OF PROSPERITY

The prevalence of such self-destructive, lifestyle-related pathologies certainly makes medicine a secure profession. Those who predicted the human race would evolve into a communal picture of nontoxic, robust heartiness have been deeply shaken by the statistics of the last few decades. Not only are health professionals still needed, but even with the addition of fringe healers from herbalists to reflexologists, we are all still working overtime.

I will not dwell further on the above litany of sorrows other than to say that, in many ways, they are further evidence of the inability of progress to solve our deepest needs. Progress brings technology, affluence, and education, but not the kind of inner discipline necessary to maintain sound physical health.

In some ways, progress is too easy on us. It caters food in overabundance, but without regard for the requirement of restraint. It provides electricity and artificial lighting, but without regard for the requirement of sleep. And it supplies transportation and convenience, but without regard for the requirement of physical activity. As a result, we eat too much, sleep too little, and move hardly at all.

THE KEYS TO PHYSICAL MARGIN

Our bodies are, in one sense, sophisticated energy machines. If we properly care for the engine and load the appropriate fuel, our machine will operate reliably. Even when called upon to double or triple its performance, the body is capable of responding by tapping into energy reserves.

These reserves can be enhanced or depleted depending upon many factors—some external, some internal, and some eternal. It is wise for us to vigilantly do all we can to protect these reserves, for if they are drawn too low, ill results follow. We are left not only exhausted but unprotected as well.

Let's take, for example, the problem of stress. According to expert Dr. Martin Shaffer, our bodies are more vulnerable to the effects of stress when our "reserves of energy have been drawn down too low. With no reserve energy available, the body cannot resist effectively, and exhaustion sets in, often accompanied by disease. . . . This scenario suggests an important principle for stress management and control: The stronger the body's reserves, the better able the body will be to resist the ravages of stress."[10]

By what methods does Dr. Shaffer propose we build up our physical margin and strengthen our reserves? "The answer is straightforward. Maximum bodily strength and efficiency depend upon three factors: sleep, exercise, and nutrition. Only a body that is well rested, properly exercised, and correctly fed will be able to maintain its energy reserves in the face of serious stress."[11]

The keys to physical margin, then, are sleep, exercise, and nutrition. Let's check the record to see how we are doing, although I suspect you already know what we will find.

PERCHANCE TO SLEEP

A recent *Time* magazine cover bemoaned "the sleep gap." We live in "drowsy America," where factories, grocery stores, service stations, and restaurants are often open through the night. "Today new cultural and economic forces are combining to turn the U.S. into a 24-hour society," explains journalist Anastasia Toufexis.[12] Sleep disorders involve more than fifty million Americans.

Many round-the-clock cities never go to sleep. After pushing the limits to the breaking point, we push some more. Students pull "all-nighters" studying for exams; nurses check on sleeping patients and watch the monitors; taxi drivers listen to an all-night station on their radios and drive denizens of the dark around town. Mothers of young children work all day in the office and then all night in the nursery.

Shift workers, a growing percentage of the labor force, miss an extra five days of work per year solely because of fatigue, notes occupational and environmental-medicine expert Joseph LaDou, M.D. In addition, they use more caffeine, suffer more drug abuse, and take four times more sleep medication than the average American.[13] Even though sleep is not optional, "evidence is mounting that sleep deprivation has become one of the most pervasive health problems facing the U.S."[14]

BEST-SELLING ADIPOSE

Technology now exists to measure the percentage of body fat in sophisticated ways. One such machine was brought to our clinic for a conference on nutrition, and I volunteered to be tested. As they entered data into the computer, I was electronically connected and laid on a special mat. The machine calculated that I weighed twenty thousand pounds and was 99.9999 percent fat. It was funny until I felt myself jiggling when I laughed.

Obesity, or the "rounding of America," is such a ubiquitous problem that one-fourth to one-half of all adults are on a diet at any given time. The list of best sellers always has at least two or three dieting books. One in five Americans is obese (defined as 20 percent above ideal body weight)—but twice that number *think* they are. What can't be dieted off is surgically removed, at an estimated one hundred tons each year. Over the last two decades, the incidence of childhood obesity is up 54 percent in ages six through eleven and 39 percent in ages twelve through seventeen. "More die in the United States of too much food than of too little," observes John Kenneth Galbraith.[15]

EXTINCT EXERCISE

Some think the cause of our adipose problem is not that we eat too much, but we move too little. Our prosperity has allowed us to be cerebral and sedentary rather than physically robust, and lack of exercise has brought problems beyond obesity. A study from the Department of Health and Human Services revealed that 80 to 90 percent of Americans do not get enough physical exercise. Of children ages six through twelve, 40 percent of boys and 70 percent of girls can do only one pull-up.

In earlier eras, the sheer harshness of existence required a physically active, vigorous lifestyle. During Revolutionary-War days, when 90 percent of our population were farmers, physical labor was an indispensable part of daily activity. Today, however, only 2 percent of Americans earn their living off the land. Most of the rest of us left our fitness behind on the farm. Now, instead of pitching hay bales, we push pencils.

And, as we sit, we thicken.

MODELS NOT TO FOLLOW

I love medicine and am continuously aware of the privilege of my profession. I do not, however, love medicine when it takes away my margin. Yet this is precisely what medicine does for nearly all students, residents, and practitioners. Don't get me wrong. I am more than willing to put in long hours and sleepless nights when it is necessary. I have done it thousands of times. But it is no longer truly necessary. The patient and illness load, if spread out among all available physicians, does not require it any more. The system, however, has not yet caught on to that fact.

From the first day of training to the last call night before retirement, the medical system is notorious for its lack of margin. Many times I have attempted to refer patients to already-swamped doctors, only to discover that they were closer to death than the patients in their swamped waiting rooms.

The medical residents I teach are a classic example of a group of people living in continuous negative margin status. They are chronically sleep-deprived. Working from 70 to 120 hours a week, they are often physically and emotionally exhausted. These young physicians eat meals irregularly and see their families haphazardly. Yet this three-year rite of passage, which so typifies the absence of margin and violates every rule of good personal health, is defended as essential to medical education. In its defense, it does accomplish the important goal of clinical experience. But isn't there something a little perverse about teaching principles of health by violating so many of them?

My own training days are vivid in my memory. On call every third night, I would work thirty-six hours without sleep. Stumbling home the following sunset, I would begin to doze midway through supper. Finally, every third evening, I would be awake enough to recognize my wife. During my busiest week in residency, I worked 129 hours. "Having too much to do seems an integral part of the physician's life from medical school on," explains David Hilfiker, M.D. "There is always more to learn in medical school than can possibly be assimilated, more to do in internship and residency training than can possibly be done in twenty-four-hour days, more problems to take care of as a practicing physician than can reasonably be accommodated."[16]

It is only a matter of time before widespread rebellion erupts concerning the stressful, marginless lifestyle of medical practitioners, and recent medical school graduates are already demanding changes. The point is, practicing medicine does not *have* to take away margin. In the past, there was too much disease in too many patients and too few physicians. But that has now changed. Doctors continue to work sixty-hour weeks, but more out of economics and force of habit than necessity.

If the entire profession would back off a little, we could work with far less pressure, sleep in after a long night on call, not be upset when the front office asks us to see a walk-in patient with chest pain, and actually take *better* care of both our patients and ourselves. We could once again have some margin for family, service, and rest. Yet because of the profession's proud tradition of being overworked, change comes slowly.

RESTORING MARGIN IN PHYSICAL ENERGY

Virtually anyone, no matter how ravaged by insomnia, intemperance, and inactivity, can take steps to reverse self-induced bodily deterioration. The rules for restoring energy to the human body are not written out in calculus and hidden in the catacombs. On the contrary, they are a matter of public record, accessible to all.

The body can bounce back; God designed it so. But not without some cooperation from its owner. "Healing is a matter of time," understood Hippocrates, "but it is sometimes also a matter of opportunity." Let's look together at some prescriptions that might help.

Rx: 1 Take Personal Responsibility
I learned long ago that I can inform but not perform that which is needed in the lives of my patients. Until we accept personal responsibility for our own health, the road to the future will remain paved with aches and adipose.

If you are underslept, overweight, and unexercised, it is your job to change. I want to encourage you that change *is possible*. And I am more than willing to provide the needed information. But just as the body is yours, so is the responsibility.

Rx: 2 Gain Physical Margin Through Emotional Margin
In this chapter we will concentrate on the physical components of restoring energy. Never slight, however, the role that emotions play in our quest. A natural, God-ordained mutuality exists between physical

and emotional well-being. We have seen how social supports, nurturing relationships, service, volunteerism, laughter, purpose, vision, gratitude, grace, faith, hope, and love are all important to emotional health. They are equally important to physical health.

I encourage seekers of physical energy to look beyond the diet and exercise books and to first seek enhanced physical vitality through enhanced emotional vitality.

Rx: 3 Change Your Habits

If you do not have margin in physical energy, you probably have habits that need changing. Poor nutrition, poor exercise patterns, and (sometimes) poor sleep hygiene are called "habit disorders." Breaking old ways and establishing new patterns are necessary.

Changing habit disorders often requires changing lifestyles. Sometimes the changes required are small. More often, however, the adjustment entails a new way of looking at and reacting to both yourself and the world around you. In making these changes, it helps to surround yourself with a subculture of people who will support the changes rather than undermine them.

THE RITES OF SLEEP

Rx: 4 Value of Sleep

Many people in contemporary society have negative attitudes toward sleep. Often these are very productive people who resent the "wasted time." They also tend to be people who need less than average sleep themselves. Unfortunately, this attitude too often forces its way into other bedrooms uninvited.

Don't get caught in a web of shame spun by other people. A good night's sleep is not an embarrassment. It is not necessary to feel guilty if you are well rested. Sleep is God's idea, not ours. He created the necessity, and "he grants sleep to those he loves."[17] The need for sleep is undeniable and should be regarded as an ally, not an enemy. To sleep soundly for a full night is a valuable restorative gift. As anyone who has read Proverbs knows, however, the sluggard is left defenseless by Scripture.

Choose to get enough rest. Determine how much sleep you need to feel your best and then determine to get it. I personally feel best with seven to eight hours of sleep, as do the vast majority of adults.

Rx: 5   Develop Healthy Sleep Patterns

Many people don't sleep well simply because they practice poor sleep habits. Develop a healthy pattern of sleep. Retire at a similar time each evening; arise at a similar time each morning. Have a quiet room and a good mattress. If you suffer from cold feet, prewarm the sheets with an electric blanket. (There is some unresolved medical controversy about sleeping under electric blankets, but there is no danger whatever in prewarming the bed.) Don't engage in disturbing conversations immediately before bedtime. Instead, begin relaxing about an hour or so before retiring. Give yourself time to unwind from the day. Don't have a big meal within two hours of bedtime. Limit the intake of caffeine in the evening and, if necessary, in the afternoon as well. If you are a clock watcher, turn the clock toward the wall.

If sleep is delayed by racing thoughts or creativity, keep a notebook or even a small tape recorder next to the bed. I have done this for years. As soon as a thought threatens my somnolence, I write it down. Then I forget it.

Rx: 6   Don't Catastrophize Insomnia

If insomnia strikes, don't panic. It happens to everybody from time to time, and one or two nights of sleeplessness do not constitute a crisis. What can become a crisis, however, is your *reaction* to the experience.

After one or two nights of sleeplessness, a pattern develops. Annoyance turns to fear, then fear turns to panic. And nothing retards sleep like panic. Trying to force yourself to sleep is the surest way of preventing somnolence. A persistent pattern of insomnia sometimes begins with exactly this reaction of desperation. "Sleep is one of the few things in life that cannot be improved upon by trying harder," explains sleep expert Dr. Peter Hauri.

If insomnia is a problem, don't stay in bed awake. Get up, sit in a comfortable chair or lie on the couch, read, write a letter, have a light snack, drink some milk, take a walk, soak in the bathtub, play relaxing music, watch television. But don't worry.

Consider turning the night into a conversation with God. Pray. Listen. Meditate. Read the Word. Begin a spiritual journal. Listen to Christian radio. And don't forget to thank Him for the special opportunity of this time together. When tiredness begins to overtake you, retire once again with gratitude for the double blessing of this night: that of fellowship and now that of sleep.

Following a night or two of sleeplessness, a common mistake is to go to bed earlier the next evening. The understandable thinking is to hope that nine hours in bed will result in at least seven hours of sleep. But this is exactly the wrong tactic. It is actually more restful to stay in bed seven hours and get six hours of sleep than to stay in bed nine hours and get seven. Go to bed later, not earlier. As the problem resolves, you can gradually resume your normal sleep schedule.

Insomnia can sometimes be a symptom of depression. Instead of poor initiation of sleep, however, the sleeplessness of depression is usually characterized by early awakening. For this condition, antidepressant medications can often be very helpful. They are not sleeping pills—although they can have a beneficial sedative side effect. They are not narcotics—although they can help greatly with chronic pain and its associated sleeplessness. And they are not addicting.

Although there are occasional indications for sleeping pills, it is not a good idea to depend on them. If you are undergoing a particularly stressful event in your life, sometimes a sleeping aid for a few days will keep sleepless exhaustion from compounding your troubles. But use them for no more than two weeks. After that time, if you try to stop taking them you will suffer rebound insomnia.

Rx: 7 Don't Oversleep
As a rule, oversleeping will make you feel worse rather than better. Extra sleeping paradoxically often causes extra tiredness. Also, headaches are more common with excess sleep.

Rx: 8 Take a Nap
Many of the world's greatest leaders were nappers. Thomas Edison is said to have catnapped up to eight times a day. John F. Kennedy napped in the White House, and Churchill took daily naps even during World War II. No doubt Jesus Himself napped.

Naps can be revitalizing. Even the Federal Aviation Administration is considering allowing the pilot to nap during long flights while the copilot takes the controls.

If you have the opportunity and need to nap, it is best to follow certain guidelines. Don't nap for more than one hour. If you do, understand that a longer nap is not necessarily more restful. The most helpful naps are in the afternoon, taking advantage of a mild drop in body temperature that induces somnolence.

A short nap in the early evening can give added stamina for the hours ahead. A longer evening nap, however, will often hinder the initiation of sleep that night.

Rx: 9 Exercise for Sounder Sleep

One of the first benefits people notice when they embark on an exercise program is sounder sleep. Healthy physical tiredness probably has no equal as a sleep-inducing sedative.

Don't, however, exercise vigorously just before going to bed. While a routine of stretching exercises or a leisurely walk can be an excellent prelude to a good night's sleep, a six-mile run is not a good idea.

THE RECIPES OF NUTRITION

Rx: 10 Decrease Intake of Fat

The typical American diet derives 37 percent of its calories from fats. This percentage should be cut to thirty or below, which means we need to eliminate two hundred to three hundred calories of fat out of our diet each day. (See figure 8.1 below.)

Figure 8.1

Current Diet	Recommended Diet
37% Fat	30% Fat
16% Protein	12% Protein
22% Starches	46% Starches
25% Sugars	12% Sugars

Of course, we all know we should eat less fat, but we eat it anyway. There are three main reasons for this: It tastes good, it is our habit, and we can afford to. In rebuttal: There are other things that taste good, we can change our bad habits, and we can't afford not to.

If you have three lumps of food sitting in front of you—one fat, one protein, one carbohydrate—all weighing the same amount, the lump of fat will have twice as many calories as the other lumps. So, using very simplistic math, if you want to eat a pound of food, it makes sense to eat a pound of carbohydrates or protein rather than a pound of fat with twice the calories. Pastries, donuts, ice cream, butter, hamburgers, French fries, steak, gravy—they all sound good, but they are all calorie-dense. Our margin in physical energy disappears as our waistline expands.

Good nutrition begins not in the kitchen but at the front door of the grocery store. If it isn't good for you, don't buy it. If everything looks too good, then shop only after a big meal when things don't look nearly as good. If you still can't help yourself, try shopping at a co-op that doesn't carry junk food. If that still doesn't work, send someone else.

Rx: 11 Decrease Intake of Sugars

Forty-seven percent of the typical diet is made up of carbohydrates. Of this, starches (or complex carbohydrates, such as potatoes, beans, wheat, and corn) make up 22 percent and sugars (or simple carbohydrates, such as table sugar, the fructose in fruits, and the lactose in milk) make up 25 percent. We need to change this in three ways: increase total carbohydrates as a percentage of our diet; double the percentage of starches; and cut the amount of sugar in half.

As a dominant component of the diet, refined sugar is a fairly late arrival in the Western world. Two hundred years ago we ate two pounds a year per person; now the figure is from 120 to 170 pounds a year (thirty-three to forty-seven teaspoons a day).

Actually, the use of table sugar has been declining. The real problem comes in the "invisible" or "hidden" sugar added during food processing. But food processors only sell us what we buy, and we only buy what our children beg for. Ninety-five percent of the food ads on Saturday morning television are for junk food: sugared cereals, candy, small cakes, chips, gum. It is little wonder that our schoolyards roll with obesity. "Most nutritionists agree that the worst influence on a child's eating habits is television," observes Sarah Eby.[18] Perhaps that applies to their parents as well.

Rx: 12 Replace Processed Snacks with Fruit

Fruits can be a good substitute for fats and "hidden" sugars. Oftentimes we bypass fruits thinking they are too expensive. Then we travel down the aisle and pick out cookies, chips, and candy instead.

To expose the fallacy of this expense excuse, Linda and I did some calculations based on average costs in our supermarket.

Item	Average Cost Per Pound
Cookies	$3.11
Candy	3.03
Crackers	2.80
Small Cakes	2.53
Donuts	2.49
Grapes	.99
Oranges	.89
Apples	.74
Pears	.50
Bananas	.39

The argument that fruits are more expensive just disappeared. Compared to other types of snack foods with lots of fat and refined sugar in them, fruits are a bargain. They are tasty, often sweet. They are liked by both children and adults. They are a good source of fiber. They are available year-round.

My advice is to spend less money on processed snack foods and more money on fruits. Have them available in a fruit bowl on the table as well as in the refrigerator. Have different forms—fruit juices, fruit leather, dehydrated fruits.

Give yourself permission to buy fresh fruits in abundance, and then give your family permission to consume them liberally.

Rx: 13 Balanced Diet

In recommending fruits, I certainly don't intend to slight vegetables. But when we search for a replacement for fats and sweetened snacks, fruits stand a better chance in the competition.

Indeed, balanced food groups are so universally recommended that they hardly need my endorsement. And in addition to balancing the food groups, also balance the three meals. Many people skip one or two meals, thinking they are doing themselves a favor. Instead, it's a disfavor. Studies indicate that a daily habit of all three meals, taken in moderation and without between-meal snacking, is the clear winner when it comes to healthy outcomes, whether in weight, vigor, or longevity.

Rx: 14 Avoid Overeating

Put smaller portions on the table. Use a small plate. Chew food longer. Set your fork down between every bite. Don't prepare the next bite until you have finished chewing and swallowing the one in your mouth. Consciously taste your food. Don't take seconds. Always sit down to eat. Eat at only one place in the house. Don't eat in front of the television. Don't snack. Bite your tongue.

Rx: 15 Garden or Buy Direct

There are two ways to process food: God's way and the factory way. God has our best interest at heart; the factories often don't.

The ground, taking its orders from God, fortunately doesn't process food the way factories do. And, generally speaking, the less factory processing, the better the food. Always protect the most direct connection from the Father's hand to your table. If there are too many steps in between, chances are the food has been unhealthified in proportion to the number of steps. If there is plastic around it instead of dirt, suspect that it didn't come directly from God.

Of course, just because food successfully bypasses the factory does not guarantee a healthy end product. For example, some garden fertilizers and pesticides are acceptable, while others are not. Without getting into an extensive discussion about chemicals and additives, suffice it to say that my main concern is the added salt, sugar, and calories found in factory-processed foods. Avoid them if you can.

Rx: 16 Drink a Lot of Water

The universal recommendation is six to eight glasses of water a day. For many, ice water is more palatable than tap water.

Drinking a large glass of water before sitting down for a meal can help keep you full and suppress the appetite.

Rx: 17 Use Exercise as Both Appetite and Weight Reducer

It is a myth that exercise increases appetite. In most cases, vigorous exercise diminishes appetite, sometimes even to the point of nausea. So if it works for you, sweat before you eat.

Also, if the goal is weight reduction, combine exercise with dieting. Dieting alone will result in the loss of not only fat but also lean body tissue such as muscle. On the other hand, exercise alone requires a huge amount of effort for a small amount of weight loss.

Every extra pound we gain equals 3,500 calories. Figure 8.2 demonstrates how many hours of various exercises are required to burn 3,500 calories for people weighing 100 pounds, 150 pounds, or 200 pounds. As you can see, relying on exercise alone for weight reduction will yield frustratingly meager results. The balanced and sensible approach, therefore, combines both calorie restriction and calorie incineration in a weight-reduction program.

Figure 8.2 - Burning 3,500 Calories

		Number of Hours		
Activity and Intensity		*100 lbs*	*150 lbs*	*200 lbs*
Walking	2 mph	29.2	19.4	14.6
Walking	4 mph	15.8	10.5	7.9
Jogging	6 mph	7.2	4.8	3.6
Running	9 mph	5.0	3.4	2.5
Cross Country Skiing	8 mph	5.6	3.7	2.8
Bicycling	13 mph	8.2	5.5	4.1
Swimming	55 yds/min	6.6	4.4	3.3
Ironing		20.1	13.4	10.1
Chopping Wood		12.0	7.9	6.0

Rx: 18   McStay at Home

There is often no comparison between the calories, fat, and sodium we consume when we prepare food at home versus dining out. For some, the difference between normal weight and obesity is the difference between eating in and eating out.

THE REGIMENS OF EXERCISE

Rx: 19   Exercise for the Heart

There are five aspects to a fitness evaluation: cardiorespiratory endurance, muscle strength, muscle endurance, flexibility, and body composition. Fitness in each of these five is recommended, but by far the most important and beneficial is cardiorespiratory endurance.

Think of your heart as a plow horse. You abuse it and abuse it and abuse it—but it never complains. And then one day in the middle of a furrow, it drops dead.

Don't abuse your heart. It is your workhorse. Every day it beats one hundred thousand times and pumps sixteen hundred gallons of blood over sixty thousand miles of vessels. Say thank you to your heart. Buy it roses. Encourage it every chance you get.

One way you can encourage your heart is by conditioning it. Through exercise, for example, you could cut your heart rate from perhaps eighty beats a minute down to sixty. In so doing, you would save your heart thirty thousand beats a day and eleven million beats a year. As a token of its appreciation, it would send you back a gift. Try it for a few months and see what the gift is.

A specific fitness program aimed at conditioning the cardio-respiratory system focuses on the body's ability to deliver and use oxygen. *Aerobic conditioning* trains your heart, your lungs, your blood, and your blood vessels in such a way that they can deliver more oxygen faster and more efficiently to the body.

How is this accomplished? By performing thirty to forty-five minutes of *sustained* exercise—walking, jogging, swimming, bicycling, etc.—three times a week.

A common misconception people have is that they already live an active life, so why all the fuss? They are on their feet all day, up and down stairs, lifting, bending, stooping, and generally on the go continuously. They always come home tired; therefore, they assume they get plenty of exercise. It is important to recognize, however, that although this might be a busy lifestyle in one sense, it is not conditioning exercise.

Note well: Of the twenty-nine prescriptions in this chapter, this recommendation will do more to establish margin in physical energy than any of the others.

Rx: 20 Exercise for the Muscles

A second kind of exercise has to do with skeletal muscle development. Despite what many falsely believe, this is not the same as cardiorespiratory conditioning. Nevertheless, muscle conditioning is important and often neglected. While weight lifting and calisthenics do not constitute overall aerobic conditioning, they can give enhanced strength, speed, agility, and self-esteem.

There are two aspects to muscle fitness—strength and endurance. In a weight-training program, for example, lifting heavier weights with fewer repetitions increases strength, while lifting lighter weights with more repetitions increases endurance. As we age, muscle strength declines more quickly than does muscle endurance.

I do not support weight training for the vanity of it. But neither should it be forsaken simply because it is misused by bronzed bodies who flaunt it. The simple fact is, progress wrongly released us from the need to use our muscles, and if we do not use them we lose them.

Rx: 21 Exercise for Flexibility

Flexibility exercising is the least demanding in terms of wear and tear. We seldom huff, puff, or sweat. Yet it can help keep us moving and decrease our aches and pains, particularly in the back.

As we age, our flexibility becomes constricted. Watch the contortions of young children and compare them to your own creaky hinges. Undergoing a program of flexibility can help regain some of the lost range of motion with laudatory results. Our bodies much prefer wearing out to rusting out.

Rx: 22 Exercise for the Mind and Spirit

One hundred percent of people who exercise to the point of cardio-respiratory fitness will experience an increased sense of well-being. "We know that people who regularly exercise say they handle pressure better, feel more confident, happier and less depressed. . . . They even say they sleep better at night," says Jackie Kuta, University of Wisconsin exercise physiologist. "There are definite benefits for the mind, too. . . . Probably the most important thing is that it allows you to focus on something besides whatever is causing your stress."[19]

Exercise has a tranquilizing effect on the body. It helps to decompress stress and is good medicine for anxiety or depression. Along with increased energy, it grants increased alertness, increased independence, increased dignity, and increased self-esteem. "Exercise isn't just for the physically unfit. It's for the mentally unfit, too. I can recommend it for anyone who's depressed," explains aerobic expert Kenneth Cooper, M.D. "If exercise benefits the body, it can do wonders for the mind."[20]

Rx: 23 Bike or Walk

When studying in Switzerland for a year, I lived with a Swiss family. My "Swiss father," a physician-researcher for a pharmaceutical company, rode his bicycle to and from work each day, including a round trip home for lunch. My Swiss mother walked to town each morning to buy groceries for the day—bread, vegetables, meat, milk. They were not alone in these habits. As I daily made my way to the study center, the streets would be crowded with bicyclists and pedestrians.

As citizens of the most prosperous country in the world, the Swiss can afford to drive, but choose not to. Although the pattern has shifted over the years to more automobile use, I will never forget the example of health that was set for me that year.

In the United States, however, we go everywhere in our cars. Vehicles have become easy chairs on wheels. We don't even use arm strength to put down the windows. And when we arrive at our destinations, we still don't disembark. Instead, we "drive up" for our banking and "drive through" for our fast food. Now we even have drive-up churches and, of all things, I once heard of a drive-up baby clinic where you lift your child through the window to a waiting pediatrician.

Climb stairs rather than use the elevator. Park a block or two from your destination. Get off the bus or subway one stop early. *Any exercise is better than no exercise*, even if it is a walk of only ten steps.

Rx: 24   Exercise in the Morning (If You Can)
Morning exercisers seem to maintain a conditioning program better than those who choose the evening hours. One study followed exercisers for a year and discovered that 75 percent of those who worked out in the morning were able to continue their regimen. In contrast, "50 percent of those who exercised at midday and 25 percent of those who exercised in the evening" were able to maintain their programs.[21]

Rx: 25   Choose What Works for You
Try to find the kind of exercise that is most practical and enjoyable for you. "The generic drug here is exercise, and running is simply a brand," explains fitness activist George Sheehan, M.D. "It's a question of finding your brand of the drug."

Don't start playing racquetball if you hate the sport. I don't enjoy swimming and get cold every time I enter the water. So if I decided to swim as my exercise, I would be guaranteeing failure. However, I very much enjoy playing basketball with my twelve-year-old son, Matt (even though this often turns into more an exercise in futility than an exercise in conditioning, with the "guaranteed failure" coming in the score).

Rx: 26   Stick with It
You will be able to find many temptations to quit any exercise program. Prominent among them are:

Fatigue—Many complain of being too tired. But when you feel too tired to exercise is actually a good time to do it. Often, paradoxically, you will feel *less* tired after the workout than before. Several nurses at one of the hospitals where I work go to the exercise lab after a long day on the wards. Are they tired? Of course they are. But do they feel better after working out for a while? Do they have a more energized, productive, and enjoyable evening? Yes.

Have you ever noticed how you can come home fatigued, only to see the exhaustion disappear soon thereafter when doing something enjoyable? I remember one evening being very tired but needing to mow the lawn anyway (something I normally enjoy doing). After fifteen minutes, I was surprised to notice that the tiredness had disappeared. Fatigue, studies suggest, often has its source in emotional rather than muscular or cardiovascular exhaustion—although this is not to deny the validity of muscular tiredness as well.

Waning enthusiasm—Another reason for wanting to quit is diminishing enthusiasm. "Be prepared for 'going stale,' that period when you begin wondering why you ever started a training program," warns Dr. Cooper. "It happens to everyone. Just sweat it out. Go through the motions. Your enthusiasm will return."[22]

Discouragement—Yet another is the feeling that all this effort is not doing any good. What you don't realize is that it is doing good—you just can't fully sense it yet. Approach exercise as an investment. If you don't begin to receive dividends within two months, you have my permission to quit.

Rx: 27 Continue It Until the Hearse Arrives
You can't store up energy or exercise benefit for the future. If you exercise six months for cardiorespiratory fitness then stop, within two weeks the benefits will begin to disappear. Once you begin a program, plan to continue it in at least some form for the rest of your life. If that sounds like a big commitment, maybe that's because it is a big commitment. The majority of recommendations in this book for restoring margin have to do with sustainable lifestyle changes rather than "momentary compliance."

"The real battle over starting to exercise," explains Dr. Don Powell, "takes place in your mind, not in your body."[23]

Rx: 28 Be Realistic
One of my patients with advanced lung cancer came in wearing a concerned look on her face. "Doctor, I had my cholesterol tested and it is

221. Is that too high?" Her death three months later had nothing to do with cholesterol. There are enough problems to worry about without adding nonproblems to the list.

▶ Focus on the important issues. If you are forty pounds overweight, don't worry about how much vitamin C is in a potato.
▶ Choose appropriate exercises. If you are elderly, it is probably best not to choose a running program. If you have arthritis or chronic low back pain, you may need to choose nonweightbearing exercises such as swimming or cycling (although a walking program is often beneficial for low back pain).
▶ If dieting, aim to lose only one to two pounds a week. Don't try to climb twenty stairs in a single bound. Slow changes are more sustainable.
▶ Be patient and persistent. "How poor are they who have no patience!" wrote William Shakespeare. "What wound did ever heal but by degrees?"
▶ Fads, scams, and frauds have a therapeutic value "as thin as the homeopathic soup that was made by boiling the shadow of a pigeon that had been starved to death," to borrow from Abraham Lincoln. Remember, *all* diets work short-term. Often the fast weight loss is water loss. John Renner, M.D., of the Consumer Health Information Research Institute, reports that there are ten thousand to fifteen thousand fad diets. If you find a new one, give him a call.
▶ Understand that this is not a definitive text on sleep, nutrition, or exercise. This chapter contains focused, practical hints that will help restore margin. Broadly applied, they can be of great help. But for more detailed information, see your physician or nutritionist.
▶ Expect to have ups and downs. Even the experts do.
▶ Set goals, but let them be reachable.
▶ Believe in yourself. I do.

Rx: 29 Give Your Body a Chance

The body is a miracle of complexity and sophistication that exceeds comprehension. Fortunately, most of it runs on automatic pilot—the heart beats, the blood circulates, the glands secrete, the enzymes catalyze, the electrolytes balance, the glucose metabolizes, the liver detoxifies. Even our thinking and breathing are largely automatic and involuntary; our brain and lungs function not because we tell them to but because God tells them to.

Describing the human body in detail would take an encyclopedia. Suffice it to say that God gave us an amazing gift, and all we are required to do is feed it, water it, rest it, and move it. Yet it needs to be the right food, water, rest, and movement.

If we perform our assignment well, we will find energy we never knew we had. We will work better, run better, feel better, heal better, and live better.

Margin in Time

Ted Anderson rose at 5:00 a.m. to howling winds and drifting snow. He washed, pulled on his work clothes and coat, and headed for the barn. Familiar with work he enjoys, Ted started feeding the 150 head of Angus cattle and attending to his other farm chores. By 7:00 a.m., he was back inside to have breakfast with his wife, Jae, and help get three-year-old Lottie Marie ready for the day. Quickly changing clothes, his next challenge on this frigid morning was to survive the icy roads into St. Paul. The usual one-hour commute to his systems-analyst job always takes longer when detoured through Siberia.

Meanwhile, Jae and Lottie Marie set off on an icy Wisconsin adventure of their own, braking and sliding the fifteen minutes to the veterinarian clinic where Jae is a full-time technician and animal groomer. Lottie has done well spending her first three years in the clinic. As a baby, she would sit in an infant seat or lay on a blanket. Now that she is older, she is always easily entertained. Each afternoon she takes a long nap in the back room.

After Ted returned home at 7:00 p.m., he finished the remaining chores on their eighty-acre farm. Most evenings, this was an hour or two of work.

Besides their own farm, the Andersons rent an additional eight hundred acres for open pasturing and for raising hay, corn, and oats. These crops have to be planted, cultivated, fertilized, harvested, baled, chopped, and stored. And, of course, the farm equipment—tractors, cultivators, balers—has to be cleaned, maintained, and repaired as well.

Anyone who would accept the job of vaccinating 150 head of cattle must be familiar with animals, and Jae is. She also has additional dogs, sheep, and horses of her own to care for.

Obviously, the Andersons are a hard-working young family. They love animals, farming, rural living, and challenges.

But they are marginless.

"What would happen if Lottie got sick?" I asked.

"She never has. We've been fortunate. She's been a great baby."

"Do you breed your herd?" I asked. "What happens during calving? How do you manage to monitor the births?"

"The Angus is famous for easy calving," explained Jae. "It *usually* just happens. All we do is check every day before and after work. Oftentimes we discover a calf that has already been born—or three or four. Then we take any newborns, weigh them, tag and vaccinate them, and give them back to mom. If any trouble arises, we have someone from the vet clinic come and help."

Lately, however, the system has been tested. This spring, the crops were planted late. Bad weather this fall delayed their harvest. The corn is now in storage, but wet with snow. They worry about mold.

A few months ago, some heifers were frightened out of the pasture by hunters. After the neighbors called, the chase was on. "We had to get help," explained Jae. "One person can't just run out and catch a nine-hundred-pound black heifer in the middle of the night without help." Some mischievous heifers continued to elude capture. Two were hit by cars on the road, necessitating police involvement.

Deciding to artificially inseminate one hundred cows this summer was a further strain. This type of breeding requires observing the herd closely. For several hours each morning and again each evening, the cows must be walked into a corral and watched. If any are in heat, they have to be separated out for insemination. This demand saw other chores suffer.

Since making the decision to expand their own family, Ted and Jae are planning some changes in their workload. "We are going to sell off at least half the cows and rent a smaller acreage next year,"

Jae explained. "And after the second baby is born, I will be quitting my job."

"How do you feel about that?" I inquired.

"Wonderful!" she explained through her fever and flu. "I love my job, and my boss is a good friend. But it will be wonderful to have more time at home."

TIME AND HOW WE TALK

Ted and Jae, along with millions of other Americans, live busy lives. Their industry and fortitude are in many ways reminiscent of the pioneer spirit that, centuries ago, carved a great nation out of a huge wilderness. They have work, a family, and a farm—all of which they enjoy. About the only thing they don't have is margin.

"I love a broad margin to my life," posited another farmer (of sorts), Henry David Thoreau. "Sometimes, in a summer morning, having taken my accustomed bath, I sat in my sunny doorway from sunrise till noon, rapt in a revery." Because his chronicles are so widely acclaimed, we think, *What a wonderful sentiment he expresses here.* But were our neighbor to seek this same reverie, we would criticize it as slothful. In contrast to Thoreau's love of a "broad margin," our modern view of time is to compress it and milk it for every nanosecond of productivity we can get.

To understand how a society experiences time, examine its operative vocabulary. We talk of no time, lack of time, not enough time, or being out of time. Trying to get more time, we borrow time only to incur a time debt and end up with even less time. Management in the workplace is so time-conscious that they practice time-management skills and time-compression techniques. They use a computerized timepiece to assure work efforts are time-intensive with no time lost. This sense of time urgency creates time pressure and time stress. Then, it's crisis time.

If God would allow us to delete any of these time phrases we thought destructive, which would you choose? If you had the opportunity of setting the time agenda for society, which concepts of time would you endorse and which would you renounce? Many executives and type As would vote to keep time linked with speed and productivity. A typical manager's view of margin? If you can catch it, kill it.

The rest of us, however, would strike these time phrases from our collective vocabulary as mortifying to the human spirit. Of course work time is important. But so is discretionary time, that is, margin. Some discretionary time would be used as leisure time, play time, free time, or time off. Some would be personal time, solitude time, fallow time, and time to think. We hope a good portion of it would be time together: sharing time, family time, couple time, prayer time.

Ideally, you see, our time should all be God's time, directed by Him and used for His purposes. It is not right that progress has tyrannized us so.

TIME AND TWITCHING

I have a fantasy: If a terrorist organization were to simultaneously trigger all the world's alarm clocks, stove timers, beepers, factory whistles, car horns, doorbells, dinner bells, digital-watch alarms, fuzzbusters, car phones, telephones, intensive-care alarms, smoke alarms, fire alarms, burglar alarms, civil-defense alarms, and sirens—namely, every manmade, adrenaline-shocking device that signals "Hurry!"—do you think it would be enough to bring Christ back prematurely, out of sheer pity?

Have you ever had a beeper go off in your ear when you were sleeping? It is one of the most horrifying experiences ever dreamed up by technology to ambush innocent, already-exhausted wretches. Although it has happened to me thousands of times, to date I have not even begun to approach psychic accommodation to the experience. It is fitting that a society with urgency as its emblem should have Valium as its addiction. Where are the noises that tell us to slow down? Which way to Lake Wobegon, that "quiet town, where much of the day you could stand in the middle of Main Street and not be in anyone's way"?

Columnist Bob Greene called it the "twitching of America." Futurist David M. Zach called it "hyperliving—skimming along the surface of life." The late Norman Cousins called it "a sprinting, squirting, shoving age." E. F. Schumacher called it "the forward stampede." From "fast food" to the "weekend squeeze" to the "Christmas rush," time has us in its grip.

CONFOUNDED SUNDIAL!

Long before our nanosecond culture, frustration with time urgency was apparent. Already in 200 BC, Plautus was cursing the sundial.

The gods confound the man who first found out
How to distinguish hours! Confound him, too,
Who in this place set up a sun-dial,
To cut and hack my days so wretchedly
Into small portions.[1]

Of course, time frenzy had barely begun, and were Plautus alive today he might run his chariot off a cliff. What was it like to have no notion of a second or a minute or even an hour? To never be late . . . or early. To not even know what late or early is. To never hear an alarm.

The first mechanical clocks were alarms of sorts, introduced in the Western world during the 1200s. Only a bell indicated time. In the 1300s, the dial and hour hand were added. "Here was man's declaration of independence from the sun, new proof of his mastery over himself and his surroundings," explains historian Daniel Boorstin. "Only later would it be revealed that he had accomplished this mastery by putting himself under the dominion of a machine with imperious demands all its own."[2]

By the 1600s, the minute and second hands were common. The invasion of the wristwatch began in 1865, about the same time Matthew Arnold penned his famous "The Scholar Gypsy"—a coincidence perhaps, but still one wonders.

O born in days when wits were fresh and clear,
    And life ran gaily as the sparkling Thames;
        Before this strange disease of modern life,
With its sick hurry, its divided aims,
    Its heads o'ertax'd, its palsied hearts, was rife—
        Fly hence, our contact fear!

In 1879, Thomas Alva Edison produced the first electric light. If the clock broke up the day, the light bulb broke up the night. Humanity was flushed with its presumed victory over yet another of nature's limitations. Yet all victories have their associated costs. The clock and the light—they gifted us with time, then they stole it away.

THE PREDICTION THAT TURNED OUT ALL WRONG

Thirty years ago, futurists peering into their crystal balls predicted that one of the biggest problems for coming generations would be what to do with their abundant spare time. I remember hearing this prediction often. In 1967, testimony before a Senate subcommittee claimed that by 1985 people could be working just twenty-two hours a week or twenty-seven weeks a year or could retire at age thirty-eight.[3]

Exactly when they stopped talking this way I am not sure, but they did stop. No one sits around today trying to figure out how to spend free time. On the contrary, the topic of conversation is usually how to get some.

According to a Harris Survey, the amount of leisure time enjoyed by the average American has decreased 37 percent since 1973. Over the same period, the average workweek, including commuting, has jumped from under forty-one hours to nearly forty-seven hours.[4] When you add the total hours worked by the dual-income family outside the home, the difference is even more accentuated.

Progress was billed as leisure-permitting and time-gifting. The opposite has been true. "The modern world of streamlined transportation, instantaneous communication, and time-saving technologies was supposed to free us from the dictates of the clock and provide us with increased leisure. Instead there seems never to be enough time," explains Jeremy Rifkin in *Time Wars*. "Tangential or discretionary time, once a mainstay, an amenity of life, is now a luxury."[5]

THE SPONTANEOUS FLOW OF PROGRESS

How can one explain this gap between the prediction and the reality? Instead of the workweek shrinking, it is expanding; instead of free time increasing, it is decreasing. And in spite of "time-saving" devices, we have less time.

To help us understand the answer, let us return to an axiom of progress:

> *The spontaneous flow of progress is toward increasing stress, complexity, and overload.*

Now we may add a corollary to this axiom:

> *The spontaneous flow of progress is to consume more of our time, not less . . . to consume more of our margin, not less.*

In other words, if we sit back, do nothing about it, and watch it happen, next year at this time we will have less time margin than we do right now. For every hour progress saves by organizing and technologizing our time, it consumes two more hours through the consequences, direct or indirect, of this activity. Because this fact is counterintuitive and subtle, we do not recognize it happening.

"People are submitting themselves to time-devouring technology," claims Todd Gitlin. This Berkeley sociologist is particularly concerned about the cellular phone craze creating more work rather than saving more time. "We're a nerve-racked society where people have difficulty sitting back and thinking of the purpose of what they do."[6]

"Paradoxical as it may seem, modern industrial society, in spite of an incredible proliferation of labor-saving devices, has not given people more time to devote to their all-important spiritual tasks; it has made it exceedingly difficult for anyone, except the most determined, to find any time whatever for these tasks," observes E. F. Schumacher. "In fact, I think I should not go far wrong if I asserted that the amount of genuine leisure available in a society is generally in inverse proportion to the amount of labor-saving machinery it employs."[7]

INTERRUPTIONS AND JUNK MAIL

Nearly all of us are caught scratching our heads about this mystery of having so little time in an era of so many conveniences and such vaunted efficiency. How can this be? To help bring this mystery to light, let us examine some of the uniquely contemporary ways we spend our time.

In a lifetime, the average American will

- Spend six months sitting at traffic lights waiting for them to change.
- Spend one year searching through desk clutter looking for misplaced objects.
- Spend eight months opening junk mail.
- Spend two years trying to call people who aren't in or whose line is busy.
- Spend five years waiting in lines.
- Spend three years in meetings.
- Learn how to operate twenty thousand different things, from pop machines to can openers to digital radio controls.

In addition, the average person will

▶ Commute forty-five minutes every day.
▶ Be interrupted seventy-three times every day. (The average manager is interrupted every eight minutes.)
▶ Receive six hundred advertising messages every day (television, newspapers, magazines, radio, billboards).
▶ Travel 7,700 miles every year.
▶ Watch 1,700 hours of television every year.
▶ Open six hundred pieces of mail every year.

What did we do with all our time before we had traffic lights, telephones and busy signals, televisions, interruptions, and cluttered desks? What did we do with our time before we spent it shopping for things we don't need? What did we do with our time before we used it to sort through forty-three annual pounds of junk mail? What did teenagers do with their time before they began listening to ten thousand hours of rock music between grades seven and twelve? Is it possible the time margin was used for things more inherently valuable to the Kingdom than commuter traffic, busy telephones, and junk mail? Is it possible the time was spent on things physically taxing instead of mentally frustrating? Is it possible the time margin was used for conversing, for serving, for resting, for praying?

True, we get to places faster—but we have more places to go. A net loss. We have devices to help us clean—but we have more things stuffed into more square footage to clean. A net loss. Hasn't the light bulb given us more time because now we can plan activities during the evening that were previously limited to daylight hours? Yes. The light bulb has given us more capacity to be busy, to produce, and to fill up schedules in the evening—when before all we could do was sit around the table and read or sit by the fire and read or sit with family and friends and visit until it was time for all to go to bed. A net loss.

Let's revisit the Third World. Here we find no televisions, no shopping malls, no traffic lights, no telephones, no cluttered desks, no junk mail. So what do people do with their time? It exists for them as margin. Some of their time is used for work—the physical work of growing food, which is good for the body and spirit. Some of their time is used for visiting the marketplace, which is good for community. A good portion of their time is for leisure. Time to watch the kids play or the donkeys bray. Or to talk to the neighbor. Or to sleep.

WORK AND TIME STRESS

When we think of time pressure, perhaps no thought comes as quickly to mind as the workplace. The stressors we experience there, according to business consultant Douglas LaBier, "are rooted in pure bombardment: the accumulation of too much work relative to the time we have, too many demands from our work and personal lives, and too many decisions facing us and not enough time to deliberate about them. In short, too much to deal with in a world which is too busy and . . . in which we all feel tremendous pressure to make the right decision right now."[8]

When appropriately undertaken, work is biblically required and an absolute necessity for healthy living. Many, however, are so driven by their work that they can never take a day off or enjoy a quiet walk in the woods. Whether we call them "type A," "driven," "workaholic," or "extra effort people," they have a problem with work addiction. They do not notice the lack of balance in their lives, for they are too preoccupied with leading our national charge toward production, expansion, and success.

Such a lopsided drive toward accomplishment lands work-addicted people top positions in nearly every endeavor. From this vantage point they often systematically remove from their employees the same freedoms they themselves have forsaken. It is common to see a worker wishing for some measure of breathing space, yet gasping for freedom because of the demands of an excessively controlling boss. These employers are so affixed on success that their lives—and the lives of those they control—contain little besides work.

Meanwhile, for the exhausted, frustration-filled employee, there are three assignments due at the same time—yesterday. Deadlines flood over them like the Mississippi at springtime. They are on the road; then they are transferred. Debt and taxes mount, so they work harder. Family and friends become strangers passing in the night. First, they miss Johnny's home run and Betsy's first step. Then, they miss John's wedding and Elizabeth's graduation.

Because financial margin is often nonexistent, people seek supplemental employment. Many work two jobs or extra shifts. Moonlighting is increasing. Work has invaded evenings, nights, weekends, holidays, and worship days. Stores and restaurants that once respected margin respect it no longer, often open twenty-four hours a day, 365 days a year. Such expansion pushes the issue to its limits and is hardly the way to gain more time margin.

Harvard economist Juliet Schor explains that the average American will work the equivalent of one month longer this year than twenty years ago. Not only are there more dual-earner families (nearly two-thirds of married American women are employed), but also we have record rates of overtime and moonlighting. Employed mothers now put in an average of sixty-five hours a week, when you combine domestic work with the hours of labor logged on their other jobs. "And my figures," Schor points out, "are extremely conservative."[9]

Now, however, for the first time in fifteen years, Americans are choosing leisure over work as the most important thing in their lives. Upon first reflection, many might attribute this trend to laziness and lament it as reflective of all that is wrong with our country. But I see it as a corrective reaction to time starvation.

NANOSECOND EFFICIENCY

Improving productivity in the workplace is the equivalent of body-building in the gym, and efficiency is the steroid. Bosses know that time pressure works, that it increases both productivity and efficiency. But who is to say when it has been pushed too far? How much can people take? Many video-display-terminal workers are now monitored electronically. Every keypunch is recorded, and if their quota is not met, their record is tainted and their job threatened.

Speed. Supercomputers operate at trillionths of a second. Do you know what that means? Neither do I, and I have a degree in physics. A trillionth of a second has no human reference.

Speed. Using electronic linkages, computers can make transactions so fast that the same dollars can finance seven different deals on the same day.

Speed. At international currency exchanges, traders watch their video-display screens as the constantly changing world-currency prices flash before them. If they move fast enough at the right moment, they can make hundreds of thousands of dollars in a couple of minutes. "For us, currencies have a value not for a day or an hour, but for a second," explained one trader.

Speed. In the past, it took weeks to send a letter by pony express. Then, it took days by mail. Then, hours by overnight jet. Now, it takes only seconds. "The fax has destroyed any sense of patience or grace that existed," says Hollywood publicist Josh Baron. "People are so crazy now that they call to tell you your fax line is busy."[10]

Speed and efficiency are the keys to productivity, and productivity is the key to success. But, of course, we must have quality. So we want more and more speed, more and more efficiency, more and more productivity, with better and better quality. In the end we have platinum products and dead workers.

"There is more to life," recognized Ghandi, "than increasing its speed."

TIME STRESS AND OUR FRIENDS

The marginless lifestyle and its resultant chronic time pressure are particularly devastating to our relationships: to self, to family, to others, to God. "I don't have time for relationships anymore," laments one business employee. "I got tired of calling up and apologizing—'Sorry about dinner; I've got to work late again.'"[11]

Everyone needs personal time. Those who say they don't need time for self are probably the ones who need it the most. We all need time to let the dust settle, to evaluate how life is going, to plan for the future, to focus on that which is spiritually authentic. "Those who are caught up in the busy life have neither the time nor quiet to come to understand themselves and their goals," quotes Robert Banks. "Since the opportunity for inward attention hardly ever comes, many people have not heard from themselves for a long, long time. Those who are always 'on the run' never meet anyone any more, not even themselves."[12]

Everyone needs family time. Families have been particularly hard hit by the time famine. Nearly every study on family stress reveals time pressures to be at or near the top. Noted family researcher Dolores Curran has found that, of the top ten family stressors, four have to do with lack of time:

- ▶ Insufficient couple time
- ▶ Insufficient "me" time

❯ Insufficient family playtime
❯ Overscheduled family calendars[13]

Consider the amount of time we spend in some of these relation-ships. Spouse-to-spouse time averages as little as four minutes a day of meaningful conversation. Parent-to-child quality time resides in the same neighborhood: between thirty-seven seconds and five minutes a day, depending on the study. "Making an appointment is one way to relate to your child," says UCLA anthropologist Peter Hammond, "but it's pretty desiccated. You've got to hang around with your kids."[14]

There are many tempting competitors for a parent's attention today, leaving us in a quandary about how much time and emotional energy we should give to child-rearing. But human children are not capable of self-rearing; they never have been nor will they ever be. "The inevitable loser from this life in the fast lane is the little guy who is leaning against the wall with his hands in the pockets of his blue jeans," explains family psychologist Dr. James Dobson. "Crowded lives produce fatigue—and fatigue produces irritability—and irritability pro-duces indifference—and indifference can be interpreted by the child as a lack of genuine affection and personal esteem."[15]

Everyone needs sharing time. We each must have time to give away in the nourishing of our relationships. Calendars today are so crowded, however, that there is no space to pencil in a friend. As a result, long-term friendships are vanishing and neighborhood identities are fading. "Neighbors no longer share common aspirations or values," explains one *Wall Street Journal* columnist. "Struggling just to maintain their standard of living, people don't have time for their families, let alone their neighbors."[16]

Everyone needs God time. Because He is not temporally pushy about His agenda, God is too easy to forget. He just waits . . . and waits. What does He think of "efficient" prayers? What happened to the "Be still and know that I am God" times? Societies that have the accelerator to the floor are doomed to become God-less. Speed does not yield devotion.

TIME AND THE INVENTOR OF TIME

Do you think Jesus would have carried a pocket calendar? Would He have consulted it before making commitments? Would He have bypassed the leper because His calendar said He was late for the Nazareth spring banquet?

Do you think Jesus would have worn a wristwatch? What would have been His reaction if the temple service extended past noon and alarms went off in the crowd? Would He have driven out the clock watchers along with the moneychangers? What would He have thought of the parishioner I knew who weekly timed the pastor's sermons with a stopwatch and reported the statistics on the way out of church?

Do you think Jesus would have carried a beeper? Would Martha and Mary have paged Him to come and raise Lazarus from the dead? Can you imagine Him being paged out of the Last Supper?

The clock and the Christ are not close friends. Imagine what God thinks of us now that we are so locked into schedules that we have locked ourselves out of the Sermon on the Mount—it is hardly possible to walk the second mile today without offending one's pocket calendar. We jump at the alarm of a Seiko but sleep through the call of the Almighty.

RESTORING TIME MARGIN

Progress tricked us into trusting it—then it exhausted us. But we are not helpless. The clock can be resisted. Time margin can be taken back. Let's see what steps we can take to restore sanity to our schedules.

Rx: 1 Expect the Unexpected
Nearly everything takes longer than anticipated. If you want some breathing room, increase your margin of error. For example, if you are chronically late, try adding an extra 20 percent time margin to your scheduled activities.

Rx: 2 Learn to Say No
As with emotional energy margin, saying no is not just a good idea—it is an absolute necessity. If there are one hundred good things to do and you can do only ten of them, you will have to say no ninety times.

Rx: 3 Turn Off the Television
As long as you are saying no, say it to your television set. For the average adult, this would gain more than thirty hours a week. No other

single effort will secure as much time margin as this simple, nearly impossible action.

Rx: 4   Prune the Activity Branches

"I view my life as a tree," explains Jean Fleming. The trunk is the anchor of her life, her relationship to Christ. The limbs represent those major focus areas that God has given her—family, job, ministry, and personal development. And the branches represent the ever-proliferating multitude of activities. "Even without special care, activity branches multiply. Soon the profusion of branches becomes more prominent than the trunk and limbs. When this happens, I feel trapped, frustrated, and empty. Why? Because my life is shaped and drained by activities that have lost their pertinence to Christ."[17]

Activities and commitments often have a way of self-perpetuating even when we are no longer particularly interested in them. It is much harder to stop something than it is to start it. Periodically, it is important to get the clippers and prune away.

Rx: 5   Practice Simplicity and Contentment

We all consume significant quantities of time in the buying and then maintaining of things. A life of voluntary simplicity and contentment, on the other hand, is opposed to the unnecessary proliferation of material possessions. It is free of the clutter much of society must sort through on a daily basis. With fewer possessions, we do not have as many things to take care of. With a simpler wardrobe, our choice of what to wear each morning becomes less time-consuming. With a smaller estate, there will be less debt bondage in our work schedule.

Recognize unnecessary possessions for what they are: stealers of divine time. At the beginning of every day we are given assignments that have eternal significance—to serve, to love, to obey, to pray. Instead, we squander much of this time on things that very soon will leave us forever.

Rx: 6   Separate Time from Technology

Remembering that technology is responsible for a great deal of our time famine, it is good to go on strike occasionally. Try disconnecting from clocks, watches, alarms, beepers, telephones, and faxes for a day, a weekend, or a week.

As an example, during our most recent trip to the developing world my wristwatch of twenty years gave out. Upon our return to the United States, I did not replace it. Without a watch it is true that I was handicapped in a certain way. But it also gave a very interesting sense of freedom. After a year, I finally purchased an inexpensive watch because my patients didn't quite know what to think of a doctor who had to borrow their watches to measure their pulses!

Cutting adrift technology is a good way to reassert our independence over the tyranny of the clock. Fasting from food leads to a starvation that purifies the body; fasting from technology leads to a margin that fortifies the spirit.

Rx: 7 Short-Term Flurry Versus Long-Term Vision

Americans are notoriously shortsighted. We live in a state of myopic mania that blurs the future. The horizon is never visible in the middle of a dust storm. But we must have a vision that extends beyond tomorrow. Living only from week to week is like a dot-to-dot life.

It is good to have five-year plans, even ten-year plans. For many these plans will be vague, for others specific. Our goals should be flexible to the redirecting God so often asks of us. But each of us needs a direction and a vision that can inform his or her focus.

Rx: 8 Thank God

If you have two meetings scheduled on the same evening, you obviously can attend only one. Don't overlook the possibility that this might be God's way of being kind to you.

Rx: 9 Sabotage Your Fuse Box

Have you ever noticed how a major storm freezes the clock? Time stands still as the whole world skids to a sudden halt. Once confident there is no danger to loved ones, we all begin to enjoy ourselves. The lights go out, and we rush for candles and flashlights. Then we sit and watch the sky or visit with each other or play board games. And sometimes we are tempted to pray that electricity isn't restored until a week from Tuesday.

Our family enjoys Wisconsin winters. A two-foot snowfall is a thrill, not a torment. When the world is snowed in, cars can't move, businesses can't open, and schools can't convene. A spirit of holiday reigns. Part of the reason for this is the unexpected gift of time margin.

"I'm not sure I understand it," commented Pastor Gordon

MacDonald after just such an occasion, "but I have this feeling that an increasing amount of conversational time between friends is spent on the subject of weariness, overcommitment, the perceived need to drop out. . . . Why on the one Sunday in five years when a New England snowstorm forced us to close down our church was it universally recognized by the congregation as the most wonderful Lord's day they had ever had?"[18]

Rx: 10   Get Less Done But Do the Right Things

Busyness is not a synonym for Kingdom work—it is only busyness. All activities need to be assessed as to their spiritual authenticity. Again, if we have one hundred things to do and can do only ten, how do we select from among them? We must have God-authored criteria with which to judge our activities, and we must be willing to use them. "The goal of much that is written about life management is to enable us to do more in less time. But is this necessarily a desirable goal?" asks Jean Fleming. "Perhaps we need to get *less done*, but the right things."[19]

Especially be on guard against the urgency we see in so much of life's flow. If this urgency regularly erodes either your time for relationships or your time for rest, reevaluation is appropriate.

Rx: 11   Enjoy Anticipation, Relish the Memories

Calendar congestion and time urgency have robbed us of the pleasure of anticipation. Without warning, the activity is upon us. We rush to meet it; then we rush to the next; and the next. In the same way, we lack the luxury of reminiscing. On we fly to the next activity.

For this reason, our family intentionally lingers on both of these relatively unremembered sources of delight. Fishing trips are planned at least six months in advance. Because our son Adam has spent the last two summers working in Alaska, this past winter I announced at a family meeting that we would be taking a trip there—in eighteen months. You can't imagine how much fun we have already had just thinking and planning.

When the activity is over, remember. Tell stories. Tell them again. Frame a picture. Mount a fish. Make a special effort to remember the funny happenings. With the gift of remembrance, we don't always have to do a lot. We can do a little and remember it a lot.

Remember that box full of old photos in your attic or basement? Gather your kids around and spend some evening arranging them in albums or picking out the best ones for collages. You won't believe the fun you'll have reminiscing together!

Rx: 12   Don't Rush Wisdom
In our current system, the decisive executive is rewarded. But seldom is true wisdom a product of speedy deliberation. As a matter of fact, wisdom is almost always slow. The more important the decision, the slower it should be made.

If life's pace pushes you, push back. Take as much time as you need for clearness to develop.

Rx: 13   For Type As Only: Stand in Line
Cardiologist Dr. Meyer Friedman, one of the first to describe the type A personality, offered this practical advice to his patients: "Practice smiling. Purposely speak more slowly, stop in the middle of some sentences, hesitate for three seconds, then continue. Purposely say, 'I'm wrong' at least twice today, even if you're not sure you're wrong. Listen to at least two persons today without interrupting even once. . . . Seek out the longest line at the bank. Verbalize your affection to your spouse [and] children."

To the physician subset of type As (a large subset), he suggests, "Trash the extraneous. Cut out some of the committees, perhaps all. Give yourself a lunch break—out of the office. Browse in a bookstore, sit in a deserted church, go to a museum. During office hours, have your secretary schedule imaginary patients, whose names you don't know. Naturally, these patients will be no-shows. You will be able to use that time to catch up . . . or best of all, renew your spirit."[20]

Rx: 14   Create Buffer Zones
If you have a busy schedule with nonstop appointments, consider creating small buffer zones between some of the obligations, a kind of coffee break for the spirit. Even ten or fifteen minutes can allow you to catch up, make phone calls, close your eyes, pray, call your spouse, reorient your priorities, and defuse your tension.

Rx: 15   Plan for Free Time
If God were our appointment secretary, would He schedule us for every minute of every day? Well-meaning Christians might differ in their answers, but by now it must be obvious that I think the answer would

be no. Many arguments could be made in defense of my answer, but perhaps the strongest is the lifestyle that Christ Himself chose. Time urgency was not only absent, it was *conspicuously* absent. And I doubt its absence had to do with cultural context.

Christ's teaching, His healing, His serving, and His loving were usually spontaneous. The person standing in front of Him was the opportunity He accepted. If He chose spontaneous living, isn't that a signal to us? Overloaded schedules are not the way to walk *In His Steps*.

"An exciting possibility is for individuals or families to arrange their schedules so one evening a week is free, not for church meetings, but for direct involvement in the lives of needy people," challenges Tom Sine. To such a suggestion one pastor responded: "There are three hundred active lay people in my congregation, and if they each volunteered one evening a week we could change the entire community!"[21]

Rx: 16   Be Available

This prescription is not a way to gain time margin, but instead a suggested way to use it up. Margin exists for the needs of the Kingdom, for the service of one another, for the building of community. It exists, just as we exist, for the purpose of being available to God.

"But it is possible that the most important thing God has for me on any given day is not even on my agenda," observes Pastor Bruce Larson. "Am I interruptible? Do I have time for the nonprogrammed things in my life? My response to those interruptions is the real test of my love."[22]

There are two ways we can be available. First, we can be willing to cancel our current activities at any time and go do what the Lord is bidding us to do. But, for obvious reasons, this seldom happens. It is understandable that we would continue with our task and say to the new need, "Sorry, I'm busy." That is part of why we make schedules in the first place, to organize our time.

For the very reason that we are seldom willing or able to interrupt our schedules, we ought to consider a second way of being available. The essence of this method is to acquire time margin and then offer it to the Father: "What do you want me to do with this time today? It would be a privilege to use it on behalf of the Kingdom." God's intention might be for us to use the time to pray, to meditate, to rest, to serve, to parent, to tell of the good news, or a thousand other ways of cooperating with His eternal purposes.

Being useful to God and other people is a large part of what life is meant to be. And yet "usefulness is nine-tenths availability." When others need help, they don't need it two days from now. "We must be ready to allow ourselves to be interrupted by God," explained Dietrich Bonhoeffer. "God will be constantly crossing our paths and canceling our plans by sending us people with claims and petitions. . . . It is part of the discipline of humility that we must not spare our hand where it can perform a service and that we do not assume that our schedule is our own to manage, but allow it to be arranged by God."[23]

DO YOURSELF A FAVOR

When flying from New York to San Francisco, we don't allow only three minutes to change planes in Denver. A much greater margin of error is needed. But if we make such allowances in our travels, why don't we do it in our living? Life is a journey, but it is not a race. Do yourself a favor and slow down.

It is not easy to reassert our right to time margin, but it helps when we are convinced that legitimacy exists for such a right. This legitimacy comes from the same God who exalts faithfulness over productivity, rest over speed, and availability over schedulability. It comes from the same God who invented time in the first place and reserves the right to set the rules for its use.

God never intended for time to oppress us, dictating our every move. That was progress's idea. Instead, time was simply His way of making sure "everything didn't happen all at once." We are free to use it, and if we are wise, we will use it with eternity in view.

Regaining margin in our use of time is one way of restoring freedom to overloaded lives. With time margin we can better enjoy what we are doing, we have a more wholesome anticipation of our next activity, we are more contemplative, we are more in touch with God and with each other, we have more time for service, and we actually delight in *looking for* the divine interruptions He sends us.

Margin in Finances

Moira was a forty-year-old overweight psychology professor from Texas. I first saw her during the second year of my residency training in Iowa, where we met over her gall bladder symptoms. Several visits later, her symptoms persisting, we decided on surgery. After a thorough history and physical, I predicted a successful operation followed by an inevitable demise. I was right. Her demise, however, had nothing to do with her physical health. Instead, she aspirated her own red ink.

Moira and her husband had no children. In substitute, they had seven cars, two boats (one that never touched water), a hot-air balloon, and a home with four thousand square feet of living space chock-full of brand-new clutter.

After bankruptcy proceedings, I happened to meet Moira downtown. "We are leaving for Texas next week," she smiled. "I was able to get a good job down there. The Lord has been good to us." I had never heard her talk about the Lord before and wondered about her theology. I also wondered if she had paid the clinic bill.

Both Moira and her husband worked. I never knew how much money they made. But however much it was, they spent more. About the closest they ever came to margin in their finances was the ledger sheet of their certified public astrologer.

THE BEST OF TIMES AND THE WORST OF TIMES

At last count, there were about 210 countries in the world. Every year, Americans spend more on trash bags than the individual gross national product of 90 of these countries. Even more astoundingly, we spend more on eating out than the individual gross national product of 200 of these nations.

Wealth. Is it the blessing of a generous God or the fast track to moral and spiritual ruin? Are we to feel guilt for the trash we put in our plastic bags or gratitude for the pizza and prime rib?

Our unprecedented affluence has brought benefits that even the most cynical ought to acknowledge. We have been able to afford education, housing, extended communications, and transportation to just about anywhere. We have health-care advancements that free us from grievous disease. Our food is plenteous. Recreational options seem limited only by the imagination. The elderly are, by and large, better-off financially than they have ever been. We even have enough to be generous benefactors, privately and governmentally, to the impoverished at home and abroad. It is clearly the best of times.

Unfortunately, however, these benefits do not constitute the whole story; luminous advancements often cast dark shadows. In the case of our economic prosperity, the shadows of debt, vulnerability, and uncertainty extend far into the future. For every positive economic indicator, there is a corresponding dismal one. We are in troubled water on nearly every financial front, and no one can confidently suggest a way out. "Serious economic experts make predictions that come up inside out," observes Norman Mailer, "and no one can quite explain why they are wrong."[1]

The major parameters of economic well-being fluctuate up and down, up and down, while millions of people in the United States nervously await each new development. How did we ever come to this state of dependence on the economy? The question ought not to be "What are the economic statistics doing?" but instead "What are the economic statistics doing to us?" Is the economy freeing us physically and spiritually and granting us a financial margin with which to serve the purposes of God? Or are we being reduced to feverish bundles of nervousness, discontent, and greed?

In fact, the debt trap set for us has a sudden spring—one that cuts off financial margin at the neck.

"BEYOND OUR MEANS"

Our list of economic woes is a long one. The ever-expanding invoice of problems requires an ever-expanding ocean of money, yet our government—along with a huge percentage of its citizens—is flat broke. As explained by *The Wall Street Journal* economist Alfred Malabre, Jr., "For a very long time, we've been living beyond our means—for so long, in fact, that now, sadly, it's beyond our means to put things right, at least in an orderly, reasonably painless manner."[2]

1. Personal, corporate, national, and international debt levels are lofting through the stratosphere. "A mountain of debt has begun to move," explains investment counselor William F. Rickenbacker. "Like some mindless blob advancing over the landscape of a horror movie, it is suffocating everything it encounters." While each of these areas is cause for great concern, nothing generates both cynicism and pessimism quite as quickly as the massive federal deficit. "There never has been anything approaching this level of debt funding in the history of mankind in so short a period of time, even on a percentage basis," observes financial counselor and analyst Larry Burkett. "The effects of this will be felt throughout the U.S. and ultimately the world's economies."[3]

2. Bankruptcies are at record levels, nearly one million each year. The rate of bankruptcy in the 1980s was quadruple what it was even in the depression-plagued 1930s. Ninety percent of these are "just plain folks" like you and me. Bankruptcy is currently the number one growth area for law firms.

3. Real estate costs have inflated so alarmingly over the last two decades that increasing numbers of Americans cannot afford to enter the housing market, even despite the volatile market correction of the early 1990s. Homeownership percentage peaked at 66 percent in 1980 and has fallen steadily since. The average mortgage today requires over one hundred hours of factory labor a month to pay, compared to forty hours two decades ago.

4. College tuition costs have consistently outpaced inflation to the point where parents can no longer afford the fees. Student borrowing

has tripled in the last decade. At current rates of increase, a college education at the turn of the century is projected to cost fifty thousand dollars for public universities (currently enrolling 80 percent of the students) and one hundred thousand dollars for a private degree.

5. The savings-and-loan industry lies in shambles. Prior to deregulation in 1982 there were 4,600 savings and loans. A decade later, there are only half as many. The government bailout will eventually cost taxpayers several hundred billion dollars—the greatest such financial loss in our nation's history.

6. Banks joined the thrifts in a decade-long morass. In the 1970s, only eighty-three banks closed their doors. In the 1980s, this number rose to eleven hundred. Overleveraged corporate takeovers, the oil bust, collapsing commercial real estate values, the farm recession, massive Third-World debt, and our sluggish economy have left the banking industry in the worst shape in sixty years.

7. Scandal and greed rock the economic world at every turn. From the excesses of Donald Trump to the exploitation of Michael Milken to the hip-pocket senators of Charles Keating, public cynicism has given way to anger. Indictments roll off the presses like a daily newspaper: cocaine on Wall Street, savings-and-loan ripoffs, insider trading, illegal loans, influence peddling, money laundering. All costs eventually come out of the taxpayers' pockets.

8. Many cities, counties, and states are scrambling to avoid insolvency. Connecticut recently was forced to cut its work force by 40 percent, while Maine entered a state of emergency. New York City laid off twenty thousand workers, while Philadelphia and Detroit staggered ever closer to the edge. Bridgeport, the largest city in Connecticut, became the first major municipality to formally seek federal bankruptcy protection. The fifty largest U.S. counties ran a total deficit of $760 million in 1991, radically up from their combined $159 million surplus in 1989.

9. Congressional spending on welfare and social programs has risen 2,000 percent since 1960. Despite this level of governmental intervention, poverty rates either remained the same or increased. Currently, one of every five children is impoverished. Unemployment and homelessness have proven once again their inextinguishability.

10. Health-care spending continues to spiral out of control. Per-capita costs were $1,000 in 1980, $2,400 in 1990, and are expected to climb to $5,500 by 2000. Total health-care spending has exploded

from $27 billion to $600 billion in thirty years, far outstripping the consumer price index. Health-care costs are without question the business community's biggest concern. With the rapidly growing elderly population, Medicare consumes ever larger chunks of the federal budget—an aggression that cannot continue much longer. Meanwhile, Medicaid is straining many state budgets perilously near to the breaking point. Hospitals, mostly rural and inner city, are being forced to close in record numbers. Our nation's 31 to 37 million uninsured is a plight unparalleled in the Western world. A philosophy professor from the University of Alabama Medical School finally threw up his hands: "I once was a liberal about financing medical care, then I became a conservative; now I am a nothing. I once thought physicians' fees caused increases in medical costs, then I blamed large institutions; now I blame everybody and nobody. I once thought escalating medical costs were a problem, later I thought they were a crisis; now I think our system may collapse before the second millennium."[4]

We are not running out of urgent projects that need expensive attention, but we are quickly running out of funding resources. "Most Americans do not want to confront the painful idea that we are headed toward the wrong future," observes former Secretary of Commerce Peter G. Peterson. "We face a future of economic choices that are far less pleasant than any set of choices we have confronted in living memory."[5]

FAMILY INCOME

Despite the tremendous increase in liabilities listed above, we have no more money to pay for it all. The federal government, state governments, and families are all swimming in the same red ink. Most citizens have given up hope for any budgetary realism to come out of Washington or state capitals, for the kind of political courage necessary to solve these fiscal problems would be not only painful for the public but also unpopular at the polls. Few politicians are willing to die for their constituency the way Jesus was.

It is therefore not surprising that governments seem so incapable of fiscal restraint. But why do families have such difficulty balancing their budgets? It would seem that family-style microeconomics should be easier to solve than the macroeconomic complexity of a $1.3 trillion federal budget or a $5.7 trillion economy.

Part of the reason families are broke is due to their unparalleled love affair with consumption. People often get into debt and destroy their financial margin simply because they buy too many things they don't need. But before we are too harsh on John and Jane Doe, let's understand another reason families find themselves in trouble. It is a matter of first grade arithmetic: Real expenses have risen and real income has not.

Median family income (adjusted for inflation) has been stalled for two decades. According to a U.S. Department of Commerce publication, "There was no increase in family income between 1973 and 1990 in real terms."[6] Perhaps even more dramatically, Harvard political economist Robert Reich explains, "Over the past 12 years, the top 20 percent of income earners in the United States have increased their real wages in the neighborhood of 8 to 12 percent. The bottom 80 percent have fallen steadily behind."[7] Understanding this, we are not surprised to discover that "the typical family now spends 30 percent [of its income] on debt service, compared with 20 percent a decade ago."[8] The number of families in debt counseling has tripled over the last decade.

It is little wonder that lack of money is the leading stressor among families. According to family researcher Dolores Curran, 58 percent of married men, 66 percent of married women, and 87 percent of single mothers list finances as the top stressor in their family.[9] When income stagnates yet expenses keep rising, financial margin vanishes along with the dreams.

DEBT WRONG

Significant controversy exists among economic experts concerning the advisability of debt. Some, such as Milton Friedman, argue that debt is the only effective restraint on congressional spending—and in that he is most certainly correct. Additionally, many economists believe that as long as indebtedness does not grow faster than the gross national product, it can prove beneficial to the performance of the economy. This is especially true if the debt, rather than wasted on consumption, is invested in our future, such as research and development, infrastructure improvement, and education.

Others remain unconvinced. Debt, they say, unavoidably imprisons the future, and the "buy now, pay later" mentality too often corrupts into "binge now, pain later."

Debt-sponsored economic theory has only been around for about sixty years. Deeply troubled by the unemployment of the Great Depression, Britisher John Maynard Keynes began urging governments to abandon Adam Smith's laissez faire approach and to become more active in regulating the economy, especially to avoid or reverse downturns. This led to the notion that it is acceptable and even fiscally wise for borrowing, credit, and interest to fuel an economy. President Franklin D. Roosevelt had no objection, for after all, we were only borrowing it from ourselves.

As a result, the national debt began its growth in the 1930s, followed by corporate debt after 1945. Shortly thereafter, personal debt began to swell. And in the mid-1980s, our international trade deficit turned negative for the first time since 1917. So popular has borrowing become that currently our total national indebtedness from personal, corporate, and governmental sources is double our gross national product. This number is alarming. Whether in the personal, corporate, or national arena, so much capital is being siphoned off for interest payments that the entire economic system is increasingly threatened with paralysis.

For my part, I don't like debt. Debt is a noose, and I don't like having my neck in a noose. I don't like my future being imprisoned. I don't like the idea that my children and my children's children will hold me to blame for their suffering. But I am not in charge, and by now, debt—that sworn enemy of margin—is everywhere.

"Let no debt remain outstanding, except the continuing debt to love one another," the Apostle Paul reminds us in Romans.[10] "God doesn't prohibit borrowing," explains Larry Burkett, "but He certainly does discourage it. In fact, every biblical reference to it is negative."[11] Why? Because, as Proverbs explains, "The borrower is servant to the lender."[12] After God paid so dearly to free us, He would prefer we not become slaves again except to righteousness.[13]

I am not an economist and can feel Luther Hodge's breath on my ear: "If ignorance paid dividends most Americans could make a fortune out of what they don't know about economics." But I would be less than honest if I didn't admit that the practice of chronic indebtedness at such levels seems unwise to me. Admittedly, this rather old-fashioned conviction might never lead to riches, but then, I don't remember Christ signaling me in that direction anyway.

PLASTIC AND THE PIT

Spending more than we make is one of those modern plastic privileges of dubious advantage. Much of this deficit spending on a personal and family level occurs because buying has become a national mania. According to studies, one-third of all shoppers experience an "irresistible compulsion" to buy. Many buy strictly out of impulse. They go to the mall with nothing in mind other than recreational shopping. Not only is it entertaining, but it makes them feel better—an antidepressant of sorts.

The average consumer enters the store carrying seven credit cards, while the average household credit-card balance is nearing $2,000 (in 1980, this figure was $550; in 1990, it rose to $1,833).[14] There are bank cards, retail cards, entertainment cards, oil cards—easy to obtain, easy to use, and hard to pay off. A recent television ad showed a Yuppie looking at his long string of credit cards and saying, "All these cards, and I'm maxed out on each one." Then comes the reassuring voice: "Now there is a new card! You cannot be excluded from obtaining it, there is no maximum on how much you can charge, and we will send it to you even if you are recently bankrupt!"

On the front side, this kind of credit is seductive. Out the back door, it is treacherous. The innocent-appearing plastic card draws its life from our financial margin, becoming more powerful as we sink deeper into debt. Soon we find ourselves looking up from a deep hole, surrounded by possessions we do not really own. "We can be poor because of the things we *have*," suggests William T. Snyder. "In debt and committed to the hilt, living from one paycheck to the next means a person has no room to wiggle!"[15]

Our love affair with plastic is one of the main reasons we have "no room to wiggle," that is, no margin. Yet we have lost interest in the discussions about caution and restraint. When it comes to fiscal matters, our skills at rationalization are so well developed we scarcely wince when God's Word counters us. We may soon learn that we followed the wrong piper, not to Paradise but to the pit.

WEALTH

"Money," the Yuppie maxim goes, "is life's report card." Our society is so captivated with earning money, having money, and spending money that we can think of little else. And what better way to gain a financial margin than to earn more money! But just as riches are not righteousness, so money is not margin.

Nothing in Scripture and in the chosen lifestyle of Christ could be clearer: Wealth is not an objective of the spiritual life. When we encounter money along the path of life, we are encouraged to do one of three things with it: turn and walk in the other direction; pick it up and give it away; or if needed, use it for the necessities of daily living. Any other interaction risks adverse spiritual consequences.

"Do not store up for yourselves treasures on earth. . . . But store up for yourselves treasures in heaven," Jesus taught. "For where your treasure is, there your heart will be also."[16] He, in fact, spent a great deal of time expounding on the issue, discussing it even more than the topic of prayer. If the ultimatum "You cannot serve both God and Money" was relevant for ancient Israel, how much more for our modern world?

Paul adds his warning in the strongest terms:

> People who want to get rich fall into temptation and a trap and into many foolish and harmful desires that plunge men into ruin and destruction. . . . Some people, eager for money, have wandered from the faith and pierced themselves with many griefs. But you, man of God, flee from all this, and pursue righteousness, godliness, faith, love, endurance and gentleness.[17]

Again and again the Word instructs us in explicit terms to distrust money. It is not that money is evil, but that the *love* of money *leads* to all kinds of evil. With sufficient wisdom and discipline, money can glorify God and be a blessing to many. But wisdom and discipline are not exactly our long suit.

THE INVESTMENT FIRM OF JOHN AND JOHN

I am not a wealthy man, and I will never be a wealthy man. This statement arises not from an inability to generate wealth. The medical profession has well-recognized income-generating abilities. I am not *unable* to be wealthy, but rather I am *unwilling* to be wealthy. Why would I—or anyone, for that matter—wish to fall into a trap, be plunged into ruin and destruction, be pierced with many griefs, and risk wandering from the faith?

Linda and I have no savings. There is an involuntary pension plan through the medical school, and our two sons have a college fund, but in our own personal account we have nothing. This, however, does not present a hardship. Quite the contrary, it represents freedom. For even as we have no savings, we also have no debt.

Please understand, I am not recommending this approach in a universal way. Most Christian financial counselors would probably gasp if I did. Given the uncertainties of our day, a savings plan is recommended for most, and I respect that opinion. Saving for housing, children's college education, and health care is not inherently wrong (or at least is not clearly wrong).

But in my own heart, where these things must ultimately be decided, I feel deeply the words of the Apostle John: "If anyone has material possessions and sees his brother in need but has no pity on him, how can the love of God be in him?"[18] That particular verse has dwelt with Linda in a closely bound friendship since her college days. Additionally, we are convicted by the example of John Wesley, who said, "If I leave behind me ten pounds for which I have no use I am a thief and a robber." It just seems to me that, according to the investment firm of John and John, the way we are doing things is the right way for us.[19]

Yes, we have financial margin because I make more than we need and our expenses are significantly less than my income. We don't buy new cars. We seldom buy new clothes. Our house is paid off. So what do we do with our margin? We like to plow it back into the fields of the Kingdom as quickly as possible.

FOR THE FUN OF IT

Any discussion of financial margin would be incomplete without mentioning the pure joy of it. There are three reasons for this joy.

First, by lowering expenses below income you live with far less stress and pressure. If the refrigerator breaks down, you don't. If your car needs new tires, you simply go out and get them. Without margin, life struggles and staggers and stumbles. But when margin is present, life flows. And flowing is more enjoyable than staggering.

Second, having financial margin allows beneficence toward others. This is one of the most rewarding of all human activities, and I am convinced it is a subset of love. Meeting the needs of others delivers us from the world of selfishness and into a world of grace and gratitude.

These two sources of joy are sufficient grounds to recommend margin. But there is yet a third, even greater, source of joy. It is a transcendent kind of pleasure that comes neither from within nor without but from above. It comes from the source of all that is right, and when you approach it you feel its warmth even from a distance. In giving, you are ushered into a world where cynicism and hatred have been banished. You are considering others before yourself. You are choosing Heaven as the place you will put your treasure. You are doing what God asked you to do, and what He did Himself. In giving, you are pleasing Him.

"It is more blessed to give than to receive," Jesus taught us through Paul. These words are not talking about a future-tense, theoretical blessing waiting for us beyond the eternal horizon, reserved there as compensation for the excruciating pain of giving today. Instead, this is a kind of joy that begins with the *thought* of giving, with the declaration of freedom in your soul that indeed you belong to God. And the joy culminates in the *act* of giving, often a secret except for the spotlight of Heaven.

The German existentialist Friedrich Nietzsche once claimed that Christians have no joy. But joy is mentioned over five hundred times in Scripture and clearly ought to be a part of the normal Christian life. If you wince because Nietzsche's dagger finds a joyless heart, restore your financial margin and then give it away.

RESTORING FINANCIAL MARGIN

Many see no way out. They have been treading water so long that they can't remember what it was like to have money left at the end of the month. They are controlled. Mammon, it seems, has won.

For all such weary debtors, take hope. A solution for our many economic burdens is possible; otherwise, God is not God. Let's see how we might go about restoring margin to our finances.

Rx: 1 Travel in the Right Direction

When making a journey of known destination, it is obviously important to start out on the right road headed in the right direction. In this case, our destination is restored financial margin. But before beginning our trip, the Father has some travel instructions for us.

If consulted, God would probably vote in favor of each of the previous three margins: emotional energy, physical energy, and time. Regarding financial margin, however, He would furrow His brow, look us in the eye, and then respond, "It depends." The issue hinges on whether or not the desired financial margin honors Him. Although each of the four margins discussed can be misused for self-serving goals, destinations involving money are particularly famous for dishonoring God. He wants to be sure before casting His vote with us.

In dealing with money, settling the issue of lordship is a mandatory first step. Otherwise, we find ourselves headed off in the wrong direction and mired in a spiritual morass that I want no part of. So, to clarify, we are not talking about restoring financial margin for the purposes of pride, of wealth, or of meeting our security needs in a way that bypasses the Father. Instead, we are talking about the kind of financial margin that honors Him.

To reach this kind of financial margin, which direction do we travel? For such an important question, contemporary Christians spend far too little time considering their answer. The choice of nearly the entire Western world is to travel down the economic road. We must realize, however, that *the economic road is not and has never been the road Jesus called us to travel.*

Economists and politicians of the past fifty years have honestly believed that economic advancement was the solution to the problems of humankind—a view shared nearly universally today. The conveniences I enjoy make me a beneficiary of such thinking. Yet if we are honest with ourselves, we should admit that the economic road was never suggested to us by Christ.

The economic answer is not the answer to our problems. Economics will solve some of our suffering, but nothing more. And solving our suffering is not the goal of the Christian life; walking in righteousness is. If we suffer, then we suffer—it is only for a season. But the economic road is not the road. The proverbial "bottom line" is not, after all, the bottom line.

If we are to restore margin to our finances, we must put first things first. Only then will we be able to break the power money holds on us and *use it instead of being used by it.*

Rx: 2 Break Its Back

Money is powerful—very powerful. It is so powerful, taught Jesus, that it competes head-to-head with God. "For Mammon's work is the exact opposite of God's work," explains French sociologist Jacques Ellul. "Given this opposition, we understand why Jesus demands a choice between Mammon and God. He is not speaking of just any other power, just any other god; he is speaking of the one who goes directly against God's action, the one who makes 'nongrace' reign in the world."[20]

Before we can accomplish anything righteous with money, we first need to understand this power, confront it, and with the help of God, demolish it. How is it possible to break the substantial power money holds over us? Very simple—give it away. "There is one act par excellence which profanes money by going directly against the law of money, an act for which money is not made," explains Ellul. "This act is *GIVING*."[21]

When we give money away, we not only neutralize its power over us, but we also bring it under the domain of the Kingdom of Light. Nongrace is turned into grace. God is honored, and His lordship is confirmed.

Rx: 3 Counter Culture

Once we are headed in the right direction and have, with the help of God, broken the power money holds over us, then we find yet another important battle in front of us: We must break the power of culture. Before we will be able to succeed in reestablishing financial margin, we must free ourselves from the dominating influences that surround us.

The way of the world is not a benign force, but instead a dictator that tells us how much education we should have; what kind of job we should seek; what kind of house, car, and clothes we should buy; who is "beautiful" and who isn't. It is rare to meet a person who isn't owned, bound, or trapped in destructive ways by a multitude of controlling cultural forces. If we remain controlled by such a culture, we will have little chance of achieving God-honoring financial margin. That same culture will demand we buy its wares and live by its rules. Acquiescing to such demands inevitably leads to margin erosion.

Willingly and knowingly we wrestle control from culture and set our orientation in the opposite direction. It is wonderful if a righteous community of believers can support one another in making such countercultural decisions. But don't wait for your friends or fellow churchgoers to lead the way or even to give you permission. This is a battle you must fight, and unfortunately, often you will have to fight it alone.

Rx: 4 "Live Within Your Harvest"

As the proverb suggests, make do with what you have. And, should you care to venture further into grace, not only make do with what you have but *accept* what you have. *More than a strategy, this is a conviction, the kind where you drive a stake and declare it so.*

Living within your harvest is possible—it just isn't popular. It conveys that we have boundaries and that we are willing to confine ourselves within the scope of these boundaries rather than pine for the putative greener grass on the other side of the fence.

Contentment and simplicity are invaluable friends in this effort, as we will see in the next two chapters. Content yourself with what God sends your way and live a simple life of righteousness. Then God, honored by your devotion, will in turn tend to both your margin and your harvest.

Rx: 5 Discipline Desires and Redefine Needs

There is great confusion abroad as to how we distinguish needs from desires. The list of what we call "needs" today is certainly much longer than the list was in 1900, which in turn was much longer than the list at the time of Christ. If the list expands each year, is this an expansion God approves of? "The cultivation and expansion of needs is . . . the antithesis of freedom," teaches economist E. F. Schumacher. "Every increase of needs tends to increase one's dependence on outside forces over which one cannot have control."[22]

It is wise to clarify this distinction between needs and desires and to be honest about it before God. Our true needs are few and basic: We need God, love, relationships with fellow human beings, meaningful work, food, clothing, and shelter. Most of the rest of what we call needs are instead *desires*, relative to the age and location in which we live.

Let me quickly state that I don't think God limits us to only our needs. He is a generous, gracious God who allows us many of our desires. So if I want carpeting in my house, I should not attempt to deceive God or myself by calling it a need. But I should also realize that God is generous and might well grant the desire.

The issue is knowing when God says "Thus far and no more." For me, when there is pride, ostentation, laziness, waste, or excessive comfort involved, then it is a desire I don't even try to bring before God.

In this process, we are greatly aided if we tune out advertisements, which are nothing more than artificial "need creation." If you listen to them and believe them, your financial margin will tend to disappear as you chase a satiation you will never find. The best advice is to turn them off. After twenty years with a small portable black-and-white television, we finally bought a color set with remote control—simply so we could turn off advertisements.

If you want to have financial margin, redefine desires and needs, using God's definition. In the process, don't listen to advertisements.

Rx: 6   Decrease Spending

Coming now to perhaps the more practical aspects of this topic, there are three ways to increase our financial margin: decrease spending, increase income, or increase savings. Among these choices, the best is to simply reduce our spending. It sounds easy, but as we all know, in practice it is hard to sustain. The context of our culture screams against restraint, and every message we receive—from the ads on television to the specials in the newspaper to our coworker's new sweater to our neighbor's new van—all urge us to cave in.

A friend, who at one time owned a catalog store, offered this interesting explanation of customer spending patterns: "When people run out of money, they stop shopping. But this only lasts about six weeks. Then, whether their financial situation has improved or not, they start buying again."

Doesn't that match what you know to be true about human nature—whether in dieting or exercise or no-shopping resolves? Understanding this simple fact of human psychology leaves us in a stronger position than we were before. *We now recognize that even our best resolves usually last only a short time and require conscious renewal on a regular basis.*

There are two facets of decreased spending: short-term and long-term. Even a short-term spending freeze—a day, a week, a month—is helpful in reestablishing financial margin. In contrast, the long-term approach requires a vastly different level of commitment and is better thought of as a lifestyle change. Short-term resolves are considerable in number but limited in effect; long-term resolves are limited in number but considerable in effect. For example, a moratorium on eating out for a month is probably sustainable and would improve the average family's financial margin by $140. But a decade-long moratorium on eating out would be very difficult for most families, even though it would improve their financial margin by over $16,000.

Rx: 7   Increase Income

Increasing income by increasing work hours is a common approach used to solve financial-margin problems. In some instances, this approach is appropriate. In most, however, it compounds marginless living. As we saw in the last chapter, most of us already have a shortage of discretionary time and are not looking to increase work hours. Yet desperation and a perceived need to consume more drive people to do strange things.

We see farmers who are now milking three times a day in an effort to increase production; service-sector workers who volunteer for overtime or weekends; spouses who violate their personal convictions to enter the dual-wage-earner role; executives who accept a promotion they don't really want; medical residents who moonlight covering emergency rooms. In each instance, these workers would rather have more time margin than more work. But their financial margin has been so eroded by the circumstances of the last two decades (stagnant family income and rising expenses), as well as personal consumption practices, that they seem to no longer have a choice.

Here we need to reconsider the problem of needs versus desires. Many people work extra and then four months later buy a new car. They have made their choices and do not have my sympathy. Others have indeed trimmed both needs and desires to bare bones. For them, increasing income seems the only option left.

The tendency of choosing more work hours in order to increase *financial margin* has a significantly negative effect on our *time margin*. On occasion, we observe that our quest for margin collides with itself, one need against the other.

Rx: 8   Increase Savings

Increasing savings is yet a third way of maintaining a financial margin. If, for example, you currently have no savings and pay expenses from a checking account that is monthly drained dry, what happens if there is an emergency—for example, medical expenses of two thousand dollars? You would need to take out a loan and enter into debt. But if you sustained a savings of three thousand dollars, you would have margin against such emergencies.

Unscheduled and unpredictable breakdowns will happen, and we should consider having some margin for them to happen in. Appliances, automobiles, lawn mowers—all wear out, usually on their own timetable. Sickness, unemployment, and sudden travel expenses are other unanticipated events. With personal and family budgets already stretched to the limits, such emergencies often result in a fiscal crisis.

The issue comes in deciding two crucial questions:

- ▶ How much savings should we have? Is one thousand dollars enough? Is fifty thousand dollars too much?
- ▶ What should the savings be spent on? What if you have a savings of twenty-five thousand dollars and God has need of it? Do you give it back to Him?

Most Christian financial counselors recommend a regular savings program: for children's college education, for exceptional medical expenses, for housing costs, for retirement. In addition, some advisors recommend setting aside a contingency fund equal to three to six months of your usual spending for unexpected emergencies. I personally do not follow this rule, preferring to live a little closer to the edge of faith. There have always been needs within the community that have taken priority over a savings program.

In the final analysis, the issue is not savings but hoarding. Moderate savings is probably acceptable to God and a good component of financial margin. Hoarding, however, is never acceptable. He is trusting us with certain resources; He as owner and we as stewards. We should never pretend that we have rights to what is not ours.

God is honored by funnels and dishonored by sponges. Be a conduit of His blessing, not a dead end. Some increased savings for known future expenses and unknown contingencies seems acceptable. But dead-end hoarding or empire building is not the kind of financial margin I have in mind.

Rx: 9 Make a Budget

Making a budget has the distinction of enjoying the most universal recommendation of all financial-margin suggestions. The scope of this book does not yield itself to the specifics of how to make a budget, and there are other books available to teach that. (I would recommend the works of Larry Burkett and Ron Blue.) But if you have trouble in the area of financial margin, the first thing you should do (that is, after solving the spiritual questions involved) is to set up a budget.

Rx: 10   Discard Credit Cards

The second thing is to cut up your credit cards. The majority of American families would probably be better-off if credit cards disappeared from the face of the earth tomorrow. They can be extremely dangerous. To be honest, I do not believe all credit cards need to be thrown away, and I personally have a credit card. I use it because I seldom carry cash and because I know I can pay it off each month.

I would strongly recommend against having credit cards if you are prone to impulse buying, if you already have excessive amounts of consumer debt, and if you cannot pay off the balance each month.

For a fairly large percentage of people, nothing would regain their financial margin faster than the simple act of destroying all their credit cards and instead paying cash for purchases. Simply stated, avoid debt.

Rx: 11   Don't Mortgage the Future

According to Christian financial counselor Larry Burkett, do not assume a mortgage of more than 40 percent of your net spendable income. (The net spendable income equals the gross income minus the taxes and tithe.) Included in this percentage are not only the mortgage payments but also the real estate taxes, insurance, utilities, and repairs.[23]

Obviously, the smaller the percentage you spend on mortgage and other associated housing costs, the larger your financial margin. Forty percent is a ceiling. Also, if you have other concurrent nonmortgage debts, this percentage may need to be decreased.

Far too many people, especially young couples, take on a mortgage that effectively deprives them of any financial margin for decades to come. When the hard reality sets in, they worry, they develop conflicts in their marriage, they begin overworking to try to make ends meet, and they deprive themselves of the joy of giving to the unexpected needs God sends their way.

Rx: 12   Resist Impulses

A large percentage of purchases are made on sheer impulse. Stores know this and stack impulse items near the cash register. These are the things you didn't go to the store to buy, but bought anyway.

If you want financial margin, don't buy on impulse. Buy only those things you know you need and can use. If you have difficulty in this area, make a list of needed items before going to the store and don't deviate from it.

It goes without saying that big-ticket items, such as a car, boat, or house, should never be bought on impulse . . . never, *never*, NEVER!

Rx: 13   Share, Lend, Borrow

Part of the reason we have our love affair with shopping and consumerism is because we think we need to personally own everything we use. This is not true. We need to develop a new depreciation of things and a new appreciation of people. Things are to be used, and people are to be served. To not allow someone to use something we own places more importance on the thing than on the person. It is a common error in our society, and one that particularly dishonors God. He feels our neighbors are so valuable that He sent His Son to die for them. But we think so little of our neighbors that we won't let them use our lawn mower. These attitudes are literally an eternity apart.

When I brought my chain saw in for repairs several years ago, the attendant offered his philosophy on lending: "Never loan out your chain saw. Other people don't take care of it." Nonsense. I haven't seen my chain saw now for the last twelve months. And I'm not worried a bit. As a matter of fact, I can't think of anything I own that I would not be willing to lend to another person. Of course, I have somewhat of an advantage in that I do not have fancy or expensive things, making me all the more willing to loan them out.

If we are willing to loan out our things, then others will not need to purchase similar items, and they will have more left over to use as financial margin.

Rx: 14   Emphasize Usefulness over Fashion

The mindless, out-of-control fashion games we play also rob us of freedom, destroy our peace, and deprive us of financial margin. Some fool or group of fools halfway around the world proclaims we must wear purple shirts and blue tennis shoes this year. Like robots we respond in unison.

Someone has to give permission for people not to follow fashion. The opinion levied over and over again by culture says that if you wear plain clothes and drive a rusty car, you should feel embarrassed. But God never said such a thing at all. As individuals and as churches, we ought to be saying the same things that God says. Does your church give people permission to live simply and not feel embarrassed? If not, then begin doing something about it. I don't mean in an institutional way that would risk legalism. Instead, begin doing something in a personal way. Go to the cross, take the embarrassment yourself, and start allowing others to follow your example of simplicity in fashion.

Rx: 15   Fast

It is healthy to periodically separate from the things of the world and do without. In traditional thinking, such fasting pertains to food. But in the context of financial margin, it is good to fast from shopping for periods of time. Use up what you have in the refrigerator and freezer. Wear out whatever clothes you have in the closet. Get along on whatever you have in the house. Remember the sampler on Grandma's kitchen wall: "Use it up. Wear it out. Make it do. Do without."

The world does not stop nor the family fall apart when we unplug from the treadmill of consumerism for a period. About the only momentous thing that will happen is your finances will be resuscitated by a much-needed transfusion of margin.

Rx: 16   Kingdom First

Jesus was distinctly unambiguous when teaching about priorities: "But seek first the kingdom of God and His righteousness, and all these things shall be added to you."[24]

All margins—in emotional energy, in physical energy, in time, and especially in finances—ought to fall within this context. All margins ought first to honor God. All margins ought to be made available for the purposes of His Kingdom.

Money belongs to God. Wealth belongs to God. The Kingdom belongs to God. We belong to God. Margin belongs to God.

Only the choice belongs to us.

PART THREE

THE PROGNOSIS: HEALTH

Health
Through Contentment

Some public health authorities estimate that only 10 percent of the indicators of health are influenced by physicians, hospitals, and medicines. What, then, influences the other 90 percent?

This book is about the building of a new, integrated health paradigm, beginning with margin.

Margin—its presence or absence—influences health. Restoring margin is a huge first step in the health direction. At least we can breathe again.

But margin cannot survive standing out there on its own. Too many forces come against it. Attempting to build a margined life without support is like attempting to build a tree house without a tree. The tree house might be just what you need for protection against the dangers of the jungle. But it must have a tree.

Contentment is willing to lend support to margin. So are simplicity, balance, and rest. Without each of these, margin has little chance of surviving. These four builders of health, however, are not very popular today. They are meek and unpretentious, greatly overshadowed by the flamboyant power of progress. So they have all been asked to eat dust.

"INEXTINGUISHABLE DISCONTENT"

Half a century ago, my grandfather might reasonably have predicted that advances in affluence, technology, education, and entertainment would bring a commensurate increase in contentment. Such has not been the case. Instead, observes historian Arthur M. Schlesinger, Jr., our society is marked by "inextinguishable discontent." For the average American, discontent has become a way of life. When we are told this is "the age of envy," the indictment does not sting. When E. F. Schumacher accuses our economic system of using "greed and envy as its motive power," our usual response is to yawn and dial our broker.

Contentment is a cause without a constituency, a virtue without a voice. No one talks about it, let alone recommends it. Books dedicated to it are rare. I cannot recall the last sermon I heard addressing it. It is understandable that secular society would not broadcast an endorsement, for secularism and contentment are enemies. But why isn't it emphasized within the church as it is in the Scriptures?

Discontent as a driving force for a society might make that society rich, but it will bankrupt it in the end. As the coffer fills, the soul empties. It's like planting a garden with weeds. Come July there will be plenty of green, but in September we'll have nothing to eat.

THE SECRET

Contentment is not only a good idea, it is our duty. If God recommends something, we *ought* to do it. If God requires something, we *must* do it. As J. I. Packer has emphasized, contentment is both commended ("Godliness with contentment is great gain") and commanded ("Be content with what you have").[1]

Such a forceful endorsement by the Almighty should make contentment a prominent concern for each of us. Instead, we make it a secret concealed by our indifference to it. When the Apostle Paul wrote, "I have learned the *secret* of being content," his use of the word secret was intentional.[2] Those things we expect to bring contentment surprisingly do not. We cannot depend upon it to fall into place through the progressive evolving of civilization, for contentment arises from a different source.

Most of us do not know how to uncover this secret and have never seriously tried. Our quest is usually not for *contentment* but for *more*. This quest brings us into an immense maze, where before us lie dozens of avenues. Some are wide, luxurious, downhill, and tempting, and we see a rush of our friends entering them. They lead to beautiful houses, comfortable cars, exotic vacations, and affluence. Other avenues, equally popular, lead to prestigious colleges, distinguished jobs, important friends, and power. Still others direct us to beautiful spouses, beautiful children, deep tans, and popularity.

All the while, off to one side, courses a narrow uphill road, unadorned and unpopular. It is dusty from its sparse use and lonely from lack of travelers. The sole treasure at its end is an elusive commodity called "godliness with contentment."

Godliness is an attitude whereby what we want is to please God.

Contentment, explains J. I. Packer, "is essentially a matter of accepting from God's hand what He sends because we know that He is good and therefore it is good."[3]

Contentment is the freedom that comes when prosperity or poverty do not matter; to accept what we have and "to want but little," as Thoreau advised. The more we choose contentment, the more God sets us free. The more He sets us free, the more we choose contentment.

FORTY LASHES MINUS ONE

The Apostle Paul lived in such a state of freedom, but that did not spare him pain. He suffered much for his faith—even more than most other martyrs. "It seems to me," he writes, "that God has put us apostles on display at the end of the procession, like men condemned to die in the arena. We have been made a spectacle to the whole universe. . . . We are weak. . . . We are dishonored! To this very hour we go hungry and thirsty, we are in rags, we are brutally treated, we are homeless. . . . We have become the scum of the earth, the refuse of the world."[4]

Comparing himself to those who boast of their spirituality, Paul further points out that he had worked harder, been in prison more often, been flogged and exposed to death many times. He had received forty lashes minus one on five occasions, been beaten with rods, three times been shipwrecked, been in the open sea overnight, been hungry, thirsty, cold, and naked, and gone without sleep again and again.[5]

Despite his suffering, this same Paul teaches us about the secret we need but know little of. From prison he writes,

> I have learned to be content whatever the circumstances. I know what it is to be in need, and I know what it is to have plenty. I have learned the secret of being content in any and every situation, whether well fed or hungry, whether living in plenty or in want.[6]

Paul emphasized the importance of contentment on two occasions (Philippians 4 and 1 Timothy 6). Yet somewhere between his theological teaching and our lifestyle application, a fog rolled in.

WHAT CONTENTMENT IS NOT

In our propensity to get things wrong, we have attributed to contentment attitudes and feelings that have nothing to do with it. Contentment isn't denying one's feelings about unhappiness, but instead a freedom from being controlled by those feelings. It isn't pretending things are right when they are not, but instead the peace that comes from knowing that God is bigger than any problem and that He works them all out for our good.

Contentment isn't the complacency that defeats any attempt to make things better, but instead the willingness to work tirelessly for improvement, clinging to God rather than results. It isn't a feeling of well-being contingent on keeping circumstances under control, but instead a joy that exists in spite of circumstances and looks to the God who never varies. It isn't the comfortable feeling we get when all our needs and desires are met, but instead the security in knowing, as A. W. Tozer reminds us, that "The man who has God for his treasure has all things in One."[7]

Finally, contentment isn't that pseudovirtue of the "American dream" where we claim solidarity with Paul from the easy chair of middle-class America. We profess to having learned the secret of contentment in all circumstances, yet we've never experienced forty lashes, stoning, shipwreck, hunger, thirst, homelessness, or imprisonment. Perhaps none of us should presume maturity until the truer tests have been endured. To snuggle up alongside Paul and profess contentment without having known want seems a bit impudent on our part. Paul's contentment in need and plenty is mostly of interest because of the need. Until we know true need and survive the test, we must not presume to be his companion.

THE LAST SHALL BE FIRST

I believe Mrs. Nguyen Thi An (a fictitious name) can claim a rightful companionship with Paul. Though she has lost everything, she has all things in One. They have taken her husband, her home, and her belongings, yet her contentment they cannot take.

Mrs. An's husband was a pastor in Vietnam. When their church was closed by police, he was thrown into prison. Without official papers, she and her children were forced to live on a balcony outside an apartment. Yet her faith has forged a sanctuary out of her surroundings, from which she greets us:

My Dear Friends,

. . . You know around here we are experiencing hardships, but we thank the Lord He is comforting us and caring for us in every way. When we experience misfortune, adversity, distress and hardship, only then do we see the real blessing of the Lord poured down on us in such a way that we cannot contain it.

We have been obliged recently to leave our modest apartment and for over two months have been living on a balcony. The rain has been beating down and soaking us. Sometimes in the middle of the night we are forced to gather our blankets and run to seek refuge in a stairwell.

Do you know what I do then? I laugh and I praise the Lord, because we can still take shelter in the stairwell. I think of how many people are experiencing much worse hardships than I am. Then I remember the words of the Lord, "To the poor, O Lord, You are a refuge from the storm, a shadow from the heat" (cp. Isaiah 25:4), and I am greatly comforted. . . .

Our Father . . . is the One who according to the Scriptures does not break the bruised reed nor put out the flickering lamp. He is the One who looks after the orphan and the widow. He is the One who brings blessings and peace to numberless people.

I do not know what words to use in order to describe the love that the Lord has shown our family. I only can bow my knee and my heart and offer to the Lord words of deepest thanks and praise. Although we have lost our house and our possessions, we have not lost the Lord, and He is enough. With the Lord I have everything. The only thing I would fear losing is His blessing!

Could I ask you and our friends in the churches abroad to continue to pray for me that I will faithfully follow the Lord and serve Him regardless of what the circumstances may be?

As far as my husband is concerned, I was able to visit him this past summer. We had a 20-minute conversation that brought us great joy. . . .

I greet you with my love.
Mrs. Nguyen Thi An[8]

Would that she could finish this chapter, and I could be her student.

THE RELENTLESS POWER OF DISCONTENT

Despite her impoverished circumstances, Mrs. Nguyen Thi An races far ahead of affluent America. Why is contentment so hard for us? For one thing, it's slippery. Contentment is not at all like cutting down a tree, which, when it is done, is done. It's more like trying to pick up mercury with tweezers—it keeps squirting away. It's like the carrot suspended two feet in front of our face that moves every time we do. We keep chasing, and it keeps dodging. "Give a man everything he wants," declared Immanuel Kant, "and at that moment, everything will not be everything."

Beyond its slippery nature, contentment is difficult to achieve because of the relentless power of discontent. The battle waged between contentment and discontent is often subtle but never soft. When we enter the material world for our contentment, it pulls us in deeper and deeper, and the pull is deceptively strong. That for which I long becomes that to which I belong.

In addition, contentment is difficult because it is a relative state—at least the world's practice of it is relative. A number of factors influence this relativism: the age in which we live, the local culture, and the lifestyle of family members and friends. If you live in New York City and all your neighbors drive Mercedes, you might feel embarrassed if you drive a pickup. Living in rural Wisconsin where many people cut firewood, however, you would find a beat-up truck more acceptable.

If we were to draw one line representing ALL THERE IS TO HAVE and another representing WHAT WE NOW HAVE, the gap between these lines would be, in most cases, proportional to our level of contentment.

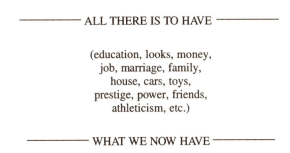

—————— ALL THERE IS TO HAVE ——————

(education, looks, money,
job, marriage, family,
house, cars, toys,
prestige, power, friends,
athleticism, etc.)

—————— WHAT WE NOW HAVE ——————

As the top line rises, the gap between what we now have and all there is to have becomes greater. Often our discontent becomes greater as well. *One of the dubious advantages progress has given us is the relentless raising of the top line.* Progress perceives this as its duty—to give us more and more. Were we free to select among the opportunities without pressure or comparison, perhaps these abundant choices would be acceptable. But humans are not like that, or at least our society is not like that. Life in the United States has become essentially a comparative experience.

With the invention of air conditioning, for example, progress raised the top line. Before the arrival of air conditioning, no one was discontented to drive in sweltering heat without it. People were miserable because of the heat, perhaps, but not discontented, because you cannot be discontented about something that doesn't exist. Yet when progress invents it for us, the level of expectation rises, and with it the level of discontent.

Living in Texas without an air-conditioned car today, you would likely be discontented. Fifty years ago you would not have been. Some might retort, "Before air conditioning people were miserable, and now, some are discontented. Isn't it about the same?" No. To be miserable with the heat is not a sin.

SET-POINTS

The relativism of contentment can be illustrated using the concept of a "floating set-point." This set-point, somewhat different for each person, is positioned at that level where you are content. If your circumstances match this set-point, you are temporarily satisfied. Once additional possibilities enter your awareness, however, your set-point floats to a new level. Then you buy a bigger house, get a better-paying job, move south, or undertake a multitude of other "improvements," and again you are temporarily satisfied.

This contentment set-point is free to float upward without limitation. There is no ceiling, and we have not tried to establish one as a matter of public policy, let alone common sense. Instead, we have fueled our economy by stimulating the set-point to rise even faster than it normally would. While this set-point is free-floating, it moves almost always in the upward direction. To see it fall voluntarily in a person's life is a wondrous thing, almost miraculous; I might even say, suggestive of godliness.

THE PROSPERITY LADDER

Another erroneous measure of contentment is the prosperity ladder. Most of us look "up the ladder" and notice that the wealthy have more than we do. This, of course, strikes a near fatal blow at one's contentment. If, instead, we reversed our gaze and looked down the ladder, our gratitude would thrive and opportunities for sharing would abound.

The pettiness of my own sources of discontent would be amusing were I not so repentant about them. I have been known to grumble when our house temperature drops to sixty degrees, yet there are untold millions in the world who do not have shelter. I have been known to complain if the day is rainy, yet a large segment of the world's land is shriveling up in drought. I have been known to groan if I miss my dinner, yet thousands who go to sleep tonight without food will not awaken in the morning. Christ came to save me from sin—not from sixty-degree homes, rainy weather, and delayed dinners.

This relativism, where the grass is greener on your neighbor's lawn, can be remedied, but first it must be confessed. We need to quit staring at those who have more than we do. We need to override the set-point by spiritual maturity, to look down rather than up the ladder, and to fix our contentment on godliness rather than relativism. It helps immeasurably if we are surrounded by a community of like-minded friends rather than a society where envy has been normalized.

THE AGE OF ENVY

The normalization of envy is yet another reason why the achievement of contentment is difficult. Historian and author Herbert Schlossberg explains why Helmut Schoeck calls this the "age of envy": "By that he means that fewer people than ever are ashamed of being envious, apparently believing that the fact of their envy is proof that social injustice has been done."9 The cultural message is strong: Why shouldn't we want what others have? We have rights, including the right to enjoy the good life. This, of course, is precisely the kind of logic that so efficiently destroys not only contentment but margin as well.

Is covetousness no longer a sin? In business we rename it ambition, making it not only dignified but exalted. "When children grab things from each other and declare, 'This is mine,' parents try to teach them to share," points out simplicity author Art Gish. "When these children grow up and grab for themselves, we praise them for being industrious."10

The advertising industry deserves a great share of the blame for consciously stimulating a chronic state of discontent. Were everyone in the United States to adopt a scripturally authentic lifestyle of contentment, we would much less often need new clothes, new toys, new furniture, and new automobiles. As a consequence, our discontent-dependent, debt-sponsored economy might well collapse on our heads.

MANUFACTURED NEED

The only way to avert this economic breakdown is to continually convince the American public that more and better is desirable. If this "need creation" is successful, it will guarantee not only economic stability but possibly even growth. Somehow in the process we forgot scriptural admonitions. I am not aware of a single person who takes seriously these words of Paul at their deepest level: "If we have food and clothing, we will be content with that."10

Two broad types of advertising deserve mentioning. The first reminds or informs: "We are having a sale this week," or "When looking for good fried chicken, don't forget us. We serve nightly until 9:00 p.m." The second type stimulates or manipulates need: "All the best athletes use Ajax breath mints," or "Use Jake's *new and improved*

fishing lure and you will never have another boring minute of fishing."
Nearly every advertisement that interrupts my consciousness (I do not
seek them out—they trespass) is of the latter type.

At first, the lying was subtle, and we overlooked it. Then it became
progressively more blatant, wrapped in entertainment. Today, the lying
is at absurd levels but goes largely unnoticed. Thus we have the intentional stimulation of covetousness through the telling of shameless lies,
both of which Scripture condemns. Yet we sit in rapt attention.

The advertisers use many additional strategies—visual stimulation
and sexual innuendo are but two of the more prominent—yet all these
are *methods*. What we really need to understand is the *message*. My
point is, the message we are given is that we need something. That we
really do not need much at all is viewed by advertisers as an obstacle
to overcome. They must manufacture need.

If we actually needed the thing, advertisers would not have to convince us of it. "The fact that wants can be synthesized by advertising,
catalyzed by salesmanship, and shaped by the discreet manipulations of
the persuaders shows that they are not very urgent," notes economist
John Kenneth Galbraith. "A man who is hungry need never be told of
his need for food."[12] We are not a hungry society; we are, in reality,
overfed. Need must be created, and discontent must be stirred up. Our
fallenness plays collusively into the hands of the enemy, and we are
easy prey.

POISON VERSUS PEACE

These manufacturers of need have been eminently successful, which
has been helpful for the economy but troublesome for veracity. In truth,
discontent has so many disadvantages one wonders why it is popular.
It can suffocate freedom, leaving us in bondage to our desires. It can
poison relationships with jealousy and competition. It often rewards
blessing with ingratitude as we grumble against God. "Discontent will
destroy your peace, rob you of joy, make you miserable, spoil your
witness," warns Packer. "We dishonor God if we proclaim a Savior
who satisfies and then go around discontent."[13] And when it has done
its work, discontent abandons us, leaving us no comfort in our indebted,
marginless, friendless self-pity.

The advantages of contentment, on the other hand, are many: freedom, gratitude, rest, peace—all components of health. They who are

content do not have to worry about the latest styles or what to wear tomorrow. They can rejoice in their neighbor's good fortune without having to feel inferior. They do not fret with wrinkles or graying because they accept what comes. They do not have to worry how they might buy this or that because they have no desire for this or that. They are not consumed with how to get out of debt because they have no debt. They have time for gratitude even in small things. They have time for relationships because possessions and the bank do not own them.

Do you see how a life of contentment both enables and supports margin? And do you see how a life filled with contentment and margin both enables and supports healthy relationships?

CONTENTMENT AND RELATIONSHIPS

God commanded contentment because He knew we would need it to anchor right relationships.

We *relate better to God* when we are satisfied with what He gives. We might say words of worship, but if our heart is not resting in the contentment of His presence, He is not fooled. "The Christian position from the beginning," contends Schlossberg, "has been that people are satisfied by becoming reconciled with God, not by acquiring wealth."[14]

We *relate better to self* when contented with our circumstances. If allowed to write a prescription redesigning our body, personality, or station in life, most of us would grab at the chance: smarter, funnier, richer, better looking, taller, thinner, more athletic. Yet none of these requests would even be an issue were it not for our comparisons with others. If we were all alone with God (which, in regard to contentment, we are), we would have a different set of values than the one society offers.

We *relate better to others* when the relationship is stabilized by contentment. If every encounter with my neighbor reminds me of something I covet, that relationship becomes tenuous. Envy makes it hard to have friends—everyone I know has something I do not.

CONTENTMENT AND MONEY

Our relationship to money is another area where contentment is essential. The poor envy the rich, while the rich envy the richer. Money gives a thrill but no satiety. The rich soon sense this and are perhaps surprised by it, but then go back to making more money anyway. Satisfaction will come later, they speculate, and if it never comes, at least there is the thrill.

Money *does seem* to meet our needs in the short term. It buys us food, shelter, vehicles, and experiences. It does not, however, meet any of our long-term needs: love, truth, relationship, redemption. This short-term deception is difficult for us to understand and is one of the reasons God spent so much time instructing us concerning money and wealth. Money is treacherous, we are told, and riches are deceitful. It is not a sin to be wealthy, but it can be dangerous. "God is merciful and can deliver the rich from the danger of being rich," observes John White. "But many of us do not want to be delivered."[15]

Many of today's rich are faced with the same depression, meaninglessness, alcoholism, suicide, and fractured relationships we see in the poor (or, for that matter, the middle class). The poor are not surprised by their plight. The rich, however, have run the rainbow out to its end and have found it an unexpectedly empty journey.

"To Americans usually tragedy is wanting something very badly and not getting it," observed Henry Kissinger. "Many people have had to learn in their private lives, and nations have had to learn in their historical experience, that perhaps the worst form of tragedy is wanting something badly, getting it, and finding it empty."[16]

Millions, as Kissinger hints, have had to discover that they can't find true contentment in important jobs and that the advertised contentment of cars, houses, and wardrobes is but a short-term hoax. The things one can buy with money are never the things that last. "Keep your lives free from the love of money and be content with what you have," we read in Hebrews, "because God has said, 'Never will I leave you; never will I forsake you.'"[17]

Did your car, your house, or your wardrobe ever say, "Never will I leave you"?

While earning money is necessary at some level, the Apostle Paul taught that seeking *wealth* would threaten us with devastation. People who want to get rich, Paul wrote in 1 Timothy 6:9-10,

▶ Fall into temptation.
▶ Fall into a trap.
▶ Fall into foolish desires.

❱ Fall into harmful desires.
❱ Are plunged into ruin.
❱ Are plunged into destruction.

And some people eager for money

❱ Have wandered from the faith.
❱ Have pierced themselves with many griefs.

Do you want to be plunged and pierced? Nor do I. But that doesn't seem to stop us from wanting to get rich. Were Paul's message not included in the biblical text, it would be out of print. No readership remains, even within the church.

THE THEOLOGY OF ENOUGH

We need contentment to relate correctly to money and, in a similar way, to possessions. The rules here are simple:

1. God comes first and possessions come second.
2. Possessions are to be used, not loved.

One of Jesus' most frightening warnings to contemporary America is His rebuke of the rich landowner in Luke 12. When the fields yielded a great harvest, the landowner proudly built huge barns and stored up his treasure for the years to come. Now, he thought, life will be easy and secure.

God's judgment was quick: "You fool!" That night the man's life was taken from him.

"Watch out!" warns Jesus. "Be on your guard against all kinds of greed; a man's life does not consist in the abundance of his possessions" (Luke 12:15). Tragically, for many Americans today, their empty lives do indeed consist in the abundance of their possessions.

"Within the human heart 'things' have taken over," asserts A. W. Tozer. "God's gifts now take the place of God, and the whole course of nature is upset by the monstrous substitution."[18] Why hasn't the Church stood against this popular error? Why hasn't there been a clear expression of a "theology of enough"? Perhaps it is because things are not evil, as stealing and adultery are; only the *love* of things, like the *love* of money, is evil. It is easy for us to say, "I don't love this thing;

it's just that I *need* it." God is what we need; things are what we use. In the words of one Christian journalist, "Contentment lies not in what is yours, but in whose you are."[19]

BOREDOM AND SUFFERING

Contentment is also helpful in enduring boredom and suffering. Children today use the word *boring* frequently. It is intended as the ultimate verbal scourge, and basically it means, "I'm discontented. Entertain me." The prevalence of this word is an unsettling indicator of where our children are in relation to contentment.

As I was growing up, we used our imagination and creativity to make our own fun. Today, electronic entertainment rides a nonstop conveyer belt directly into the dormant souls of the young. It is not a favorable development. I cannot be optimistic that this trend will miraculously result in a mature sense of contentment in later years. Over time, a decaying log will not turn into a house. All you get is a bigger pile of rot.

> A man said to the universe:
> "Sir, I exist!"
> "However," replied the universe,
> "The fact has not created in me
> A sense of obligation."[19]

In his famous poem, Stephen Crane reminds us of an important truth: God is not indebted to us. If life is boring, then it is boring. We work to make it better, but our duty throughout the working is contentment. If life is tough, so it is tough. Our duty is contentment. If there is suffering, why would we expect anything different? Our duty is contentment.

Life can be painful. Most people do not choose this pain; it comes with living. Contentment, however, is different. Contentment or discontent is a matter of the will, a choice. When we choose obedience, God, in His wonderful way with surprises, can redeem the pain and suffering in our lives and can turn the destruction into benefit.

DON'T WAIT—WORK

No formula exists for finding contentment other than obedience. Remember, it is a secret. It won't make sense to worldly thinking, and it won't be discovered by scientific study. First you must seek it. Then it will be revealed to you.

This, of course, is no excuse to sit around waiting to hear from Heaven. There are steps you can take, acts of your will, which point you in the right direction. You always have a better chance of discovering the secret if you're in the vicinity of its hiding place. The following nine steps will start you on your way.

1. Get to work. The conflict between contentment and discontent is a struggle format. It requires much effort on our part. You cannot get from New Orleans to Minneapolis on the Mississippi except by paddling.

2. Divorce your thinking from society's relativistic standards. God says, "Be content," not "Be content if . . ." Never allow the affairs of others to influence your contentment.

3. Turn off the ads and tune out the lies. If you wish to preserve your financial margin, cast your lot with contentment.

4. Defer to God's opinion concerning your family relationships. How often, particularly in modern America, have we seen the devastation visited upon families through the "if only" syndrome? Emotional margin is an early casualty with such discontent as, "If only my wife were more appealing or more sexually interested," or "If only my husband made more money or had more hair." Infidelity, even in thought, is greener grass only because it's been spray painted by the Deceiver himself. Contentment keeps our eyes on the right side of the fence.

5. Set new standards for your contentment using the truth of Scripture. God has long desired to teach us these principles, but it has not been an easy task for Him.

6. Develop "counter-habits," as John Charles Cooper calls them. Instead of getting, try giving. Instead of replacing, try preserving. Instead of feeling covetous, try feeling grateful. Instead of feeling inferior before men, try feeling accepted before God. Instead of being ruled by feelings, try enjoying the freedom of contentment.

7. Subtract from your needs. Make a list of all the things you need and then start crossing things off. It might at first be painful, but after a while it becomes fun. "There are two ways to get enough," G. K. Chesterton has pointed out. "One is to continue to accumulate more and more. The other is to desire less."

8. Accept from God's hand that which He gives—not resignation, not complacency, but contentment. All that is needful He will supply.

Even pain and suffering that seemingly cannot be corrected, He can redeem.

9. If you still do not feel the stirrings of contentment within, argue with yourself and tell yourself the truth. We discover contentment, according to Packer, "by learning to talk to ourselves in a good Christian way. You listen to God in Scripture and then tell yourself what He said. If your emotions disagree, you argue with your emotions. And if you find unbelief in your heart, you argue with that unbelief and drive it out by appeal to God's truth."[21]

DISLOCATION OR DELIGHT?

Is contentment, then, a move in the health direction? Let's ask the masters.

"Discontent doth dislocate and unjoint the soul, it pulls off the wheels," advises Thomas Watson in *The Art of Divine Contentment*. "Discontent is a fretting humour, which dries the brains, wastes the spirits, corrodes and eats out the comfort of life."[22]

"Christian contentment," counters Jeremiah Burroughs in *The Rare Jewel of Christian Contentment, "is that sweet, inward, quiet, gracious frame of spirit, which freely submits to and delights in God's wise and fatherly disposal in every condition."*[23]

When I get sick, I want to go to their clinic. They never knew about penicillin. But they sure knew a lot about health.

Health
Through Simplicity

T hough it has been variously commended and practiced for centuries, simplicity has seldom been more needed than it is today. Health requires it. Sanity demands it. Contentment facilitates it. "Simplicity is crucial to progress," observes complexity expert Duane Elgin, "for without simplicity we will be overwhelmed by massive social and material complexity."[1]

If overload is sabotaging our equilibrium, simplicity can help. If we find ourselves being detailed to death, simplicity can restore life. If we find ourselves overextended in our emotional, financial, and time commitments, simplicity is one of the best ways to reestablish margin. "Do not underestimate the delight of real simplicity in your life style," advises stress expert Hans Selye, M.D.[2]

GETTING AWAY FROM IT ALL

We hear frequent talk about the rat race and the treadmill, about stopping the world to let people off. Many fantasize about walking away from their jobs, throwing away the television, and moving to a cabin in the woods. Indeed, in the last few decades, many have acted upon the fantasy. "Former city dwellers are said to be opting out by the hundreds of thousands in search of clean air, safe streets, more time for family—in short, a simpler, slower pace of life," reports John Naisbitt.[3]

The reasons people feel like "getting away from it all" have already been explored. Given the complicated, rushed nature of daily life in modern America, it is not surprising that many are looking for the exit door. The solution, however, for our stress-overload-pain triad is not so much escaping as it is transcending: The solution is simplicity. Simplicity does not guarantee margin, but it is helpful.

NOT A MODERN INVENTION

In our age of frenzied distress, large numbers of contemporary think-ers have begun discussing and writing about the concept of a simple lifestyle. We encounter with regularity such phrases as "the plain life," "plain people," "intermediate technology," "intentional com-munities," and "contrast culture." We are enamored by the Amish lifestyle, wanting to tour their villages, eat their food, and bring home their quilts. Even the popular "country look" in home decorating has become, at least in part, a manifestation of the nostalgia many share about things simple and past. In much of the United States now, glitz and gaudiness are out; fireplaces, rocking chairs, and cross-stitch are in.

Despite its attractiveness and timeliness, simplicity is not a new concept. The spiritually minded have long sought it as a way of facilitating the contemplative life. The monastic orders and the Desert Fathers practiced simplicity, often including vows of poverty, extreme asceticism, and complete separation from the world.

Through the seventeenth and eighteenth centuries, many of those who traveled to the New World in search of religious freedom, from the Puritans to the Quakers, sought a simple, godly lifestyle. America of the nineteenth century also saw its simplicity movements. Perhaps the most lasting impressions were made by the Transcendentalists, a group who were in many ways spiritually motivated but not within the context of orthodox Christian doctrine. Two of their number, Ralph Waldo Emerson and Henry David Thoreau, were articulate prophets for this "plain living and high thinking," and their legacy continues to influence many today.

The modern era has witnessed such simplicity causes as the hippie communes and cultural dropouts. In addition, there has been significant activity within the Church, although not always mainstream. From the International Consultation of Simple Life-Style to the Mennonite Central Committee, some in the Church seek to find the posture of proper theological balance in an age of affluence and complexity.

Austere separatists such as the Amish, once widely scorned for being so backward, now garner more respect. "We should look again at the life styles and beliefs of the Brethren, Mennonites, and Amish," encourages author John Charles Cooper. "They do not pollute the earth. They do not waste food. They concentrate on the care of the earth and the care of their families. They have no ambitions for wealth or status. They harbor no political lusts to control the lives of their neighbors. All they ask for is the right to live simple, godly lives. The joy of these plain people lies in their communion with Christ and with one another."[4]

CHRISTLIKENESS

Even if I were not a Christian, the notion of stepping off the treadmill would sound attractive. Yet for adherents of Christianity, a stronger pull motivates: To be a follower of Christ means we should *follow* Him. No one lived a simpler, more unencumbered life than He. His birth was in spartan conditions, and His life was free from the ties of possessions or money. He was born with nothing, lived with little, and died with nothing. His simplicity was not accidental. Jesus could have chosen any standard, yet He chose to live simply.

In the Sermon on the Mount, Christ told us not to worry even about food and clothing and not to worry about tomorrow. That He did not seek luxury is a statement to us who follow Him. When He demonstrated servitude by washing the feet of His disciples, He explained, "I have set you an example that you should do as I have done for you. . . . No servant is greater than his master."[5]

The Apostle Peter instructs us to walk after the example of Christ in enduring suffering.[6] Paul teaches us to follow after Jesus' example of humility.[7] "Does the Bible infer that we are to live like *a king* or like *the King*?" asks Rev. Tom Allen. "The simplicity, sacrifice and servanthood of Jesus Christ should be our way of life, too."[8]

INTERNAL ANCHOR, EXTERNAL JOY

All external manifestations of the Christian life require internal foundations, and simplicity is no different. The external practices are important, but the internal requirements are essential. For simplicity to bring us the lifestyle rest we are searching for, the internal truths must be confirmed by our own will. They have to do with the lordship of Christ. This means seeking the Kingdom first, thus giving over our plans, our expectations, our future, our family, our reputation, and our possessions to Him. Once these conditions are met, then we are free to begin seeking the external practices.

With the internal issues settled, the external practices are a joy. Loaning or giving away our possessions is not anxiety-producing because we are only stewards anyway, and the true Owner has told us to give generously. We are free to wear older clothes or to live in modest homes because God doesn't care. We no longer need to impress. With the internal truth anchored, the external simplicity of our lives is a celebration. Without this anchor, however, the external workings become a chore, a set of rules, and often degenerate into legalism.

WHAT IT IS

Simple living over the centuries has been variously defined. "The precise meaning of the simple life has never been fixed," explains historian David Shi. "Rather, it has always represented a shifting cluster of ideas, sentiments, and activities."[9] Certain common threads, however, can be identified. The simple life is:

Voluntary—If the simple life is forced, it ceases to be simple. Involuntary impoverishment, for example, makes it difficult for people to *choose* simplicity. This is not to say it is impossible. But the plain life is far more profitable when it is chosen as an act of the will.

Free—One of the key features of simplicity and, at the same time, one of its principal advantages is that it is a life of freedom. It is free from anxiety—about our reputations, our possessions, our tomorrows. It is being controlled by that which is life-giving and refusing to be controlled by that which is destructive.

Uncluttered—Realizing that psychological and material clutter impedes our journey, simplicity seeks to unclutter. Emotionally, we release our worries, we reconcile our relationships, we forgive our enemies, and we begin anew each day. Materially, instead of possession gluttony, we practice de-accumulation. Like runners of old, we strip down to that which is authentic so that we might run the race effectively.

Natural—We respect the natural order—the things God has created and the job God has given humankind within that order. We don't just return to nature; we return to the God who created nature.

The simple life understands that natural beauty exists and that it penetrates deeper than the adornments of humankind. The real beauty of another human exists within the spirit and consists of virtue and purity.

Creative—Life is not boring just because it is simple. Simplicity sets the imagination free to work and to enjoy. Passive entertainment can dull the sense of wonder God has placed within us. The simple life, however, affords an opportunity to rediscover the joys of creativity.

Authentic—A simple lifestyle must distinguish between the spiritually authentic and spiritually inauthentic aspects of life and be devoted to the former. Biblical authenticity includes those things God has told us to focus on, those things that have eternal, God-assigned value: people, love, service, worship, prayer, self-denial, relationships, contentment, freedom, rest.

Focused—Understanding the significance of spiritual authenticity, we focus on it. We lock in on what is good and true. We bind ourselves to that which has eternal value. This does not mean we do not wash our car or take out the garbage. But it does mean that we understand who God is and what His priorities for our lives are—and then follow them. It does mean that we focus intensely on seeking the Kingdom first, and on loving God and man. Without such focus, we drift.

Margined—Because the simple life is focused, it is able to distinguish the things that truly matter from the imposters. It can tell the difference between the authentic and that which is only attractive. Thanks to such visionary wisdom, simplicity recognizes the importance of margin and seeks to protect it. Together margin and simplicity are allies in a hostile world. Like a team of oxen straining against the storm, they will not be beaten back by the forces that seek to crush them both. The pace might plod. But they are a reliable team, always pulling together. Given time, the work will get done. Thanks to their efforts, health has a better chance to reach its final destination—relationships.

Disciplined—Restraint is necessary for successful living, and all the more for simple living. Comfort is not a legitimate primary goal—authenticity is. Understandably, then, those seeking simplicity may experience discomfort. Doing without is often necessary. Inasmuch as the simple life is an obedient life, and obedience requires discipline, we will not be able to thrive without it.

Diligent—The simple life knows how to rest, but it also knows how to work. One of the benefits of simplicity is a return to human labor. It is time to rethink the notion that small-scale, labor-intensive production is undesirable. It is good to be physically active. It is good to work with our hands. Human energy, unlike coal, natural gas, or oil, is renewable and nonpolluting. It is good to start and end the work ourselves and to have pride in the process and the product. It is good to plant our own food, to sew our own clothes, to cut our own wood, to walk to work.

Healthful—A life voluntarily chosen and lived in freedom; a life uncluttered and natural; a life that is focused, diligent, and disciplined; a life characterized by creativity and spiritual authenticity—is not this a healthy life?

WHAT SIMPLICITY ISN'T

Misconceptions abound about the simple life. We can clarify simplicity as much by explaining what it isn't as by delineating what it is. And it is not:

Easy—Many equate "simple" with "easy" and become disillusioned with simple living when they find out how hard it can be. To bake your own bread or cut your own wood is not always the easiest way to provide food and warmth. But doing these chores yourself allows an often hard-earned independence that can facilitate simplicity.

Legalistic—Legalism is the trap I dread more than any other. Those who choose to live a simple lifestyle often set a standard of judgment for the lives of others. Such legalism does not liberate; it kills. It destroys the joy of both the accuser and the accused. The message of simple living is better spread by invitation than by judgment.

Proud—While simple living is intended to be a vehicle for virtue, it can deteriorate into the vice of pride. This we might call "reverse pride." It is possible, and even tempting, to wear patches on your clothes as self-awarded badges of righteousness. It is possible to practice self-exaltation for the rust on your car or the stone-ground whole-wheat bread in your oven. All of these highly visible "sacrifices" serve to elevate your (perceived) righteousness level several notches above that of your inferiors. Jesus, of course, dealt with this attitude in Matthew 6 (giving, fasting, praying) and no new teaching is needed.

Impoverished—Taking a vow of poverty does not guarantee that spiritually authentic simplicity will follow. Simplicity does not reject money and ownership—it merely subjugates it. All money goes quickly to the purse of the Father for use in our lives and the lives of others according to His wishes. We don't seek wealth as a goal in itself, not only because it is sinful to do so, but also because money cannot buy what we need. Yet money is received and used, for the Father knows how to control it for the purposes of His Kingdom.

Ascetic—Asceticism rejects all possessions and argues that "things" are spiritually handicapping. While it is true that things can become spiritually inauthentic, they are not an *a priori* evil. God is a good Creator, and He has created a whole world full of good things. It is not wrong to use them—they were made to be used. But our material appetites must be controlled.

Neurotic—Some adherents live a simple life but know nothing of its freedom. They tilt toward spartan asceticism because they feel unworthy of any blessing or they feel responsible for all the poverty in the world. Such a guilt-driven lifestyle is not simplicity. It is neurosis. God blames us only for what we are to blame for, and He took it all away when we asked Him to. Now that the slate is clean, we choose simplicity, not out of guilt but out of sensitivity and devotion.

Ignorant—Simple livers are not to be simpletons. We don't achieve such a lifestyle by burning our books and burying our heads. On the contrary, one of the main advantages of such a life is the opportunity it provides for study, discussion, and meditation. God created our brains just as surely as He did our hearts, and He expects us to use them both for His glory. Ignorance is not the essence of simplicity—it is an enemy.

Escapist—"The grass is greener on the other side of the fence" is 98 percent lie. We don't attain the simple life by throwing away our cars and phones and running off to live in the woods. Clearly, for some people the simple life is facilitated by moving from an overmortgaged house or departing a traffic-paralyzed city. But simple living is not a location; it is an attitude. It is not escaping; it is transcending. It is not separation; it is sanctification.

A RETREAT TO THE PAST?

Many among us might wish to turn back the clock, to retreat to a simpler, easier time. We long for the quiet of nature rather than the blast of rock music and car horns. We want to be more directly involved in the elements, whether planting the seed that feeds our family or digging the worms that catch our fish. Perhaps we even long to raise our own animals or build our own log home.

Much debate continues over such nostalgia. Is it healthy, or is it escapist? Is sentimentality an ally or a deceiver? We often forget the horrid problems of the past, and in the process, also overlook the blessings of today. "Too often the past seems far more virtuous, simpler, and happier than it actually was," reminds historian Shi.[10] Our historical memories are selective. To pine for a misrepresented dreamland is not a spiritually authentic thing to do.

In addition to calling such nostalgia irresponsible, some argue we could not reverse the process of history even if we wanted to. These critics maintain that the forces which have steamrolled us to this point are far too strong to be turned back. Such a longed-for retreat to the past is not only irresponsible—it is impossible. Progress, they say, cannot be stopped.

Progress *is* very strong. Yet we must be careful here. To say that history and progress must flow in only one direction is to give those forces the power of gods. In exposing such thinking, Herbert Schlossberg points out, "One of the most common [examples of historicism] is the saying, 'We can't turn back the clock.' The progressive connotations of this saying are wholly illusory. . . . In refusing to believe that an identified historical trend may be challenged, the historicists have divinized history."[11] Nothing is so embedded that it cannot be dislodged. No momentum is so great that it cannot be redirected. Otherwise, God is not God.

When Art Gish was confronted with the question of turning back the clock, his answer was enlightening: "The analogy of a clock is not helpful. It is not the question of a clock, but a compass. The issue is not chronology, but direction. And that we can decide. . . . We are not retreating, but looking ahead to perceive what is important.

Simplification implies leaving things behind and moving to a new future."[12]

Progress *can* be suspended and reversed on an individual level, and, for that matter, even on a societal level (although admittedly, with great difficulty). But is that the best direction for our simple-life search? Instead of escaping, can we not transcend? Selectivity is an important concept here. Can we not hold on to what is good and reject what is destructive?

THE DIFFICULTY OF SIMPLICITY

What factors make the simple life hard to obtain? If we embark on this journey, let's first decide how much of the currency of fortitude we need to bring with us. There will be tollbooths all along the route, with the costs often quite steep.

No sooner have we started out the gate then we encounter our first problem: society's disrespect. If we choose to ignore fashion and status, we will not gain the admiration of our peers. From the outset, we need to decide who it is we are trying to please.

To further illustrate this roadblock called social respectability, let me suggest a story and then ask a question. Suppose one day you went exploring in a cave near San Francisco. When you came out, shockingly you discovered that everyone had disappeared from the face of the earth, transported away by invading aliens. As you search for an automobile, you find that they too have been removed. By linking your cam-recorder to a fax machine and then running both through a satellite dish, you cleverly locate the only two cars left in the United States. The first, a ten-year-old Chevrolet with ninety thousand miles, is near San Diego and could be reached in three weeks by walking. The other car is the same model Chevy, only brand-new. It is on the outskirts of New York City and would require six months of walking to reach. Which would you choose?

Perhaps you already suspect my point. Given this scenario, virtually all of us would be content with the older car. We would not walk an extra 161 days just for a shiny paint job and new interior. Yet this is commonly what we do in our society—work six months for a new car instead of three weeks for a functional older one. Why do we do this? Is it because we get tired of paying for repairs? No. We buy new cars primarily for one reason: *because of the presence of other people*. We desire respectability in the eyes of others. Appearance—not function—rules us.

Continuing down the narrow road of the simple life, we keep encountering another problem: our expectations. After decades of convenience and affluence, we not only desire but *expect* ease and satiation. Gratification of our appetites has become a widespread goal not seriously challenged by the church. If we do not reprogram such expectations, we will experience recurrent frustration in our search for simplicity.

Our lack of discipline presents us with yet another obstacle. We have not needed much discipline during this era of abundance, and we have lost interest in it as a component of lifestyle. Most of us have grown soft. But the simple life is not easy, and discipline is necessary.

Finally, our own mistaken opinions of how things ought to be also trip us repeatedly. Theological confusion has permitted us first to look at what we want and then to build a theology that justifies it. For example, very little money is needed to live a fully God-honoring life. Yet somehow we have incorporated the presumed need for money into our theological construct. True enough, we need a lot of income to live as our society does, to partake in the many benefits of our age. But it is not true that we need a lot to live on.

SUGGESTIONS

The following are suggestions that will assist in simple living. Beware of the distinction between suggestions and rules, for if you make them rules, you will have converted simplicity into legalism and defeated its purpose before even beginning.

Possessions and Finances

- Cultivate contentment, desire less.
- Resist covetousness.
- Resist consumerism.
- Wage war against advertisements.
- Buy things for their usefulness rather than their status.
- De-accumulate.
- Develop the habit of giving away.
- Share possessions.

▶ Offer the use of your possessions—don't make others ask.
▶ Develop a network of exchange.
▶ Avoid overindulging—for example, toys, food, movie viewing, etc.
▶ Avoid impulse buying.
▶ Don't buy anything if the time and money spent on it compete with family, service, and God.
▶ Avoid debt if possible.
▶ Don't buy now, pay later.
▶ Avoid credit cards if they are a problem.
▶ Reject fashion, especially fads.
▶ Deemphasize respectability.
▶ Simplify your wardrobe—give away excess.
▶ Learn how to make do with a lower income instead of needing a higher one.

Pace and Atmosphere

▶ Slow down.
▶ Do not exhaust your emotional bank account.
▶ Lie fallow.
▶ Say no.
▶ Enjoy peaceful music.
▶ Control/restrict/eliminate television watching.
▶ Get a remote control set and turn off advertisements.

Relationships

▶ Cultivate a closeness with God.
▶ Schedule "simple" dates with your spouse.
▶ Teach your children.
▶ Enjoy family field trips.
▶ Practice regular hospitality.
▶ Help each other, emphasize service.
▶ Encourage others.
▶ "Always speak the truth and you'll never be concerned with your memory."
▶ Don't judge.
▶ Learn to enjoy solitude.

Appreciation

- Send cards of encouragement and appreciation when others are not expecting it.
- Be grateful for things large and small.
- Emphasize a joyful life.
- Appreciate creation.

Spiritual Life

- Make the Word central.
- Meditate, memorize.
- Pray.
- Encourage simple worship.

Activities

- Make your commitments simple.
- Don't overwork.
- Fast periodically from media, food, people.
- Elevate reading, go to the library.
- Simplify Christmas.
- Write down those things you need to remember and forget everything else.

Nutrition and Exercise

- Exercise.
- Bike or walk.
- Make your recreation active rather than passive.
- Develop healthy sleep habits.
- Avoid overeating.
- Frequent a co-op.
- Whenever possible, buy food directly from those who grow it.
- Garden.

FAD OR THE FUTURE?

Is simplicity a trendy fad? Will it fade in significance as did the hippie communes, or is it destined to grow in importance? Simple lifestyles, or something approximating that idea, will only continue to increase in importance. Our age is ever becoming more complex and diffusely overloaded, and simplicity is a movement whose time has come.

One hundred years ago, the most popular spokesman for simple living was the writer John Burroughs. Naturalists and students, journalists and politicians (including Theodore Roosevelt) wore a path to the door of his rustic New England cabin. Humble and self-effacing, he was an eloquent spokesman for unencumbered living.

> I am bound to praise the simple life, because I have lived it and found it good. When I depart from it, evil results follow. I love a small house, plain clothes, simple living. . . . To see the fire that warms you, or better yet, to cut the wood that feeds the fire that warms you; to see the spring where the water bubbles up that slakes your thirst, and to dip your pail into it; . . . to be in direct and personal contact with the sources of your material life; to want no extras, no shields; to find the universal elements enough . . . to be thrilled by the stars at night; to be elated over a bird's nest, or over a wild flower in spring—these are some of the rewards of the simple life.[13]

Do these strike you as sentiments that future generations will scoff at—or yearn for?

I agree.

WHAT DOES THE LORD REQUIRE?

The simple life will not sound attractive unless you are in love with the Truth. If you have such a love, however, anything that distracts you from it is gladly cut adrift. Then, after you have been freed to pursue your path unencumbered, you will not desire more from your days on earth than simply to act justly, to love mercy, and to walk humbly with your God.[14]

Health Through Balance

The human body is a universe. Made up of 10^{28} atoms, we each contain millions of times more atoms than there are stars in space (10^{20}). Ninety percent of these atoms are replaced every year, and virtually 100 percent are replaced every five years. Thus our physical beings are continuously tearing down but also continuously building up. From dust we have come and to dust we return—continuously.[1]

Veritable factories that never shut down, our bodies exhibit a complexity beyond human comprehension. We each are made up of trillions upon trillions of working units, all perpetually moving, metabolizing, combining, interacting, adjusting, purifying, purging, building, and decaying. Yet everything must function in *balance*. If this balance is disturbed, disease is the result. We get sick. We feel pain.

When organ systems are functioning in a balanced manner, physicians say they are "compensated." To be decompensated—that is, out of balance—is to be ill. Likewise, in the area of mental health, when someone is functioning poorly, he or she is said to be "unbalanced." For physiology to avoid becoming pathology, balance is essential. It is no different in the broader context of life.

THE BALANCING ACT

The balanced life today seems inaccessible: too many activities, too many choices, too many decisions, too many commitments, too many expectations, too many people, too much hurry, too much change. Overload, stress, complexity—all are unbalancing pressures. Their effect is to cause ever-increasing disequilibrium in systems and people. Of the many problems compounded by this mischievous triad, imbalance is prominent among them.

The average conscientious American wants to be committed as a spouse, responsible as a parent, faithful in the church, successful in the workplace, and active in the community. Family, church, community, self—each one is a legitimate pull. Indeed, life is full of tugs:

Work	Leisure
Action	Meditation
Leading	Following
Speaking	Listening
Handwork	Headwork
Productivity	Recreation
Intensity	Idleness
Serving	Waiting
Giving	Receiving
Applying	Learning
Structure	Spontaneity
Assertiveness	Submissiveness
Confidence	Humility
Judgment	Grace
Analysis	Synthesis
Specialization	Integration
Society	Solitude
Laughter	Solemnity
Duty	Freedom
Joy	Sorrow
External life	Internal life

How does one find the balance? When life is so correctly constituted of both sides, by what criteria do we make decisions? Is balance appropriate? Is it possible?

As we have illustrated, medicine has become very specialized. More and more is known about the details of health and disease, and specialists are required for such detailed understandings. Yet the kind of investigation that dissects organs and cells will never lead to an understanding of the *person*, and generalists are needed to put it all back together. Specialization versus integration, analysis versus synthesis—how do we balance?

Are we to pray or to serve? To work or to rest? To rejoice at the goodness in people and the great goodness in our Creator, or to sorrow at the pain so evident all around? Life requires both. Balance has always been necessary and will always be necessary. It is just becoming more difficult.

BALANCE OR EXCELLENCE?

Much is made today of the virtues of excellence. But what does this mean? Often the excellence described is only in one narrow corridor of life: virtuosos who exist only for their music, or corporate executives who live at the office.

What do these passionate high achievers think of balance? For many, it is an enemy. Single-minded fervency is their standard. One-hundred-percent effort is the minimum, and those who question such asymmetrical dedication are distrusted and unpromoted.

While undivided devotion to one cause can bring great success and vault a person into prominence, such a priority structure often leaves the rest of that person's life in a state of disorder. Thus it is not uncommon to discover a physician who fails as a parent, an entertainer who fails as a spouse, a pastor who neglects personal health, or an executive who fails at all those other areas. Traditional wisdom has told us not to put all our eggs in one basket. Yet, in pursuit of excellence, we often discard this basic wisdom. Balance is not the goal; preeminence is the goal.

I am not advocating halfheartedness and mediocrity, for we always ought to do our best. But "doing our best" has limits. Our rush toward excellence in one quadrant of life must not be permitted to cause destruction in another. "We need," as Norman Cousins explains, "to be more proportionate."

Those who go all out for success in one endeavor, points out physicist/engineer Richard H. Bube, risk failure in other important areas of life. "Not only is the ability to exhibit excellence in other fields decreased, but in several fields the net consequence is to produce what we may colloquially call 'negative excellence.'" Bube recommends "a more balanced approach."[2] This principle is demonstrated in figures 13.1 and 13.2 (adapted from Bube).

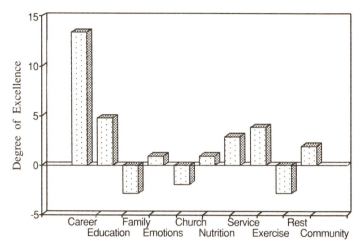

Figure 13.1 - Excellence Plus Failure

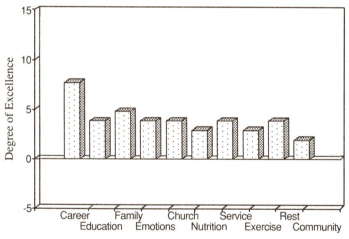

Figure 13.2 - Balance

Schematic illustrations of choice patterns in major fields of a persons endeavors. The ten bars represent individual areas that require time and effort and in which it is possible to establish excellence. (a) This set of choices represents those made by a person who strives for such a high degree of excellence in one area that other areas may actually experience "negative excellence," i.e. failure. (b) This set of choices represents those made by a person who strives to avoid failure in any area and therefore does not achieve quite as high a degree of excellence in any one area as the person represented in (a). Limitation of time and resources make it necessary for every person to choose between some degree of (a) and (b).

The person in figure 13.1 has chosen to strive for such a high degree of excellence in one area that other areas reveal little excellence or even "negative excellence" (that is, failure). Consequently, this person has achieved excellence in the career area but, at the same time, has suffered failure in the other important areas of family, church, and rest.

In contrast, the person in figure 13.2 has chosen to live a balanced life and has therefore avoided "negative excellence" in any area. As a consequence, no outstanding level of excellence has been achieved. On the other hand, no failure has been experienced either.

If you wish to achieve excellence but also to have life balance, beware. Those who advocate excellence at all costs often do not believe in "outside interests" and may not tolerate them. Family, friends, church, as well as margin in personal time and emotional health—all are luxuries that may compete with a stellar performance in a single area. If, then, we are forced to choose between excellence or balance, how do we choose? Once we understand that God expects us to act responsibly in each area of life, it is easier to discern the problems associated with one-track excellence.

A MATTER OF PRIORITIES?

If we accept that balance is important, especially in light of avoiding "negative excellence" in any area of life, how do we achieve it? Since each of us lives according to a set of priorities—whether we are aware of it or not—perhaps that is the place to start.

What does your priority list look like? For those committed to ultraexcellence, one goal stands alone on the top—perhaps wealth, power, athletic success, academics, or political victory. Sequentially beneath this exalted goal are myriad subordinate goals. These form a constellation of priorities for each person. If written down, one list might look something like this:

1. God
2. Spouse/marriage
3. Children
4. Self
5. Work
6. Church

7. Friends, neighbors
8. Health
9. Security
10. Civic duty

Does creating such lists help us solve our problem and lead us to biblically authentic decision making about balancing priorities? I think not. "A list of priorities doesn't make sense!" observes J. Grant Howard in *Balancing Life's Demands*. "No matter how you define and describe your particular approach, if it is a sequential approach, it is loaded with contradictions."[3]

We cannot achieve balance by stacking our priorities one on top of another, even though this is a common practice. As Dr. Howard goes on to advise, it fits better to think of God as *central* to everything and then build outward from that point. We do not love God, *then* spouse, *then* children, *then* self, *then* church. We love God, spouse, children, self, and church all at the same time. Similarly, we do not love God 100 percent, spouse 95 percent, children 90 percent, church 80 percent. God's standard requires that we love all of them all of the time.

One of the interesting things about love is that it is not a mathematical entity. When divided, love multiplies. However we attempt to factor it, love remains an intact whole. For example, if we have one child in our family, we might be singularly devoted to that child and love him or her 100 percent. If we have a second child, does that mean we love each child only 50 percent? Of course not. We would love each child 100 percent even if there were ten of them.

God has suspended the laws of mathematics in allowing love to expand infinitely. In so doing, He has delivered us from the need to prioritize our love sequentially.

THE APPORTIONMENT OF TIME

It does not make sense to have sequential priorities in terms of love or even in terms of commitment. We love each person fully. Additionally, we are committed to doing good in all areas of life. Priority thinking *is* appropriate when we speak of *time*, however.

Time is the context within which we all must work. In any given year, no one is granted more time than another person, and no one is granted less. Time cannot be stretched or borrowed. It is a universal given, and it is in apportioning this time that balance and priorities become very important.

Time, then, is the key. When we couple it with our goals, desires, and responsibilities, we have some priority decisions to make. It is unwise to give all our time to work and family, but none to personal health. God created us to need health, and it is not wrong to seek it. Likewise, God created us to need each other in relationship. It is not wrong to dedicate time for that. He created us with duties toward nature, work, and government, and it is not wrong for us to focus on these duties. *But the time devoted must be balanced, for if we give too much in one area we neglect our duty in another important area and fail God's requirements for balanced living.*

RESTORING BALANCE

Partitioning our time is probably the most important practical issue in achieving balanced living. Yet rationing it wisely presents a dilemma for each of us. How do we do it? First and most important, balance cannot be achieved unless we are willing to say no.

It is not easy to say no. Anyone who has eaten in a buffet restaurant knows what it is like to face a long table of inviting foods: salads, potatoes, gravy, rolls, corn, chicken, shrimp, roast beef, and pie. It is difficult to go down this line without saying yes to too much. In life, as in the buffet, our plates fill up sooner than we realize. In attempting to be sociable we try to accommodate everyone's invitations. In attempting to live a full life we taste every experience. In attempting to be good parents we try to give our children more opportunities than we had. In attempting to be compassionate we want to help with everyone's problems. In attempting to be good providers we accept extra work assignments.

At this point we need to remember discussions from earlier in the book. With each passing year, modern-day life spontaneously becomes more stressful, more overloaded, and more complex. No one controls all this change—it is simply the way progress unfolds. As we are presented with more decision and activity overload within an increasingly complex and stressful context, balance becomes more difficult. We cannot resolve this problem without saying no—even to some very good things. Saying no, then, is the first step. But what comes next?

What follows are four additional steps to restoring balance.

1. It is important that we gain control over our own lives, for only then will balance be a possibility. If our schedules are ruled by the urgent and tyrannical, we will not have the control necessary for substantive changes. Each of the chapters in parts 2 and 3 is intended to help us gain a measure of control and reorient our lives in a God-given rather than society-driven direction.

2. We must place God at the center of all things, and build outward from there, rationally and consistently. We know which areas of living God has told us to focus on—in particular, loving relationships. Making our choices in the light of accepted limits, we reassess regularly and defend each area of importance against the onslaught of other demands.

3. We must beware the trap of trying to solve the problem of imbalance by becoming even *more* imbalanced. Sometimes it feels like we are in a Chinese finger trap—the harder we try to pull free, the worse we become entrapped. If already maximally scheduled, we cannot give added attention to one area unless we subtract from another area. "We respond to our sense of imbalance by committing *more* time and energy to an area in which we feel deficient," warns physician George Rust.[4] Yet when the rain barrel is full, it is full. We cannot put another drop in unless we first take a drop out. As elementary as this principle is, its application escapes the majority of modern-day people.

4. We must accept the no given us by others. We ought not to feel offended when another person is merely attempting to achieve God-honoring balance and margin. Let's beware of forcing our expectations upon our friends. Give them the freedom to maneuver within the complicated context of their own lives. "Be kind," someone once said, "for everyone you meet is fighting a hard battle."

If we insist on unbalanced living (for example, working fourteen-hour days or being involved in six church programs simultaneously), at least we should allow those around us to seek balance should they so desire. Even as we reap the rewards for our area of excellence, we will also reap the penalties for the areas of negative excellence. Others might not desire this same scenario.

A FEW SHELLS

One of the most charming books written about balance and simplicity is a small volume by Anne Morrow Lindbergh. Well known as wife of the famous pilot Charles Lindbergh and daughter of the diplomat Dwight Morrow, Anne Lindbergh was a celebrity in her own right as aviator and author. Probably her most famous book, *Gift from the Sea*, was written during an island retreat off the New England coast. Our personal copy is a 1957 edition, and by that time—two years after first publication—more than one-half million copies had been printed. She wrote,

> For the natural selectivity of the island I will have to substitute a conscious selectivity based on another sense of values—a sense of values I have become more aware of here. Island-precepts, I might call them if I could define them, signposts toward another way of living. Simplicity of living, as much as possible, to retain a true awareness of life. Balance of physical, intellectual, and spiritual life. Work without pressure. Space for significance and beauty. Time for solitude and sharing. Closeness to nature to strengthen understanding and faith in the intermittency of life: life of the spirit, creative life, and the life of human relationships.[5]

GOD UNDERSTANDS

Balance is necessary and attainable. Not easy, but possible. When we understand that we are finite and that it is okay to be finite, then we can begin to accept our limits with comfort.

God expects us to perform well in many areas of life. But when He gave us the limits of time and finiteness, at that moment He also built in the necessity of balance. We work hard to please our Master, but we also rest confidently knowing that He understands our condition.

What we do we do well—but we do not do it all.

Health Through Rest

Three-year-olds seldom sit still. Bundles of energy tightly wound, they dash from here to there, leaping over toys and ricocheting off walls. Church services—as every parent knows—were not designed with these squirmers in mind. Each Sunday the rear of the sanctuary witnesses the sixty-minute ritual of parent against child; the one trying to survive, the other trying to escape.

My eldest son, Adam, was once such a wiggly three-year-old, and I was more than once the embarrassed parent. A particular service stands out vividly. His restless noisiness was not in the least malicious, but it was distracting nevertheless. Attempting to maintain quiet, I lifted him onto my lap and held him loosely in my arms. The wiggling, however, did not stop. Now, instead of random wiggling, there was willful wiggling. He and I were soon doing battle. Adam was intent on freedom. I was intent on containment.

Finally, after twenty minutes, that blessed moment arrived. As if someone had thrown a switch, he suddenly melted into my arms and fell asleep. The tug of war ended. Adam had yielded and was now at rest. As the struggling ceased, my attitude also changed. The frustration of the previous moments vanished, and in its place was a deep protective love.

This, I thought, is as it should be—not striving, but nestling. I would have moved mountains at that moment to defend him.

Rest. In the arms of a loving Father.

WEARINESS

The patients who come to my office do not seem rested. For that matter, neither do most physicians. The medical residents I teach often are five minutes away from collapse. Many people I meet look haggard and worn-out.

Often-used descriptors of our society include active, busy, driven, fatigued, tired, exhausted, weary, burned out, anxious, overloaded, or stressed. But seldom do you hear our society described as "well rested." We are a tired generation, one for which Matthew Arnold's "hurry sickness" has become a way of life. Our carburetors are set on high, and our gears are stuck in overdrive. Our lives are nonstop.

We have leisure but little rest. The pace, the noise, the expectations, and the interruptions of modern life have not soothed the soul nor brought refreshment to the burdened spirit.

FROM JET TO DONKEY

Earlier in the book we took a short trip abroad, visiting Africa and the Caribbean. Let's again pack our bags and head off on another fact-finding mission, this time watching closely for signs of cultural and personal restedness. Even though we board a DC-10 in New York, be prepared to disembark from the back of a camel in the middle of nowhere.

The first thing we notice is that the pace of life in such places is decidedly slower than ours. The people have much more time to visit with their neighbors, walk to town, or stop and leisurely watch the children rolling a hoop down the middle of the main street. No one seems in a hurry (except, that is, when they drive).

Just your presence in town brings the entire society to a curious halt. The children flock around and almost all of them are giggling. In the market, everyone is talking—but only a fraction of the exchange is commercial. If you ask for directions, you will have twelve volunteers.

On the main street, men sit on barrel tops and talk. Women lean out of shop windows to visit with the closest passerby. Kids try to hawk their trinkets or beg for money—but often with just the hint of a smile at the corners of their mouths. If you go to the bank for a transaction, you might wait interminably for even the smallest request. But no one else seems to mind, and no one looks at the clock. Oh, the frustration we feel when our paperwork is processed with the speed of a glacier.

Despite such an accumulation of anecdotal evidence, sociologists will still want more hard data. And skeptics will scorn my sentimentality. In fairness, I want to be honest. When abroad in more primitive conditions, I often miss modern conveniences—like a cold glass of milk or bathrooms without cockroaches and tarantulas. But what I *don't* miss are telephones, televisions, stoplights, video games, watches that beep during pastoral prayers, and boom boxes on the beach.

I have not gone so far as to suggest that the way of life in developing countries is superior or preferable to that of developed ones. I am only making the observation that these refreshingly gracious and hospitable people are not exhausted, in body or spirit, whereas we often are. Those who would maintain that progress brings rest are wrong. We may have education, affluence, technology, leisure, and conveniences— but the only experience many of us have with rest today is the first half of restless.

God, however, has commanded us to rest. A biblically authentic and balanced life will include time to be still, to remember, to meditate, to delight in who He is and what He has made. But a large obstacle stands in our way: There is no glory in rest. No social acclaim. We are never a hero because we rest. We can only be still and better wait upon the Lord. We can only meditate upon the Word more. We can only have more margin with which to serve our neighbor. These things, however, are not socially reimbursable.

BURNING UP THE ENGINE

The healthiest lifestyle comes equipped with four gears. The first is *park* for the contemplative times. This gear is to be used for rest and renewal. It is the gear we use to recharge our margin batteries. This is where we do much of our thinking about values and spirituality, as well as much of our Scripture study and prayer. It is the gear we plan to use as we pick up a novel and head for the hammock, or as we sit on a stump and watch the wildlife.

The second gear is *low*. This gear is for relationships, for family and friends. This is the gear we use when talking with someone, and it prevents us from being distracted and nervously moving on to the next activity while still in the middle of a conversation. This is the gear we use when the children ask for a story or a back rub. Or when they ask about the death of pets, or sex, or God. No hurry here: just quality.

The third gear is *drive*. This is our usual gear for work and play. This gear uses lots of energy, and the faster speed feels good because it is productive. It gets us from place to place quickly. This is the gear we mow the lawn in or exercise in.

The fourth gear is *overdrive*. This gear is reserved for times that require extra effort. If we have a deadline coming, we kick into this gear. If we are playing a basketball game, we call upon overdrive to energize us. This is the gear I use during flu season when my schedule is double-booked. This is the gear most families use getting ready for church.

Unfortunately, many in our society do not shift down from overdrive. Our cars are not meant to race at high speeds continuously—the engine would burn up. Neither are our bodies or spirits. Yet to slow down for some is unthinkable and for others, impossible.

In our everyday lives, most of us need rest in three areas:

▶ Physical rest, the least important of the three.
▶ Emotional rest, more important by several orders of magnitude.
▶ Spiritual rest, which, though widely neglected, is of supreme importance.

PHYSICAL REST

Constant activity is a characteristic of our age. If we are not active, we feel slothful. If we are not productive, we feel guilty. A healthy twenty-eight-year-old man sitting on a lawn swing for an entire Sunday afternoon would more than likely feel the need to apologize to his neighbors should they discover him.

Such busyness does not come because our bodies can't help themselves. We cannot blame our thyroid or adrenal glands. Nor does it result from a theological teaching. It comes from a cultural value system that idolizes productivity.

I am not saying that productivity is wrong. I am only saying it must not be idolized. Productivity has no more spiritual value than does rest and, as a matter of fact, probably less. Industriousness might be good for an economy, particularly one like ours. But that does not mean it is healthy in all respects.

As a physician, I clearly affirm that physical activity is not only good, it is necessary. But so is physical rest. Our bodies were designed to need rest. Sleep is the clearest example, and one that cannot be violated. Many Americans, however, get the activity-rest cycle out of balance. Millions get too little activity, and millions more get too little rest. Type As, as an illustration, refuse to rest: to them it is an enemy. Also, those around them are made to feel weak if they desire a pause. Consequently, life is lived full speed ahead. They work hard, they play hard, and they even Sabbath hard.

Restless Work

Work in our culture often dominates other areas of life. To be sure, work is very important. But other activities are more important. The people who work the hardest and rest the least naturally rise to the top, from where they drive the entire work system. They set the rules, which maximize productivity. Even love and relationship come far down the list. Little wonder rest cannot find a resting place.

"People in the Western world have leisure. We do not need to slave every minute in order to eat. But only a few appear to have rest," observes Mennonite author Doris Longacre.

> Profit-making work began to swallow Sundays and holidays. No wonder everyone has been getting so tired.
>
> Obviously much of this fatigue takes place in the name of making more money, even though the pantry's already stocked. After all, by burning a little more gas and working one more evening a week, it *is* possible to chase down one more account, open another store, or farm another field. But it may not be possible to love a spouse, children, and the friendless poor at the same time.[1]

God has instructed us that life is more than work. It includes relationships, worship, and yes, even rest. "A rest-less work style produces a restless person," notes Gordon MacDonald. "We do not rest because our work is done; we rest because God commanded it and created us to have a need for it."[2]

Lethal Leisure

Leisure might be the name we give our time away from work, but it is not a synonym for rest. Many can't understand why they are so tired after a vacation. The reason is because our vacations and weekends have ceased to be restful. "It is ironic that our society, so addicted to pleasure and 'leisure,' knows so little of what it means to rest," observes lawyer and pastor Jim Buchan. "We are often more tired after the weekend is over than before it started. We come back from our vacations feeling as if we need some time to rest."[3]

Americans do not tolerate an activity vacuum well. The slow, contemplative life is largely foreign to our experience. Therefore, when "leisure time" appears on our schedule, we select from the many activity options society offers. This is not inherently wrong. Neither is quiet, introverted reflection always right. But when we work hard and then play harder, no wonder we feel fatigued so often.

Technology does not answer our need for physical rest. Labor-saving devices help in some respects, but curiously, those cultures that have the most laborsaving devices are the most hectic and the least rested. We often wonder why the homemaker remains so tired despite all the household appliances and conveniences. We forget to calculate that for every minute of time saved, our society offers hours of new activities, each with noise, expectations, and complexities of its own.

Although progress may not approve, *it is okay to rest physically*.

EMOTIONAL REST

More important to our overall health than physical rest is the resting of our emotions. Ask physicians about the frequency of anxiety or depression they find in their patients, and you will be stunned to learn how few in our midst are emotionally healthy and well rested. We worry about our jobs, our marriages, our children, our looks, our age, our health, and our future. The unacceptably high rate of tranquilizer use is a reliable indicator of our lack of emotional rest.

Physical rest and emotional rest often go hand in hand, but we have no guarantee the resting of our bodies will produce rested psyches. The stilling of outward activity does not always assure a commensurate quieting of inward activity. Nevertheless, if we would rest our emotions, a wise first step would be to seek out quiet. Unfortunately, Walden is rarely found; lights and noise are to our right, people and action are to our left. With each successive decade, the ambient environmental noise level increases. Even within the four walls of home, televisions blare seven hours a day. Rock music has defrauded an entire adolescent generation out of anything even approximating emotional rest.

The majority of each day is spent with people. While that is exactly where we should be most of the time, it can be quite draining. For many, occasional solitude is a prerequisite for emotional resting, but where does one find privacy and silence?

Even the privilege of royalty doesn't always assure the privacy of rest. Near the end of his reign, England's King George V was asked what he would do if he could do whatever he pleased. "He replied that he would take his biggest car and drive and drive as far as it would take him. There he would find a little farmhouse, and in the farmhouse there would be a small, clean, whitewashed room, furnished only with a bed and an open fire. He would lie down on the bed, and lying so, alone in the small, clean room, he would look at the glowing coals of the fire, and the flames playing blue about them—and so he would rest. For once in a royal lifetime he would rest."[4]

Contemporary Commotion

If you think about it, you can find many reasons for the absence of emotional rest in our midst—so many, in fact, that it would be surprising to discover true restedness among us. Noise deprives us of rest, yet we have more noise today than ever before. Activity overload deprives us of rest, yet we are busier than ever. Inappropriate expectations deprive us of rest, yet our culture advertises: "You *deserve* the best." Pride deprives us of rest, as we worry about every wrinkle we have and every piece of clothing we wear. Discontent and covetousness deprive us of rest, yet our culturally sanctioned advertising intentionally stimulates discontent. "The proud man and the covetous man never have rest"; noted Thomas à Kempis, "but the meek man and the poor in spirit live in great abundance of rest and peace."[5]

Preoccupation with success deprives us of rest—always climb a little higher and get a little more. So does preoccupation with power. Yet success and power are two cogs of the "American dream," and we are reluctant to let them go. Debt deprives us of rest, yet our debt is at unprecedented levels. We worry about our image and our reputation until we have no rest.

As A. W. Tozer observed, "The heart's fierce effort to protect itself from every slight, to shield its touchy honor from the bad opinion of friend and enemy, will never let the mind have rest."[6]

Restless Relationships

Perhaps the greatest root cause for the absence of emotional rest in our society is fractured relationships. When there is fighting in the workplace, contention in the community, bitterness in the church, and combat in the home, we won't find rest. The saddest of these, of course, is the home. It was intended by God as a haven of peace and security. But when strife enters, rest flees.

"If we don't deal with our unresolved conflicts, they'll deal with us," counsels Tim Kimmel. "Are there people whom you need to forgive? Do yourself a favor. Give them something they don't deserve but desperately need. Give them the gift of forgiveness. It's a gift that, once given, offers something in return. Your spirit gets a rest."[7]

If we would avoid the many unexpected pains of our day, we must discipline our expectations, tame our discontent, and mend our relationships. For *it is important to rest emotionally.*

SPIRITUAL REST

When our bodies find rest, we feel refreshed. When our emotions find rest, our countenance is lifted. Yet relaxed muscles and minds are of little worth unless our souls also find rest in the acceptance of God. Such a rest transcends the problems of our world and shelters us where no injury can follow. As the psalmist tells us, "He who dwells in the shelter of the Most High will rest in the shadow of the Almighty. I will say of the LORD, 'He is my refuge and my fortress, my God, in whom I trust.' "[8] The shadow of the Almighty is impregnable; His rest ultimately the only dependable rest.

We should be concerned with at least two types of spiritual rest. God calls us to *Sabbath rest.* And He offers us *surrendered rest.*

Sabbath Rest

Someone once remarked, "God rested—and He wasn't tired." After creating, even the Almighty rested: "God blessed the seventh day and made it holy, because on it he rested from all the work of creating that he had done."[9] He looked on what He had made and delighted in it, and He has commanded us to do the same.

At Sabbath rest we don't simply rest the body—although that is important. Also, we don't primarily rest the emotions—although we would be wise to discover such rest in our Sabbaths. Instead, *it is a remembrance*. Moses writes, "Remember that you were slaves in Egypt and that the LORD your God brought you out of there with a mighty hand and an outstretched arm. Therefore the LORD your God has commanded you to observe the Sabbath day."[10] This same God who rescued the Israelites from their slavery in Egypt is the One who rescues us from our bondage to sin. Remember.

At Sabbath time we suspend dominion work and instead worship the dominion-Maker. We cease reaping for our own cupboards and instead bring an offering to Him. We rest not because we are tired. We don't cease our labor because it is finished. We don't worship because now there are grapes on the vine and cattle in the stalls. We rest and worship one day in seven simply because He is the Lord.

Remembering, worshiping, and resting are acts of contemplation. Yet churches today, for the most part, have not developed a practical theology of contemplation nor a practical theology of rest. "It is my own conviction that the church, and humanity at large, neglects inwardness at its own peril," warns philosopher Nicholas Wolterstorff. By inwardness Wolterstorff means contemplation. "It seems to me that amidst its intense activism, the Western world is starved for contemplation."[11]

The Sabbath rest is an opportunity for contemplation, an opportunity to remember our roots.

Surrendered Rest

"Softly and tenderly Jesus is calling"—but the world is shouting and waving its hands. Sometimes, over the din, it is hard to hear His invitation: "Ye who are weary come home." The Sabbath rest is a rest He *calls* us to, but the surrendered rest He *offers* to us. The Sabbath rest we enter out of obedience; the surrendered rest we enter out of our need. The Sabbath rest arises from the good and perfect law of God; the surrendered rest arises from the good and perfect grace of God. The Sabbath rest is remembrance; the surrendered rest is meekness. Both provide soothing, God-ordained healing.

High on my list of favorite scriptures are Jesus' words in Matthew 11:28-30: "Come to me, all you who are weary and burdened, and I will give you rest. Take my yoke upon you and learn from me, for I am gentle and humble in heart, and you will find rest for your souls.

For my yoke is easy and my burden is light." These words draw weary people everywhere. Yet, per usual, Jesus leaves us scratching our heads. What does He mean, to take His yoke? I'm not sure that sounds restful. It sounds more like hard work and suffering. "I see pastors wanting to follow Christ and taking up his yoke, but somehow not finding the rest," pastoral counselor Louis McBurney points out. "Instead of a lighter load, they have a heavier one."[12] Where is rest hiding?

MEEKNESS

The answer lies in meekness. In this passage, Christ calls Himself "gentle and humble"—meek. He came not to judge but to die. He came not to shout and defend the honor of the Father but to die. He came not to fight but to die. No persecution could disturb Him for He came to suffer. Yet all the time He was suffering, He knew He was winning.

We, too, can suffer and win. We can live with love even when others hate—all the time knowing that love wins. We can respond with grace when others fight, knowing that grace wins. When we come to Him and surrender, accepting His yoke, we accept full vulnerability to the onslaught of the world. Yet, at the same time, we are assured that nothing can separate us from the victorious love of Christ. This rest is a self-weakening unto God-strength. It is a self-emptying unto God-fullness. It is the rest of full surrender.

"Jesus calls us to His rest, and meekness is His method. The meek man cares not at all who is greater than he, for he has long ago decided that the esteem of the world is not worth the effort," teaches Tozer. "The rest [Christ] offers is the rest of meekness, the blessed relief which comes when we accept ourselves for what we are and cease to pretend. It will take some courage at first, but the needed grace will come as we learn that we are sharing this new and easy yoke with the strong Son of God Himself."[13]

In an age of strife and unrest, when our bodies are weary and our spirits are frenzied, "Don't worry, be happy," will not rescue us. I prefer Corrie ten Boom's "Don't wrestle, just nestle." Even when I feel inferior, even when I have been victimized, even when the pace and pressures of life bring me to the point of collapse, Christ brings me to His rest. When my surrender is completed and His yoke is accepted, then my soul will find rest. And *it is imperative, in such an age as ours, that we rest spiritually.*

Pain, Margin,
Health, and Relationship

History is something that happens to people; what happens
is always different from what people would rather have
done. . . .We have made great progress—for which we also
have paid a price.[1]

—Claude Lévi-Strauss,
French anthropologist

Humans are passive agents. It is true that, from time to time, we make
small and even a few large changes attempting to improve matters. But
mostly our lives are filled with passivity.

At this juncture, however, allowing history to just "happen to us"
is unforgivably foolish. For no matter what their ideological bent, the
trend watchers are united in one opinion: Something is afoot. Along
with much of the rest of the world, the United States is in a period
of profound disequilibrium. Having never been through a disjuncture
of such dimension or consisting of such particulars before, we are not
quite sure in what condition we will find ourselves when it leaves off.

In this unfolding of historical change, we have been guided by the
process of history called progress. In many respects, progress has done a

good job, bringing us places previously reserved for fantasy writers. And at such speed! But progress has been especially painful of late.

WHAT TO DO WITH PAIN

At times it appears as if the cumulative weight of suffering and sorrow will sink the entire world. People hurt, families hurt, friendships hurt, churches hurt, communities hurt, nations hurt. Some hurt more than others, but nearly all hurt to some degree. Many have hurt for so long it seems as if the pain will never end. What should we do about all this pain?

First, let's thank God for it. Anything that redirects us to Him is of benefit.

Second, let's repent. Not the "ineffectual, unfervent prayer of an unrighteous man availeth little" kind of repentance, but the kind that means something and costs something. The kind of repentance where you conduct business with God and whereafter life has actually changed and you are headed in a different direction.

Third, let's do some surgery. There is a lot of pruning that needs to be done and abscesses that need draining. Let's prune away the time cancers, amputate the energy tumors, and drain the debt abscesses. Don't cringe—God is a great physician, and it is good to be pruned and drained. We ought to do it more often. For without surgery, margin and health will not return.

Fourth, let's cooperate with God. Our hope for the future is only valid because of one fact: God is still around, and what's more, He's still interested. Our success or failure will hinge on our cooperation with Him. "When this little life is over, nearly all that makes the headlines in the newspapers or fills the bulletins on the radio will seem to be of purely temporary significance," notes J. B. Phillips. "But the work of those who have cooperated with God will remain, for it is part of his everlasting purpose."[2]

SHORT TERM, LONG TERM

When we contact God to tell Him we are ready to cooperate, He will give us a two-term plan: short and long.

For the short term, we need worry only about today. Isn't that good news? Isn't that hopeful? Plan for tomorrow, to be sure. Be concerned for tomorrow. But worry only about today.[3]

You see, our responsibility is to do what is right today. Of course the future is important; of course we are concerned about what kind of society we end up with; of course we must plan intelligently and prayerfully. But we can only get there one day at a time, and today is the day to do what is right.

Today we must begin valuing the things God values and cease valuing those things of no value to Him. Today we must agree that our choices *do* make a difference—whether we live without margin, work two jobs, build an expensive house, overload a friend, don't spend time with our children. Today let's decide to invest in relationship, to encourage someone. Today decide to love, the sacrificial-service kind of love. Today forgive someone who should have been forgiven long ago. Today light one little candle and stop cursing the darkness.

For the long term, God would have us set about rebuilding using the instructions previously given. He has already told us what to do—now we just have to do it.

Let me tell you another hopeful secret about God's plan. He wants us to reclaim society, but not necessarily as the first order of business. Redeeming what we can of progress will be a huge job, but we can work on that tomorrow. For now, we have enough work at home to keep us occupied. So put away the newspaper, turn off the nightly news, and *forget about the despair of problem mountain.* We will return to them later. It is time to put on the work clothes and report for duty in the front yard.

Here God awaits us, with the confidence of a Leader who has been through it all before. As we become teachable—even desperate—what will be His advice? He has, of course, already given us lots of instructions, all of them valuable. But if we were to boil them all out, one principle would rise to the top: the priority of relationship.

GOD'S REPORT CARD

If God's greatest commandments are as inclusive as I believe they are, when life is over and we receive our report card, it will have only one category—relationship. There will be three lines:

▶ How did we relate to God?
▶ How did we relate to ourselves?
▶ How did we relate to others?

We know that relationship is so important to God because *He does all His work there. That is why progress missed Him.* Progress kept telling us to search for buried treasure inside bank vaults, while all the time God had it buried in the heart of our neighbor.

Even if we have little time for healthy relationships, we all instinctually understand their importance. Due to the antagonistic influences of marginless living, however, they are an increasingly rare commodity. Overloaded contemporary life attempts to de-relationalize us, which is perhaps the English equivalent of the German word *Zerrissenheit*— "torn-to-pieces-hood." Today, it is possible to live in a city surrounded by one million people and be alone for a lifetime. We become a number, and no one ever loved a number. The systems of modernity swallow us alive. Bureaucracies, corporations, institutions—all conjure up images of structures that inhale people and exhale cement.

God, however, is a personal God, and relationship is very important to Him. He created us as relational beings—not because He had to but because it suited Him. We are relational and dependent whether we acknowledge it or not, whether we want to be or not. We ought not kick against this, however, for it was meant as a gift. God gave us to each other for reasons of benefit, not torture.

RELATE TO WHOM?

How do we know that God's report card contains three categories? Jesus told us so. When asked outright by the Pharisee, Jesus answered that, of course, the Shema was the greatest commandment: "'Hear, O Israel, the Lord our God, the Lord is one. Love the Lord your God with all your heart and with all your soul and with all your mind and with all your strength.'" However, He did not stop there: "The second is this: 'Love your neighbor as yourself.' There is no commandment greater than these!"[4]

In so answering, Christ laid out for us the greatest imperative of eternity: to love God, our neighbor, and our self. This commandment must be the first guideline for all of life's decisions and actions. Nothing is to come before it.

Love the Lord your God. God is our Creator, which means we were related to Him even before birth. He yearns for our broken relationship to be reconciled. He went 99.99 percent of the way and extends a nail-pierced hand for us to grasp. His patience has given us much space to repent. We live in a world that promotes distance, builds fences, buys locks, and doesn't talk on elevators. But God, in Christ, says, "Come."

Love yourself. God assumes we love and care for self. Some people, however, have no relationship with themselves. To leave them alone in solitude for a day would be punishment. That we are worthy of love is demonstrated by the fact that God loves us. His love validates our worth and, as a matter of fact, provides the only basis for it. Without that validation we stand undeserving. Some are so broken by this unworthiness that they get stuck in it. The concept of unworthiness is a wonderful thing to grasp and is the first step in setting things right. But getting stuck in it is a spiritually neurotic thing to do and is not God's will. The call to spiritually accurate self-love is not a denial of our unworthiness but is instead the result of a journey that goes through unworthiness to God.

Love your neighbor. Created incapable of meeting all our own needs, God gave us others, in relationship, to help. Despite the fact that each individual is of more value than all the careers, education, and money in the universe added together and multiplied times infinity, right relating to others seems to be the most difficult item on the contemporary agenda.

QUIET KINDNESSES

God has shown us the road to health, the path to blessing—it is the way of relationship. Do you see now why careers, degrees, and estates can never quite get the job done? Somehow we just keep taking our expensive automobiles to our posh offices to make another hundred thousand dollars, while all the time our relationships vaporize before our eyes and our loneliness deepens.

But we are not helpless. Progress does not own us. We do not have to let history "happen to us." We are free to change. And God is still interested in lending a hand.

We can focus on relationship and create a margin for it. We can simplify and balance our lives so that relationships have some space. We can invest ourselves in other people. When we don't feel like it, we can still do it. Even when we can't find anyone else interested in friendship, we can always start spreading around quiet kindnesses, *expecting none in return.*

Soon, love will begin to flow out from us, and with the flow there will also come a flowing back. For love, you see, is "the most excellent way."[5]

LOVE

All the commandments in Scripture reduce to Christ's Great Commandment, and the Great Commandment reduces to one concept: love.

God is in love with His creation. The creature has something of the Creator in him, and God has loved us from the beginning. Even when the creature turned his back on Heaven, yet God loved him: "I made you, and I will carry you. I don't hold anything against you. Let me rescue you."

The history of the world reduces to this: your being pursued by love. He courted you; He followed you; He loved you. If you go to work or school or church, He is there. If you go to the edge of the universe or to the borders of hell, He is there. If you go deep inside yourself, He is there. In the dark of the night, in your depression, He is there. On your deathbed, when you don't want anybody to leave you, He is there. If you look behind you or before you, He is there, waiting to be allowed entrance into your life.

In the economics of eternity, God paid a great price. If we only better understood the cost, we would also better understand our worth.

THE ECONOMICS OF THE RELATIONAL LIFE

Love is the currency of the relational life. In the relational life, we spend love and receive love. That was God's idea from the beginning. It is what He taught us, and it was what He showed us. God wants us to spend love freely, even generously. When we do, everyone becomes rich. It is the primary currency of God's economics.

As you can see, love is not like other resources. There is an infinite supply. You can use it and use it and use it. Yet there will still be more left over. As a matter of fact, *the more it is used, the more its supply increases.*

Some guard their supply of love, doling it out in portions. But this kind of thinking works with money, not with love. With money, the more you *hoard*, the richer you become. But *with love, the more you spend, the richer you become.*

Spending and receiving love is the best part of Kingdom work. It is also the best part of doctoring.

FLOWERS FROM THE OTHER SIDE OF THE GRAVE

Eileen was sixty-three years old and already had advanced cancer when I first met her. Following surgery, there was little that could be done.

She healed nicely from her operation but, some months later, developed a persistent cough. "It is probably the tumor, Eileen," I said. "We should get a chest X-ray to be sure."

"No, doctor," she replied. "I don't want to know anything about it." Soon, however, her shortness of breath left us no choice but to investigate.

"It's as we suspected," I said. "Your X-ray shows a large amount of fluid in the right lung. If you would like, we can make you more comfortable by draining some of the fluid off here in the office. It really doesn't hurt much, and you should be able to breathe easier."

Under normal circumstances, tapping the lung is always followed by an X-ray to make sure the lung has not been punctured or deflated during the procedure. But after three uneventful taps in the clinic, I decided to deviate from protocol and do the procedure in Eileen's home. By now, she was having great difficulty getting around.

Each time I went to her home, I would first sit on the bed and we would talk. Then I would examine her lungs, position her for the procedure, paint her with Betadine, and introduce the needle into her chest.

On the third visit, I held her hand for a while, and together we looked out the open window. Perhaps we both sensed the end was near.

"Those are beautiful lilacs," I said, noticing for the first time the flowers hardly a foot or two outside her open window. They were just coming into full bloom, and the room was full of their fragrance.

"Lilacs are my favorite," she replied. "That is why I wanted to be down here, close to them. I love them."

After draining another quart of fluid off her lung, I left the house for the last time. A week later she died.

Shortly after Eileen's death, her daughter came to the clinic carrying a huge bouquet of deep purple lilacs in a blue mason jar. She asked the receptionist to bring the flowers to my office, explaining that it would be too hard for her to see me just then.

This note was with the lilacs:

> Words do seem inadequate to express our thanks for all you have done for our family. Because of your kind, caring ways Mom was able to stay in her home and be as comfortable as possible.
>
> Mom wanted the "Best Doctor in the World" to enjoy her special lilacs. God bless you!

I have received many expressions of thanks from the relatives of deceased patients. But this was the first time I had been given flowers from the other side of the grave.

I am not the "Best Doctor in the World." But at least for a moment, I felt like it. Medicine can be a grinding profession when money is the only reward. But when love is the currency of exchange, gratitude alone can pay the debt in full.

MUST WE LOVE?

I did not drain the fluid off Eileen's lung because I am a technician who enjoys doing procedures. I did not visit her in the home because I am a businessman looking for increased revenue. Instead, I cared for her because I allowed her ache to enter my heart.

Eileen was suffering, and I had the skills to help. I reached out to her, not as a proceduralist or a profiteer, but as a physician. My reaching is what I call love. Why should I work just for money when I can work for love? And from the other side of the grave, Eileen reached back. I call that love too. Relational economics.

Somehow, we just can't wrap our minds around this idea of love. We can't nail it down and say, "There, I've got you." Yes, love is strange. It is weak yet tough, vulnerable yet strong. It chooses to lose but can never be beaten. It puts itself last yet always leads the way. It is mysterious, yet it came in flesh and stood before us. It is death—yet it is life.

God's love is commonly undervalued and always underestimated. No virtue can compete with it, and no vice can defeat it. God ordained that it should be so, and He stands guard to see that no one changes the order of things.

Must we love? That is a nonsensical question. It is like asking, "Must we breathe?" No, we do not have to breathe, and no, we do not have to love. But the consequences of both those decisions will be the same.

ARE YOU READY?

Pain surrounds us all. Much of this pain comes from progress's blatant disregard for our need of margin. And much of this pain—far too much of this pain—is because of neglected and broken relationships. It is difficult to be healthy in a society where relational, emotional, and spiritual sickness is endemic. If you live in a swamp, malaria has a head start.

But do you know what? Malaria can be treated, and so can pain. Margin can be restored. Broken relationships can be healed. It takes work. It takes love. It might even take going to the cross. But healing is worth it. I have never seen a truly healthy person who didn't derive that well-being from the benefits of intact, loving relationships.

Are you ready to commit to relationship in love? This is not like asking, "Would you go to the store for some milk?" but more like, "Are you ready to lay down your life for your friends?"[6]

If you are, then do everything you can to travel in the health direction. If stress crushes your spirit by poisoning you with despair, then either conquer stress or walk away—but don't stop relating. If overload destroys your relationships, then dispatch overload to the far side. If that malignant, universal enemy of relational health, marginless living, leaves you panting for air and desperate for space, then go and take margin back. Hack it out of your cultural landscape. And guard it for the sake of your God, yourself, your family, and your friends.

Health cannot be far behind.

Appendix

The graphs on the following pages visually demonstrate the rapid and unprecedented changes within American society. A few guidelines will help make their interpretation easier and more accurate.

The slope—It is important to note the slope of the curves. As explained in chapter 3, curves that slope upward rapidly are called exponential. Some of the graphs appearing here are true exponential slopes, while others only approximate exponential slopes for a period of time. The point is, all these graphs illustrate rapid, radical change.

The reason margin disappeared as quickly as it did is because of the type of exponential slopes found on these graphs. Remember: straight line graphs represent historical transition; exponential curve graphs represent historical disruption.

Extrapolation—If you want a glimpse into the future, take the most recent portion of these curves and extend it for another twenty-five or fifty years. For example, if you were to do this with the graph of health-care costs it would become quickly apparent why so many people are worried.

S-curves—Several of the curves (for example, divorces) already demonstrate a tailing off, and this is reassuring. Nevertheless, during the time when these slopes were climbing rapidly, the amount of change experienced in our society was dramatic.

Time frame—Most graphs have a standardized time frame, from 1900 to 2000. A few, however, go back much farther.

Not all are negative—Not all of these graphs represent problems—for example, the number of new books or the gross national product. Most of the graphs, however, have at least some negative repercussions.

Logarithms—With two of the graphs, the change was so dramatic that it had to be scaled logarithmically. I have provided some additional explanation with these graphs to help in understanding the startling dimensions involved.

Generic graphs—The first three graphs listed are generic: *complexity, information,* and *change.* The type of data represented by these topics is hard to quantify. Nevertheless, I believe them to be in essence true.

Graphs Illustrating Increase

Despite the absence of objective parameters for the y-axis, generic graphs are perhaps the most important in the appendix to understand. The slopes here represent *my estimates*, and some would take issue with the exact shape of the curves. But no one can deny that each of these areas has experienced rapid and historically unprecedented increases over the last century.

Graphs Illustrating Rapid U.S. Economic Change

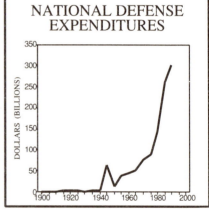

Graphs Reflecting Financial and
Economic Difficulties

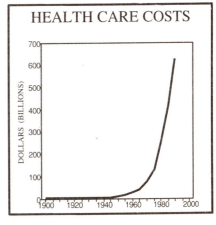

Graphs Reflecting Various Social Problems

NUMBER OF PRISONERS
State and Federal

DIVORCES

U.S. DISTRICT COURT
Civil Cases Commenced

BIRTHS TO
UNMARRIED WOMEN

Graphs Illustrating Change in the Mail
and the Media

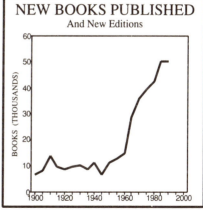

Graphs Illustrating Change in Travel and Mobility

Note that the graph representing passenger cars registered is actually more linear than exponential. It is included, nevertheless, out of respect for the tremendous role the automobile has played in dissipating margin and bringing about unprecedented societal change.

Graphs Reflecting Various Demographic Changes

Note the different time frame on the x-axis.

Logarithmic Graphs Illustrating Technological Power

These two graphs are the most dramatic of all those in this appendix, which is why the logarithm scale is necessary for the y-axis. As you can see, the maximum speed of vehicles has increased over one thousand times, while the explosive power of weapons has increased nearly ten billion times!

Notes

CHAPTER 2—THE PAIN OF PROGRESS

1. Robert Nisbet, *History of the Idea of Progress* (New York: Basic Books, 1980), pages 4-5,7.
2. Nicholas Wolterstorff, *Until Justice and Peace Embrace* (Grand Rapids: Eerdmans, 1983), pages 64 and 25.
3. David H. Hopper, *Technology, Theology, and the Idea of Progress* (Louisville, KY: Westminster/John Knox, 1991), pages 126-127.
4. Nisbet, page 9.
5. Christopher Lasch, *The True and Only Heaven: Progress and Its Critics* (New York: W. W. Norton, 1991), page 13.
6. Jeremy Rifkin, *Entropy: A New World View* (New York: Bantam, 1980), page 3.
7. Dennis Meadows, et al., *The Limits to Growth* (New York: Universe Books, 1972), page 23.
8. Mihajlo Mesarovic and Eduard Pestel, *Mankind at the Turning Point: The Second Report to the Club of Rome* (New York: New American Library, 1974), pages 1,129.
9. Robert L. Heilbroner, *An Inquiry into the Human Prospect* (New York: W. W. Norton, 1975), page 22.

10. Alvin Toffler, *The Third Wave* (New York: Bantam, 1980), page 350.
11. Mark Rosin, "The Family of the Future," *Parents*, March 1982, page 67.
12. John Naisbitt, *Megatrends: Ten New Directions Transforming Our Lives* (New York: Warner Books, 1982), pages 279,283.
13. Norman Mailer, Interviewed, "Something Has Been Stolen from Us That We Can't Name," *U.S. News and World Report*, 23 May 1983, pages 73-74.
14. Mesarovic and Pestel, page 11.
15. Harry Schwartz, "Solzhenitsyn Without Stereotype," *Saturday Review World*, 20 April 1974, page 24.
16. Lasch, page 168.
17. Karl Löwith, as quoted by Bob Goudzwaard in *Idols of Our Time*, trans. Mark Vander Vennen (Downers Grove, IL: InterVarsity, 1981), pages 12-13.
18. Goudzwaard, pages 50-51.
19. Robert N. Bellah, et al., *Habits of the Heart: Individualism and Commitment in American Life* (New York: Harper and Row, 1985), page 277.
20. Micah 6:8.
21. Bellah, page 284.
22. E. F. Schumacher, *Small Is Beautiful: Economics as if People Mattered* (New York: Harper and Row, 1973), page 157.
23. William Wilberforce, *Real Christianity: Contrasted with the Prevailing Religious System* (Portland, OR: Multnomah, 1982 [first published 1829]), page 91.
24. "This is what the LORD says: 'Let not the wise man boast of his wisdom or the strong man boast of his strength or the rich man boast of his riches, but let him who boasts boast about this: that he understands and knows me, that I am the LORD, who exercises kindness, justice and righteousness on earth, for in these I delight,' declares the LORD" (Jeremiah 9:23-24).
25. Wilberforce, page 123.

CHAPTER 3—THE PAIN OF PROBLEMS

1. Alvin Toffler, *Future Shock* (New York: Bantam, 1970), page 186.
2. Mark A. Noll, George M. Marsden, and Nathan O. Hatch, *The

Search for Christian America (Colorado Springs, CO: Helmers and Howard, 1989), pages 152 and 148.

3. Harry Clay Blaney III, *Global Challenges: A World at Risk* (New York: New Viewpoints, a division of Franklin Watts, 1979), page 8.

4. J. Scott Armstrong, *Long-Range Forecasting: From Crystal Ball to Computer* (New York: Wiley, 1985), page 102. Note: A piece of construction paper is .016 inches thick. If doubled ten times, the pile of paper would be 16.38 inches thick. If doubled another ten times, it would be 16,777 inches, or 1,398 feet. If doubled another ten times, it would be 1,431,552 feet, or 271.1 miles. And if that were doubled ten times, the result would be an amazing 277,606 miles! The distance to the moon is 250,000 miles.

5. Barry B. Hughes, *World Futures: A Critical Analysis of Alternatives* (Baltimore: The Johns Hopkins University Press, 1985), page 149.

6. Hughes, page 4.

7. Robert N. Bellah, et al., *Habits of the Heart: Individualism and Commitment in American Life* (New York: Harper and Row, 1985), pages 285 and 277.

8. George Gallup, Jr., with William Proctor, *Forecast 2000* (New York: Morrow, 1984), page 12.

9. Gallup, pages 155,156.

CHAPTER 4—THE PAIN OF STRESS

1. Richard Trubo, "Stress and Disease: Cellular Evidence Hints at Therapy," *Medical World News*, 26 January 1987, page 26.

2. Christiaan Barnard, M.D., "Medicine Negated," *Living in the Future*, ed. Isaac Asimov (New York: Beaufort Books, 1985), page 226.

3. Hans Selye, M.D., *Stress Without Distress* (New York: New American Library, 1974), page 14.

4. Selye, pages 93-94.

5. Selye, pages 28-29,94-96,136.

6. David Elkind, *The Hurried Child: Growing Up Too Fast Too Soon* (Reading, MA: Addison-Wesley, 1981), page 26.

7. Eileen Rockefeller Growald and Allan Luks, "Good Samaritan Has Big Heart, Healthier Body," *St. Paul Pioneer Press Dispatch*, 21 March 1988, section B, page 1.

8. Selye, pages 73-74.

9. E. F. Schumacher, *Good Work* (New York: Harper and Row, 1979), page 25.

10. Allan V. Abbott, M.D., and Ruth K. Peters, "Type A Behavior and Coronary Heart Disease: An Update," *American Family Physician*, November 1988, pages 105-108.

11. Quoted in Thomas B. Graboys, M.D., "Stress and the Aching Heart," *The New England Journal of Medicine*, 30 August 1984, page 595.

12. Carol Tavris, "Coping with Anxiety," *Science Digest*, February 1986, page 51.

13. Jon Johnston, "Growing Me-ism and Materialism," *Christianity Today Institute*, 17 January 1986, page 16-I.

14. Ann Tyndall, *Longevity Lifestyle* (San Bernadino, CA: Borgo Press, 1986), page 111.

15. Selye, page 68.

CHAPTER 5—THE PAIN OF OVERLOAD

1. Bob Sakamoto, "Bear Secondary First Rate," *Chicago Tribune*, 13 October 1990, section 2, page 1.

2. Alvin Toffler, *Future Shock* (New York: Bantam, 1970), pages 351-352.

3. *Resident Mental Health* (Kansas City, MO: American Academy of Family Physicians, 1988), page 6. The human function curve is found in *Stress and Women Physicians* (New York: Springer-Verlag, 1985) by Marjorie A. Bowman, M.D., and Deborah I. Allen, M.D. Used by permission.

4. John Townsend, *Hiding From Love: How to Change the Withdrawal Patterns That Isolate and Imprison You* (Colorado Springs, CO: NavPress, 1991), page 77.

5. Richard J. Foster, *Freedom of Simplicity* (New York: Harper and Row, 1981), page 91.

6. Edward Wenk, Jr., *Tradeoffs: Imperatives of Choice in a High-Tech World* (Baltimore: The Johns Hopkins University Press, 1986), page 51.

7. Quoted by Mihajlo Mesarovic and Eduard Pestel, *Mankind at the Turning Point: The Second Report to the Club of Rome* (New York: New American Library, 1974), pages 151-152.

8. Philippians 4:13, NKJV.

9. Roberto Vacca, *The Coming Dark Age,* trans. J. S. Whale (Garden City, NY: Anchor Books, 1974), page 8.

10. Robert Banks, *The Tyranny of Time: When 24 Hours Is Not Enough* (Downers Grove, IL: InterVarsity, 1983), page 45.

11. Arthur M. Schlesinger, Jr., "The Modern Consciousness and the Winged Chariot," *The Personal Experience of Time*, eds. S. Gorman and A. E. Wessmann (New York: Plenum, 1977), page 269.

12. Toffler, page 269.

13. J. Grant Howard, *Balancing Life's Demands: A New Perspective on Priorities* (Portland, OR: Multnomah, 1983), page 144.

14. Aleksandr I. Solzhenitsyn, *A World Split Apart: Commencement Address Delivered at Harvard University, June 8, 1978* (New York: Harper and Row, 1978), page 27.

15. Vacca, page 111.

16. Terri Lackey, "Churches Can Add to Family Stress," *Twin Cities Christian*, 13 December 1990, page 9A.

17. Louis McBurney, M.D., with David McCasland, "The Danger of Aiming Too High," *Leadership*, Summer 1984, page 30.

18. Theodore Berland, *The Fight for Quiet* (Englewood Cliffs, NJ: Prentice-Hall, 1970), page 200.

19. Ronald A. Taylor, "What All That Noise Pollution Is Doing to Our Lives," *U.S. News and World Report*, 16 July 1984, page 50.

20. Donald A. Norman, "Infuriating by Design," *Psychology Today*, March 1988, page 53.

21. J. D. Runions, as quoted by J. R. Kriel, M.D., in "Le Syndrome Du Bon-Dieu: A Fatal Malady Affecting Doctors," *Christian Medical Society Journal*, Winter 1983, page 26.

CHAPTER 6—MARGIN

1. Russell D. Robinson, *An Introduction to Helping Adults Learn and Change* (Milwaukee: Omnibook, 1979), page 38. Idea credited to Howard McClusky.

2. Mildred Tengbom, "Harried Lives: If You're a Frenzied Mess, It's Time to Decide What's Really Important to You," *Focus on the Family*, October 1985, pages 11-12.

3. Robert F. Greene, M.D., "True Confession: I Enjoyed My Year

Abroad as a Short-Term Missionary," *Christian Medical and Dental Society Journal*, Winter 1990, page 17. Reprinted by permission. The Society is a fellowship of Christian physicians and dentists representing Jesus Christ in and through medicine and dentistry. P.O. Box 830689, Richardson, Texas 75083-0689.

4. John W. Burnside, M.D., "A Piece of My Mind: Deserted Island," *The Journal of the American Medical Association*, 265, 6 February 1991, page 589.

CHAPTER 7—MARGIN IN EMOTIONAL ENERGY

1. Louis H. Evans, Jr., *Covenant to Care* (Wheaton, IL: Victor, 1977), pages 80-81.

2. "Attempted Suicide Among High School Students—United States, 1990," *Morbidity and Mortality Weekly Report*, 20 September 1991, page 633.

3. Alvin Toffler, *The Third Wave* (New York: Bantam, 1980), page 365.

4. Tom Sine, *The Mustard Seed Conspiracy* (Waco, TX: Word, 1981), page 81.

5. Jack Dreyfus, *A Remarkable Medicine Has Been Overlooked* (New York: Simon and Schuster, 1970), pages 26-27.

6. Nancy Livingston, "Out of the (Agent) Blue Come More Suicide and Depression," *St. Paul Pioneer Press Dispatch*, 13 January 1987, section C, page 1.

7. Gerald L. Klerman, M.D., and Myrna M. Weissman, "Increasing Rates of Depression," *The Journal of the American Medical Association*, 261, 21 April 1989, page 2234.

8. Walter E. Afield, M.D., "Managed Mental Health Care: Curbing Costs in the 1990s," *Medical Interface*, March 1990, page 26.

9. Frederic Flach, M.D., *Resilience: Discovering a New Strength at Times of Stress* (New York: Fawcett Columbine, 1988), page 35.

10. "The LORD is close to the brokenhearted and saves those who are crushed in spirit" (Psalm 34:18).

11. "God opposes the proud but gives grace to the humble" (James 4:6).

12. Willard Gaylin, as quoted by Bill Moyers in *A World of Ideas* (New York: Doubleday, 1989), page 120.

13. "Laughing Toward Longevity," *University of California, Berkeley Wellness Letter*, June 1985, page 1.

14. In research conducted at the University of Pittsburgh, Margaret T. Crepeau studied 137 males and females to determine both attitude (meaning) and behavior with respect to weeping. Three groups were included: healthy patients, colitis patients, and ulcer patients. The healthy patients scored higher (at a statistically significant level) on both the meaning scale and the behavior scale than did the ulcer or colitis patients.

15. John Townsend, *Hiding From Love: How to Change the Withdrawal Patterns That Isolate and Imprison You* (Colorado Springs, CO: NavPress, 1991), pages 80-81,82.

16. Quoted by Arthur F. Holmes, *Contours of a World View* (Grand Rapids: Eerdmans, 1983), page 12.

17. S. D. Gaede, *Belonging* (Grand Rapids: Zondervan, 1985), page 56.

18. Thomas à Kempis, *The Imitation of Christ*, trans. Richard Whitford (New York: Washington Square Press, 1953 [1424]), page 3.

19. 1 Corinthians 13:13, emphasis added.

20. Flach, page 259.

21. Armand Mayo Nicholi II, "Why Can't I Deal with Depression?" *Christianity Today*, 11 November 1983, page 40.

22. Nicholi, pages 40-41.

23. Diogenes Allen, *Christian Belief in a Postmodern World: The Full Wealth of Conviction* (Louisville, KY: Westminster/John Knox, 1989), pages 5,126.

24. Romans 5:2-5.

25. Colossians 3:14.

26. Hans Selye, M.D., *Stress Without Distress* (New York: New American Library, 1974), page 124.

27. 1 Corinthians 13:13, emphasis added.

CHAPTER 8—MARGIN IN PHYSICAL ENERGY

1. Judd Allen and Robert F. Allen, "From Short Term Compliance to Long Term Freedom: Culture-Based Health Promotion by Health Professionals," *American Journal of Health Promotion*, Fall 1986, page 40.

2. Quoted in Don R. Powell, *A Year of Health Hints* (Emmaus, PA: Rodale Press, 1990), page xxi.
3. Marcia F. Goldsmith, "Risk Assessment, Management Addressed at 'Prevention 85,'" *The Journal of the American Medical Association*, 254, 20 September 1985, page 1421.
4. Arthur J. Barsky, M.D., "The Paradox of Health," *The New England Journal of Medicine*, 318, 18 February 1988, page 414.
5. James O. Mason, M.D., "From the Assistant Secretary for Health," *The Journal of the American Medical Association*, 263, 26 January 1990, page 494.
6. Susanna McBee, with Sarah Peterson, "How Drugs Sap the Nation's Strength," *U.S. News and World Report*, 16 May 1983, page 57.
7. Armand M. Nicholi, Jr., M.D., "The Nontherapeutic Use of Psychoactive Drugs," *The New England Journal of Medicine*, 308, 21 April 1983, page 931.
8. Byron J. Bailey, M.D., "Tobaccoism Is the Disease—Cancer Is the Sequela," *The Journal of the American Medical Association*, 255, 11 April 1986, page 1923.
9. Jimmy Carter, "Closing the Gap: The Burden of Unnecessary Illness," *The Journal of the American Medical Association*, 254, 13 September 1985, page 1359.
10. Martin Shaffer, *Life After Stress* (New York: Plenum Press, 1982), pages 91-92.
11. Shaffer, page 92.
12. Anastasia Toufexis, "Drowsy America," *Time*, 17 December 1990, page 84.
13. "Woes of Night Work Vary Among Patients," *Medical World News*, 10 August 1987, page 22.
14. Toufexis, page 78.
15. John Kenneth Galbraith, *The Affluent Society* (New York: Mentor Books, 1958), page 103.
16. David Hilfiker, M.D., *Healing the Wounds: A Physician Looks at His Work* (New York: Pantheon, 1985), page 137.
17. Psalm 127:2.
18. Quoted by Doris Janzen Longacre, *More-With-Less Cookbook* (Scottdale, PA: Herald, 1976), page 15.
19. Karen Walsh, "Exercise Can Be the Great Escape," *Wisconsin Week*, 26 November 1986, page 3.

20. Kenneth H. Cooper, M.D., *Aerobics* (New York: Bantam, 1968), pages 62,107.
21. Don R. Powell, *A Year of Health Hints* (Emmaus, PA: Rodale Press, 1990), page 96.
22. Cooper, page 158.
23. Powell, page 94.

CHAPTER 9—MARGIN IN TIME

1. Quoted by Daniel J. Boorstin, *The Discoverers* (New York: Random House, 1983), page 25.
2. Boorstin, page 39.
3. Nancy Gibbs, "How America Has Run Out of Time," *Time*, 24 April 1989, page 59.
4. Gibbs, page 58.
5. Jeremy Rifkin, *Time Wars* (New York: Simon and Schuster, 1987), page 19.
6. Quoted by Frank E. James, "Battle of Miniature Cellular Telephones Heats Up with Launch of Motorola Model," *The Wall Street Journal*, 8 May 1990, page 30.
7. E. F. Schumacher, *Good Work* (New York: Harper and Row, 1979), page 25.
8. Douglas LaBier, *Modern Madness: The Emotional Fallout of Success* (Reading, MA: Addison-Wesley, 1986), page 98.
9. Juliet B. Schor, *The Overworked American: The Unexpected Decline of Leisure* (New York: Basic Books, 1991), pages 21-31.
10. Gibbs, page 60.
11. Richard Phillips, as quoted in "The New Workaholics," *St. Paul Pioneer Press Dispatch*, 5 January 1987, section D, pages 1,3.
12. Quoted in Robert Banks, *The Tyranny of Time: When 24 Hours Is Not Enough* (Downers Grove, IL: InterVarsity, 1983), page 66.
13. Dolores Curran, *Stress and the Healthy Family: How Healthy Families Handle the Ten Most Common Stresses* (San Francisco: Harper and Row, 1985), page 157.
14. Quoted in Gibbs, page 61.
15. James Dobson, *Dr. Dobson Answers Your Questions* (Wheaton, IL: Tyndale, 1982), pages 27,28.
16. Alex Kotlowitz, "Changes Among Families Prompt a Vanishing

Sense of Community," *The Wall Street Journal*, 11 March 1987, section 2, page 33.

17. Jean Fleming, *Between Walden and the Whirlwind: Living the Christ-Centered Life* (Colorado Springs, CO: NavPress, 1985), page 40.

18. Gordon MacDonald, *Restoring Your Spiritual Passion* (Nashville: Oliver-Nelson, 1986), pages 24-25.

19. Fleming, page 43.

20. Nancy Yanes Hoffman, "Meyer Friedman: Type A Behavior Cardiovascular Research Continues," *The Journal of the American Medical Association*, 252, 21 September 1984, pages 1392-1393.

21. Tom Sine, *The Mustard Seed Conspiracy* (Waco, TX: Word, 1981), page 129.

22. Bruce Larson, *There's a Lot More to Health Than Not Being Sick* (Waco, TX: Word, 1981), page 114.

23. Dietrich Bonhoeffer, *Life Together* (New York: Harper and Brothers, 1954), page 99.

CHAPTER 10—MARGIN IN FINANCES

1. Norman Mailer, Interviewed, "Something Has Been Stolen from Us That We Can't Name," *U.S. News and World Report*, 23 May 1983, pages 73-74.

2. Alfred L. Malabre, Jr., *Beyond Our Means: How America's Long Years of Debt, Deficits and Reckless Borrowing Now Threaten to Overwhelm Us* (New York: Random House, 1987), page xii.

3. Larry Burkett, *The Coming Economic Earthquake* (Chicago: Moody, 1991), page 121.

4. Gregory E. Pence, "Everyone's Entitled to Blame for Soaring Health Costs," *The Wall Street Journal*, 22 December 1983, page 24.

5. Peter G. Peterson, "The Morning After," *The Atlantic Monthly*, October 1987, pages 58,64.

6. U.S. Department of Commerce, Bureau of the Census, *Money Income of Households, Families, and Persons in the United States*, 1990 Series P-60, No. 174, August 1991, page 9.

7. Robert Reich, as quoted by Susan Dentzer in "Harnessing Human Capital," *U.S. News and World Report*, 22 April 1991, page 46.

8. Mortimer B. Zuckerman, "The Free Ride Is Over," *U.S. News and World Report*, 15 October 1990, page 136.

9. Dolores Curran, *Stress and the Healthy Family* (San Francisco: Harper and Row, 1985), page 62.

10. Romans 13:8.

11. Larry Burkett, *Major Purchases* (Chicago: Moody, 1991), page 19.

12. Proverbs 22:7.

13. Romans 6:18-19, 1 Corinthians 7:23, Galatians 5:13.

14. Jo Ann Tooley, "Database," *U.S. News and World Report*, 22 October 1990, page 16.

15. Doris Janzen Longacre, *Living More with Less* (Scottdale, PA: Herald, 1980), page 97.

16. Matthew 6:19-21.

17. 1 Timothy 6:9-11.

18. 1 John 3:17.

19. Additional verses that speak to this issue are found in Proverbs 3:27-28: "Do not withhold good from those who deserve it, when it is in your power to act. Do not say to your neighbor, 'Come back later; I'll give it tomorrow'—when you now have it with you."

20. Jacques Ellul, *Money and Power*, trans. LaVonne Neff (Downers Grove, IL: InterVarsity, 1984), page 88.

21. Ellul, page 110.

22. E. F. Schumacher, *Small Is Beautiful: Economics as if People Mattered* (New York: Harper and Row, 1973), page 33.

23. Burkett, *Major Purchases*, page 53.

24. Matthew 6:33, NKJV.

CHAPTER 11—HEALTH THROUGH CONTENTMENT

1. 1 Timothy 6:6, Hebrews 13:5.

2. Philippians 4:12.

3. J. I. Packer, "The Secret of Contentment," Address given at Wheaton College, Wheaton, Illinois, 27 February 1984.

4. 1 Corinthians 4:9-13.

5. 2 Corinthians 11:23-27.

6. Philippians 4:11-12.

7. A. W. Tozer, *The Pursuit of God* (Harrisburg, PA: Christian Publications, 1948), page 20.

8. Nguyen Thi An, "A Letter Written to a Vietnamese Friend in

Canada," *Alliance Life*, 10 December 1986, page 17. Used by permission.

9. Herbert Schlossberg, *Idols For Destruction: Christian Faith and Its Confrontation with American Society* (Nashville: Nelson, 1983), page 103.

10. Arthur G. Gish, *Beyond the Rat Race* (New Canaan, CT: Keats Publishing, 1973), page 130.

11. 1 Timothy 6:8.

12. John Kenneth Galbraith, *The Affluent Society* (New York: Mentor Books, 1958), page 128.

13. Packer, "The Secret of Contentment."

14. Schlossberg, page 136.

15. John White, *The Golden Cow: Materialism in the Twentieth-Century Church* (Downers Grove, IL: InterVarsity, 1979), page 61.

16. Quoted by L. S. Stavrianos, *The Promise of the Coming Dark Age* (San Francisco: W. H. Freeman and Company, 1976), page 165.

17. Hebrews 13:5.

18. Tozer, page 22.

19. Doug Trouten, "Discontent Is the New Spirit of the Age," *Twin Cities Christian*, 13 September 1984, page 6.

20. Joseph Katz, ed., *The Poems of Stephen Crane* (New York: Cooper Square Publishers, 1966), page 102. Originally published in Stephen Crane's book of poetry entitled *War is Kind*, 1899.

21. Packer, "The Secret of Contentment."

22. Thomas Watson, *The Art of Divine Contentment* (Glasgow, Scotland: Free Presbyterian Publications, reprint of 1855 edition), pages 16,22.

23. Jeremiah Burroughs, *The Rare Jewel of Christian Contentment* (Edinburgh, Scotland: The Banner of Truth Trust, 1987 [1648]), page 19.

CHAPTER 12—HEALTH THROUGH SIMIPLICITY

1. Duane Elgin, *Voluntary Simplicity* (New York: Bantam, 1981), page 16.

2. Hans Selye, M.D., *Stress Without Distress* (New York: New American Library, 1974), page 142.

3. John Naisbitt, *Megatrends: Ten New Directions Transforming Our Lives* (New York: Warner Books, 1982), page 136.

4. John Charles Cooper, *The Joy of the Plain Life* (Nashville: Benson, 1981), page 106.
5. John 13:15-16.
6. "To this you were called, because Christ suffered for you, leaving you an example, that you should follow in his steps" (1 Peter 2:21).
7. "Your attitude should be the same as that of Christ Jesus" (Philippians 2:5). "But made himself nothing, taking the very nature of a servant, being made in human likeness" (verse 7).
8. Tom Allen, "Living Like the King," *Alliance Life*, 10 June 1981, pages 5-6.
9. David E. Shi, *The Simple Life: Plain Living and High Thinking in American Culture* (New York: Oxford University Press, 1985), page 3.
10. Shi, page 18.
11. Herbert Schlossberg, *Idols For Destruction: Christian Faith and Its Confrontation with American Society* (Nashville: Nelson, 1983), page 15.
12. Arthur G. Gish, *Beyond the Rat Race* (New Canaan, CT: Keats Publishing, 1973), pages 73,74.
13. Quoted by Shi, page 200.
14. "He has showed you, O man, what is good. And what does the LORD require of you? To act justly and to love mercy and to walk humbly with your God" (Micah 6:8).

CHAPTER 13—HEALTH THROUGH BALANCE

1. David M. Baughan, M.D., "Contemporary Scientific Principles and Family Medicine," *Family Medicine*, 19, January/February 1987, page 42.
2. Richard H. Bube, "On the Pursuit of Excellence: Pitfalls in the Effort to Become No. 1," *Perspectives on Science and Christian Faith*, June 1987, pages 70-71. Used by permission.
3. J. Grant Howard, *Balancing Life's Demands: A New Perspective on Priorities* (Portland, OR: Multnomah, 1983), page 37.
4. George Rust, M.D., "The Balancing Act," *Christian Medical Society Journal*, Winter 1983, page 8.
5. Anne Morrow Lindbergh, *Gift from the Sea* (New York: Pantheon, 1955), page 120.

CHAPTER 14—HEALTH THROUGH REST

1. Doris Janzen Longacre, *Living More with Less* (Scottdale, PA: Herald, 1980), pages 210-211.
2. Gordon MacDonald, *Ordering Your Private World* (Nashville: Oliver-Nelson, 1984), pages 166,174.
3. Jim Buchan, "Grinding the Gears," *Focus Ministries*, March 1984, page 4.
4. Marjorie Barstow Greenbie, *In Quest of Contentment* (New York: McGraw-Hill, 1936), page 57.
5. Thomas à Kempis, *The Imitation of Christ*, trans. Richard Whitford (New York: Washington Square Press, 1953 [written in 1424]), page 13.
6. A. W. Tozer, *The Pursuit of God* (Harrisburg, PA: Christian Publications, 1948), page 112.
7. Tim Kimmel, *Little House on the Freeway: Help for the Hurried Home* (Portland, OR: Multnomah, 1987), pages 63,66.
8. Psalm 91:1-2.
9. Genesis 2:3.
10. Deuteronomy 5:15.
11. Nicholas Wolterstorff, *Until Justice and Peace Embrace* (Grand Rapids: Eerdmans, 1983), page 146.
12. Louis McBurney, M.D., with David McCasland, "The Danger of Aiming Too High," *Leadership*, Summer 1984, pages 34-35.
13. Tozer, pages 112,116.

CHAPTER 15—PAIN, MARGIN, HEALTH, AND RELATIONSHIP

1. Claude Lévi-Strauss, as quoted by Linda Rogers, "'Passive' Progress," *World Press Review*, December 1983, page 41.
2. J. B. Phillips, *For This Day*, ed. Denis Duncan (Waco, TX: Word, 1974), page 180.
3. "Therefore do not worry about tomorrow, for tomorrow will worry about itself. Each day has enough trouble of its own" (Matthew 6:34).
4. Mark 12:29-31.
5. "Now I will show you the most excellent way" (1 Corinthians 12:31).
6. See John 15:13.

Index

Author

Richard A. Swenson graduated Phi Beta Kappa with a B.S. in physics from Denison University in 1970 and received his M.D. from the University of Illinois School of Medicine in 1974. Following five years of private practice, Dr. Swenson accepted a teaching position with the University of Wisconsin Medical School, where he is currently Associate Professor, Clinical Health Sciences.

Dr. Swenson has traveled extensively, including a year of study in Europe and medical work in developing countries on several occasions. He has special interests in societal trends, information management, complexity, and international health issues. He is actively involved in a local church, both as a teacher and an elder. Dr. Swenson and his wife, Linda, live in Menomonie, Wisconsin, with their two sons, Adam and Matthew.